The Decline of Pleasure

WALTER KERR

Simon and Schuster · New York ·

FOURTH PAPERBACK PRINTING, 1968

A portion of this book has appeared in
Horizon *and* American Scholar.

Library of Congress Catalog Card Number: 62–9607
Manufactured in the United States of America
By American Book–Stratford Press, Inc., New York

for my sister

CONTENTS

1

Some Observations on the Oddness of Our Lives

I AM GOING to start out by assuming that you are approximately as unhappy as I am. Neither of us may be submitting ourselves to psychiatrists, neither of us may take an excessive number of tranquilizers each day, neither of us may have married three times in an effort to find someone who will make us happier. We are not desperate, but we are, vaguely, dissatisfied. The work we are doing is more or less the work we meant to do in life; it does not yield us the feeling of accomplishment we had expected. The family pattern we have created around us, with wife and children arranged neatly in a home, would pass muster in a magazine series devoted to typical American domestic relationships; it leaves us tense. We own the car, the television set, and the encyclopedia that are generally suitable to our better than modest station, and we are neither terribly envious of those who have accumulated a greater number of these things nor terribly determined to acquire very many more for ourselves; these things have given us some pleasure and some feeling of competence, but not so much that we are convinced that all felicity lies in acquiring more of them. By the standards of another generation, and by the standards of the present generation in an alien three-quarters of the globe, we might be forgiven for thinking ourselves rich; and we are restless.

Restlessness, and even unhappiness, is in some measure an excellent thing. Any species that is wholly contented, perfectly adapted to its environment, runs a real risk of extinction; or so Lecomte du Noüy has told us. Absolute felicity is fatal. The wholly contented creature vanishes into the soil around it, victim of that immobility that comes of never having to lift a finger. Toynbee has added a graphic description of the spurs, and the winters of discontent, that are essential to a civilization if that civilization is to advance: what mankind requires is a decent challenge, a serious but not overwhelming source of worry, that may in turn provoke a decent, vigorous, creative response.

The question to be answered about our own restlessness is whether it is a creative restlessness or an enervating one. I shall say quickly that it seems to me to be an enervating one, self-feeding, on the way to being self-destructive, unproductive of either the general happiness or the specific satisfactions it seems to seek, random, objectless, at sixes and sevens with itself and with everything about it. I believe that our dissatisfaction is both real and damaging and that it may be progressive: that it may, at some future time, do total damage to the human personality. If I were required to put into a single sentence my own explanation of the state of our hearts, heads, and nerves, I would do it this way: we are vaguely wretched because we are leading half-lives, halfheartedly, and with only one-half of our minds actively engaged in making contact with the universe about us. I know this seems an odd thing to say about a generation that has learned more about the universe in a shorter time, and made more efficient use of what it has learned, than any generation before it. But the special nature of our achievement has in itself helped create the climate of our malaise. The astonishing work we have done is the half-life we have led, brilliantly. The disappointment and distress we feel in the face of our accomplishment is the result of its having engaged only one-half of our faculties, while the other half of our instincts, affections, and energies was permitted to atrophy. It is as though we had used our right hands exclusively for a great many years, so exclusively and for so long that our left hands had withered; and we now wanted to play the piano.

It will take something more than a paragraph to make the point properly clear. And clarity will come hard unless we can first clear away a certain underbrush of assumptions, certain habits of thought that conceal from us the true contours of our prison and hold us immobile, though fretting, inside it.

Something of our frustration may stem from continuing to believe what is no longer quite so, or perhaps never was; casual beliefs casually acted upon may be pushing us further in the direction of our dismay.

I should like to begin, a bit deviously and in a fashion that may at first sight seem irrelevant, by raising a few questions about the shape of our days, by examining a few commonplace assumptions that may quietly have turned into ironies. To do so, it will be necessary to speak briefly of matters personal and domestic. It is in the privacy of our passing from kitchen to bedroom, and from the party to the car, that we are now most conscious of a fundamental unease. We can distract ourselves while we are publicly occupied; the sense of going nowhere overtakes us precisely when we are going home. My own observations on matters personal and domestic cannot, of course, be offered as though they constituted any sort of statistical proof; but it is always possible that what has surprised me has also surprised someone else and that together we may make a statistic. It is not, in any case, statistics we are after; we are after some reassurance that we are not statistics.

☼

It is ungrateful of me, but I am disturbed by something that should please me: the temper of mind of the children I meet.

I meet children because I have children, and I try to see them as the most worried and prophetic minds of our time wish me to see them: as intellectually undisciplined and emotionally overindulged, as soft products of a school environment in which the learning processes are corrupted into play projects and of a home environment in which too much permissiveness permits them to become flaccid captives of television.

The alarums that are most often sounded obviously have some basis to them. Twentieth-century parents have been taught by psychologists that feelings of insecurity are damaging to the preschool infant: in terror of rearing insecure children, a good many parents have lavished forgiveness and love where some strictness was wanted. Strictness has all but vanished from contemporary teaching, in the classroom work itself and in the grading systems that measure that work.

"Whenever possible," Jacques Barzun has ironically reminded us, "the menace of drudgery, that is, of work, must be replaced by an 'activity.' To be ingenious about devising activities is the mark of the 'imaginative' teacher. In the 'living-museum' class (elementary biology) for example, the eleven-year-olds are divided into two groups. Those in one group draw and color a picture of a microscope, paste it on a piece of cardboard, and cut it up into a jigsaw puzzle for the others to put together. Meanwhile, few in the group learn to focus the 'living' microscope; it takes practice and concentration and is not a rousing activity."

John Bainbridge has uncovered a school group in Texas in which the teaching of arithmetic was made a rousing activity by having a single class cut out of paper one million imitation dollars. That our children are playing at learning, or playing when they should be learning, is a real fear.

It is not removed by monthly reports from the teacher in which no grades of any kind are given to indicate the child's relative skill in language or in mathematics but in which encouraging comment is made on his "maturing as a personality in relation to music" or discouraging comment is made on his "tendency to detach himself from the group." The fear is certainly not removed when such reports, of which I have received one and seen others, contain two or three words misspelled by the teacher.

The situation at home is, if anything, worse. An unfortunate medium called television has been invented just in time to take up the slack that has developed since educators decided against the wisdom of giving homework. Left to his own devices throughout the late afternoon, and having been taught to pursue his natural instincts rather than to think, the child lounges about reading comic books or sprawls in a chair before the television set. If his intellectual tone is limp from lack of exercise anywhere, his body tone is no better. This creature is sponge from head to foot.

At least that is the picture we paint of him when we are having one of our nightmares. And when one or another community or national crisis arises—a sharp increase in delinquency, a rumor that Russian children are managing calculus with ease in fifth grade—the portrait seems grimly confirmed.

Now I must say that the exceedingly permissive rearing of the young has always appalled me. The abandonment of the intellectual and moral disciplines in school seems to me a sorry mistake. But without surrendering either of these views, and while acknowledging that I may simply have been lucky or may simply have not looked far enough, I am in honor bound to report that I have never yet met the nightmare we are so fond of describing, and I doubt very much that you have. The children I know, for instance, are in no real sense captives of television.

They look at television, of course, and will snap on the set just as often as permission is granted. When permissions are restricted, they will beg to have them increased. If you were to ask them whether they liked or disliked television, they would say that they liked it. In every formal sense they treat it as though it were a luxury, a joy, and a right.

But a captive is someone who cannot wrench himself loose from whatever it is that confines him. The children I know are not only able to free themselves at will from what is presumed to be spellbinding but are also able to free themselves without the least sign of wrenching. The drift from the set is the most casual thing in the world. The young television audiences with whom I am familiar are vaguely mobile. They snap on a program, watch it for a while, wander off, wander back, exchange places from time to time. It may be during a television show that "detachment from the group" occurs most often. I am sure that the casual housekeeping gesture *I* perform most often is that of snapping off the set because no one is looking at it just now.

This can become a kind of game. Snap off the set and the probabilities are that, within a minute or two, it will be snapped on again by a nomadic child who has returned to the room and is conscious of his rights during the hours of permission. Having found the set turned off, he is likely to stay a little longer this trip. There are occasions, too, when an entire group will remain closeted with the set for an hour or more. But once again the probabilities are strong that during that hour or more the dial will be abruptly, skiddingly turned a half dozen times—sustaining the easy, fragmentary character of ordinary, in-and-out viewing. On the whole, I would say, the children of my acquaintance are fond of television as one is fond of an undemanding dog or a familiar cat, and they "watch" it in something of the way they watch adults: now and again in passing, as though mostly to make sure they are there.

Certainly it is the child that dominates the experience, not the experience the child. One is almost tempted to read contempt into so cavalier a treatment of so much expensive entertainment—an adult who wandered in and out of a concert or even a movie thus freely would be thought to be showing contempt—but that is going too far. The child does not feel superior to what he is seeing; he simply feels surprisingly objective about it.

I do see children reading comic books, perhaps especially when they are watching television. I also see them reading books. The books they read most eagerly are not what our image of the generation as uninformed and irresponsible would suggest: they are not even the contemporary equivalents of the Victor Appleton or Joseph Altsheler thrillers you and I might have wasted time on. The books they read are *The Monitor and the Merrimac, All About Snakes, The First Book of the Early Settlers, Getting to Know Malaya, The Story of Geology,* and *Thomas Jefferson, Father of Democracy.*

As publishers have learned, the contemporary American child will read any volume in the Landmark Series or any other historical, biographical, geographical, or otherwise useful treatise on the true. Mr. Barzun, in his lament over the follies of twentieth-century teaching, has concluded that any modern child who becomes truly educated will have to have become self-educated. The sales records of books sold to the young— especially in series that are resubscribed year after year—suggest that self-education is now beginning early and that the young are handsomely compensating for the defects of their mentors. Publishers who have dared work against this grain, who have issued handsome series of once-standard children's classics or fresh retellings of age-old myths, have sold some copies: they have sold them to adults with long memories who have sentimentally wished to pass cherished delights along to a new generation—and who have failed. Success has not attended the attempt to revive interest in the idly imaginative; where such series survive, they survive as prestige appendages to the line of "scientific" books that sell.

If there is any question about what has happened to publishers and booksellers, consider a circular I recently received from the finest suburban bookstore I know.

"You are most cordially invited," the message began, "to a very special event at our bookstore—at 4:00 P.M. on Thursday, October 6.

"On that day we will be privileged to initiate the first SCIENCE MATERIALS CENTER in Westchester—indeed, in the nation. I believe this is an event of great importance to all of us who are concerned with the problems of education in an age of science.

"The Center will make available to our youngsters a remarkable collection of 'Portable Laboratories,' created by teams of eminent scientists and educators—specifically to stimulate an awareness of the facts, the methods and the language of science.

"I know that you will enjoy seeing youngsters demonstrate these remarkable kits, which are really precision scientific equipment. Won't you join a group of neighbors in the educational, civic and scientific fields to mark this occasion? (Refreshments will be waiting.)"

Should anyone wonder why a "bookstore" should find it necessary to add to its already abundant supply of children's atlases, oceanic studies, and primers of anthropology an actual stock of laboratory equipment, it will be well to remember that what used to be called "children's fiction" is now difficult to sell not only to children but also to libraries. A few years ago, for instance, there was a widespread campaign to remove the *Oz* books from the shelves of public libraries. As reported by Martin Gardner in the *Saturday Review*, librarians had decided that such fantasies were "untrue to life, sensational, foolishly sentimental and consequently unwholesome for the children in your community." Nor was the removal of many volumes due solely to the conviction of prim authorities that the works of

L. Frank Baum and his colleagues gave youngsters "a distorted view of the universe." The youngsters themselves were in part responsible. "Kids don't like that fanciful stuff any more," it was explained; "they want books about missiles and atomic submarines." No protest from children was ever recorded.

It would seem that contemporary children are a good bit freer of the television opiate and a good bit more dedicated to sober inquiry than our sometimes panic-stricken outcries proclaim them to be. I find that their conversation reflects the essential seriousness of their preoccupations. I am not myself particularly good with children; when one of my own brings a friend to the house, I am often distressed by my inability to hit upon a genial opening that will let him know he is officially welcome. But I have grown better at this lately, because I have learned what to talk about. If, instead of asking artificially cheerful questions about his vacation or his prowess at fishing, I adopt an entirely adult tone and draw him into a discussion of the now-vanished land mass by means of which the original Eurasian tribes crossed the Bering Straits to Alaska during the fourth glacial period, I can establish almost immediate *rapprochement*. The problem after that is to get away from him.

If I am myself now interested in paleontology, it is because the children I meet have made me so. Having been made uncomfortable at the dinner table by my obvious ignorance of the finds at Altamira, having heard no more excited cry in the household than a shrill and happy "Hey, *Darwin!*" when an issue of *Life* devoted to the voyage of the *Beagle* was discovered in the mailbox, and having realized that in no time at all I should be unable to advise my own children on anything because of a loss of intellectual standing, I began to read up on the matter. The reading has ended in an enthusiasm: I cannot wait to visit Crete, and I have already made a considerable and tiring detour in order to see the cave paintings at Lascaux. The self-educated are educating me, and in more than one sphere.

Though I have never made an investment in the stock market, I know something about the stock market: I have had to learn something about it so that I could answer the questions of eleven-year-olds.

Am I deceiving myself about children, generally, because I have met no more than a gaggle of them? Apparently not. It is impossible to go into toy stores nowadays, in search of fatherly or godfatherly birthday gifts, without coming upon windup dinosaurs, rubber molds for making plaster of Paris brontosauruses, plastic pterodactyls—all in massive supply. The passion must be close to universal. Reach to the game shelf and you are likely as not, really more likely than not, to take down something playfully entitled "Rich Uncle" but actually built around stock-market speculation.

Whenever we do notice that our children aren't wholly committed to television, that they aren't willing to offer it their firm concentration for any length of time, we wonder if this isn't one more symptom of their rootlessness, their restiveness, their eternal distractibility. It isn't. Though the twentieth-century child can be rather easily distracted from certain of the experiences available to him, he is fiercely tenacious about others. His attention can be held. It can be held by facts, by what is demonstrably true rather than by what has been only dramatically imagined. Hitler's Germany, the depression of 1930, the battle of Antietam, the rate of bank interest, the action of sperm cells are subjects of endless fascination. When a child is found truly intent upon the television screen, the odds are great that he will be watching a stop-motion film in which the stamen and pistil of a flower are seen in the process of growth.

If these things are as true as they seem to me to be—if our children are psychologically free to take or leave entertainment and deeply drawn to sources of factual knowledge—what is there left for a father and a citizen to worry about?

It is precisely this inversion of the expected that disturbs me. I am disturbed by what may seem a small thing and may seem a sentimental thing but is nevertheless a real thing: by the fact that the modern child's mind is not susceptible to the attractions of free narrative.

By free narrative I mean storytelling for its own sake; storytelling that stands independent of any historical, scientific, or otherwise factual relevance and that finds its exhilaration within its own shapely, suspenseful patterning; storytelling that draws upon what is instinctive in the child and not on what is provable in the world about him. I mean the sort of "fiction" that takes its energies and its power to compel from a profound, though playful, tapping of the child's intuitions.

We all of us have our nostalgic pockets of memory, and we perhaps ought to distrust them because they are nostalgic. But they did exist, and they do cling. I can remember my passion for movies, a passion that began the moment I saw one and remained at white heat, in spite of too much movie-going, for almost twelve years. I badgered my parents for permission to attend movies in just the same way that contemporary children beg for television time. There, however, the resemblance between us ends. For when I was given permission, I *attended* the film. I invariably arrived early at the theater, perfectly willing to wait, for there was one moment I particularly did not want to miss: the moment when a rectangle of light struck the curtains *before* they parted. The thought that I might thereafter leave my seat until "The End"—or "Finis," as they were fond of saying in those days—appeared on the screen never entered my head.

I can still recall, with an absurd vividness, the shock I felt one Saturday afternoon when the projectionist's shutter sliced blackly across the screen exactly in the middle of *Robin Hood*. I had seen *Robin Hood*, with Douglas Fairbanks, Sr., several times before. I had, in point of fact, seen it once before that afternoon. But my sister and I were in the habit of "staying," and neither of us was prepared to have the Earl of Huntingdon's career cut short at the very moment he was returning from the Holy Land. He hadn't even slid down the five-story castle drapery yet. We were stunned, uprooted, in effect decapitated.

We remembered, after a moment's bewilderment, that it was the custom at this particular movie house to suspend showings at six o'clock so that the projectionist could go out for dinner. But common sense did not remove the sense of violation we felt. Mine, it would seem, has never vanished entirely: when I paid a loyal visit to a showing of *Robin Hood* at the Museum of Modern Art a few years ago and the film arrived at the moment of Huntingdon's return, the echo of a shutter bleakly dousing this world of light leaped instantly into my head.

If this foolish fear, this experience of loss, remains with me, merely waiting to be summoned up again, it is because my sister and I had a habit of making a pact with a narrative. It was our practice, and our delight, to enter into a rhythmic commitment with an unfolding image that we meant to honor and to have honored. Nor was my own inability to detach myself from something I'd made an enchanted bargain with confined to Saturday afternoon thrillers or Sunday Harold Lloyds. I was thirty years old before I could choose not to finish a book.

Neither my own children nor the children they bring home with them make any such commitments, at least none of this particular kind. They seem content with a sampling of frag-ments: a fast flash of horses racing into a gulley toward a rendezvous they may not be around for, a man walking into a district attorney's office to report a crime they may or may not wish to hear solved, one-sixth of a wrestling match, the irising-out of an animated cartoon, the first roar of a cataract that would have ended as a commercial—a clattering continuum that need never become a continuity.

A passion that gave me great pleasure—and that led, in time, to many other pleasures—is no passion, no irresistible pleasure, for them. Their commitments lie elsewhere. It can, of course, be argued that their relative indifference to free narrative comes from having had too much of it. Television is omnipresent, its wares are repetitious, overexposure has wearied the appetite. These things must to some degree be true. It is clear to me, for instance, that my own youthful pleasure was increased by the fact that I had to wait a week for it.

But as the child turns from a form to which he has been overexposed and begins to investigate one far less familiar—as he turns to books, let us say—there is no fresh, native, innocent leap to the excitements of fiction. He is no more compelled by *Kidnapped* or *Heidi* or *The Prince and the Pauper* than he was by the ubiquitous Lone Ranger. Given a choice between a road map and *Robinson Crusoe*, he will elect the road map; I have seen the choice made. Publishers and booksellers have seen the choice made.

I am not convinced that it is a satiety born of too much television that has killed a generation's taste for fable, for fantasy, or for fiction of a most human kind. I do not think that it has been killed in the child at all. I think he was born without it, or at best with an extraordinarily limited appetite. In our time, something has happened to the tides.

The contemporary child is a stranger to me, and not because he is coddled or spongelike or irresponsible. He is no prisoner of television; he is close to patronizing about it. He is no woolgatherer; he is a "factgatherer." His habits are his own, obviously not the result of indoctrination: instead of being the victim of pedagogical tyrants determined to teach him useful things, he seems to have reversed a too indulgent pedagogical system and set about informing himself. His mind is naturally bent in a given direction; he likes that bent and he pursues it because he likes it. He does not long for greener, gayer hills. He is happy that his view of the universe is less "distorted" than mine was, and is; happy that he knows more about the moon and pterodactyls than I do. He is, in his particular commitments and in the intensity with which he pursues them, admirable.

Making whatever exceptions or qualifications one wishes to make, it is impossible to conceive of this child as essentially pleasure-mad. He is not even especially tempted to what you and I would once have called pleasure. He is soberly devoted, for the most part, to what you and I still call work.

Does it matter that this curious transposition of interests should have taken place? Before saying why it seems to me to matter very much, I should like to inquire whether some of the commonest assumptions we make about the adult world are not similarly misleading.

One of the first great adult dreams of the twentieth century was the dream of leisure. The nineteenth century, in its rush to colonize and to supply, to industrialize and to market, left the laborer, the bookkeeper, and even the man who was known as the boss with very little time to enjoy his achievements. The working day was long: most men were up at dawn, if not well before it, and most men plodded home in the dark, to eat, to discuss with their wives the price of pork, and to get to bed early enough to be able to rise again. Work was virtually uninterrupted: carpenters brought their lunches with them and ate them on planking while a foreman stood by silently urging them back to their awls; no bookkeepers took coffee breaks; few employers permitted themselves festive two-hour lunches—preceded by Martinis—in fashionable restaurants. Wives washed their own dishes, baked their own bread, sewed clothes for the children, made patchwork quilts, walked to market, entertained very rarely and then most modestly, saw little of their husbands and shared interests not at all, and were glad enough to fall exhausted into bed at the necessary hour. Of sweatshops, child labor, and the nose to the grindstone we have all heard enough. "We never sleep" and "the sun never sets" were phrases coined in the period.

In due time the conscience of the world was aroused. Children were snatched from their shoe-blacking benches and sent off to the schoolhouse and the sunshine. Bertha, the sewing-machine girl, joined a union and found herself with a two-week paid vacation in the Catskills. The carpenter began work an hour later, stopped work an hour earlier, demanded Saturday afternoon for himself and then Saturday morning as well. The boss, perhaps the last to surrender his prerogative of unceasing labor, discovered not only the two-hour lunch but the five o'clock cocktail, the Friday night flight to his farm in Connecticut, and the fact of Florida. Wives demanded not only the vote but the right to play bridge: some other arrangement would have to be made about the bread, the dishes, and the darning.

A dream stirred. What had been the point of all the work if no one was ever going to derive any pleasure from it? The very purpose of work was to create occasions for ease. The moment had come now to seize them: the world was well mechanized, the money could be made during a five-day week, gracious living required only that we stop, breathe, smile, and buy appliances. Might we, given just a bit more ingenuity and a few more years, never have to work again? In his 1932 film, *A Nous la Liberté*, René Clair showed us just what we had in mind: the factories were able to run themselves and the men who had once manned them were free forever; we saw these exuberant souls, fishing on a riverbank, their bread and cheese beside them, singing the livelong day. As M. Clair simultaneously mirrored and mocked our vision we may have grinned at the absurdity of the image. But it is clear today that, absurd or no, we did not give it up.

Everyone knows how far we have pushed the promise. The forty-hour week is no longer accepted as ideal; Boris Pregel, past president of the New York Academy of Sciences, has predicted that it will soon be reduced to twenty. Even now, no bookkeeper need stay after twilight; IBM machines are swift to the touch. The junior executive can afford to commute; the world will not fall apart if he appears shortly before ten. From four o'clock onward the highways are anthills of Chevrolets and Buicks, employers and employees jostling one another in the race to the suburban back yard and a cool glass of beer or to the exurban terrace with its twist of lemon peel in an appropriate drink. Lunch hours are comfortable at all levels, and at some they are invitations to indolence. A month in Europe is a gleam in many a wage earner's eye; trips to Canada, to Mexico, and to Disneyland are commonplace.

Domestic duties need detain no one. Dishes may be left to the dishwasher. Clothes may be passed into a machine that will wash them and dry them in a single cycle. Should any of the clothes need pressing, an electric mangle will do the job swiftly and effortlessly; because so many clothes are being made of materials that fall into shape without coaxing, there is less and less work for the mangle to do. A disposal unit will crush and carry off the garbage. Toasters, knife sharpeners, electric ranges, electric frying pans, and Waring Blendors nestle beside one another on easy-to-clean counters, each of them reducing in its own efficient way the time a wife must spend in her kitchen. Shopping need be done no more than once a month: an intelligently-stocked freezing unit will carry a family comfortably for four or five weeks. The hours that have now been spared to the housewife need never be passed in discomfort; air conditioning will see to it that her leisure is unruffled.

The homebound husband and the chore-free wife are at liberty to enjoy their release in a variety of ways. They may elect for solitude, but they are not bound to it, as their relatively immobile forebears so often were. Friends may be summoned or reached: the telephone will do one in an instant and the automobile the other in a pleasant half hour. No one need be starved for conversation or for the companionship of kindred spirits. If one prefers physical to intellectual pleasures, there are bowling alleys within walking distance, golf courses within driving distance, and boats of all sizes for those who live within fifty or sixty miles of a lake or the seacoast.

When he does choose solitude rather than company, the twentieth-century man discovers that nearly every form of delight yet devised has been built snugly into his home. He has very little call, for instance, to hie himself to a public library: the masterpieces of the past and the best sellers of the present are available to him in paperback reprints so inexpensive as to make everyman's bookshelf a potential Bodleian. Everything from Aristotle to Agatha Christie is at his finger tips. Should his taste turn from reading to the contemplation of color and form, he knows perfectly well that he is in easy possession of that "museum without walls" André Malraux promised him in *The Voices of Silence*. Grünewald, Picasso, and the contents of the Louvre are handsomely at hand as they have never been before—in reproductions that may be hung in his rooms and changed as frequently as he likes, in substantial volumes whose color plates have been made with an exacting fidelity to the originals. Should he be willing to settle for a lessened fidelity and some reduction in size, he can have the best of Goya for thirty-five cents. No treasure is kept from him behind the portals of the Prado.

In another mood he has but to snap on the television set to see and hear Leonard Bernstein conducting the Philharmonic, Agnes De Mille arranging a new dance, Sean O'Casey chatting informally about the glories of his back garden, Mary Martin or Ethel Merman or Fred Astaire or Gene Kelly romping through the materials that have made Broadway glow brightest.

He can relax with *Oedipus Rex* or *The Maltese Falcon,* more or less as he likes.

If Bernstein's selections on a given Sunday afternoon do not happen to be the selections best suited to the state of his mind and nerves, he has no difficulty in suiting himself. The record cabinet is well stocked, *The Emperor Concerto* has become his for merely joining a cut-rate club, and the automatic changer on his phonograph assures him of what has been called "uninterrupted listening pleasure." Nor need he discommode himself should his fancy shift from one kind of melody to another. If it is verse he wants, verse he can have: poets will read their poems for him on another set of records, as actors will act Shakespeare and Goldsmith and Sheridan and Shaw at the drop of a needle. The resources of the lecture platform, the concert hall, the Broadway stage, the best-stocked library, and the range of galleries from the Uffizi to the Museum of Modern Art are at his leisurely beck and loving call.

The twentieth century has not only realized, within reason, its dream of leisure time but has also supplied the riches with which to fill it.

It will be obvious at once that not all of the treasures vouchsafed to modern man are being put to extensive use, and it is not my point at the moment to bewail the fact that neither *Oedipus Rex* nor the Philharmonic has ever been found among the "top ten" on a television rating log.

Recordings of Shostakovich's Fifth Symphony probably do not sell as well as the "Dance Party" records of Lawrence Welk. Indeed, there is a serious fear in some quarters that the same mass methods that have made Dante and Debussy available to everyone have ended in producing a mass culture that does not know Dante except as an admirer of Beatrice and that does not know Debussy except as a strain on a sound track for a Warner Brothers film. The term *kitsch* has come into almost deafening use among critics. *Kitsch* is composed of "popular,

commercial art and literature with their chromeotypes, magazine covers, illustrations, ads, slick and pulp fiction, comics,
Tin Pan Alley music, tap dancing, Hollywood movies, etc.,
etc." It is, as Clement Greenberg points out in *Mass Culture*,
"a product of the industrial revolution which urbanized the
masses of western Europe and America and established what is
called universal literacy." A universal love of quality has not
followed directly upon universal opportunity. Let us acknowledge the fact and not—just now—dwell on it.

Before asking what twentieth-century man has done with the
treasures bestowed upon him, it may be proper to phrase a more
fundamental question: What has he done with the time bestowed upon him?

I would like to consider, briefly, a man I know. This man
lives in the suburbs, earns a satisfactory salary in an investment
house, is educated and intelligent, gets along well with his wife
and three children, has his evenings and Saturdays and Sundays
at his disposal, and possesses many of the machines invented
to assure him of leisure and pleasure. For a while, several years
ago, he developed a surprising habit; perhaps I should say he
developed a habit that is not at all uncommon among twentieth-
century middle-to-upper-class men but that was surprising at
the time to his family. Three or four times a year, in a rhythm
too erratic to be easily understood, he would lose himself for a
long weekend in a succession of bars. These periods of escape
did not seem to be related to domestic crises or office tensions;
they did not spill over into Monday mornings but were cut off
sharply and quite soon enough to enable him to return to work;
the classic symptoms of an incipient alcoholism—self-pity, indifference to family, fear of faltering in a career—were nowhere in evidence. The problem was not acute, but a problem
existed.

The problem was ultimately solved, as it is now so often
solved, by the purchase of one more machine for the home. This

man bought himself a power saw and installed it in his basement. Certain supplementary tools were added a little later. With his new equipment, the essentially responsible husband and father transformed a rather dingy room that had been used for laundering into a pine-paneled breakfast nook, which is both charming and useful. Having completed the task, he transferred his attention to an unfinished attic, gradually turning it into a cheerful hideaway for the children to use whenever one of their rooms is pre-empted by house guests. During the coming spring he intends to devote his free evenings to the construction of an outdoor terrace, with access from the dining room, so that the summer may be made pleasanter with frequent cookouts.

There are two things to be said about his present condition. One is that the drinking bouts have ceased. Nor is there anything in his eye to suggest that the old impulse is apt to erupt again; his activity is not feverish; the strange destructive strain that led him headlong to liquor has been assimilated and in a sense exhausted by his new interest. The second thing to be said is that he does not look particularly well. He seems tired.

It is not unreasonable that he should be tired. He is now working five days at the office and two days and five nights at home. Where his nineteenth-century ancestor worked sixty hours a week, he works approximately seventy-one. It is difficult to say whether the lines in his face are deeper on Friday night or Monday morning. Still, he goes on, content to have been rescued from his aberration.

What released him from his aberration was renewed labor. I cannot say precisely how typical this man is of twentieth-century Americans in general. I have been able to watch him, and a few dozen like him, but my range of observation is limited by the circumstances of my own life. It is clear to me, however, that the therapy of the power saw is a specific in more cases than I am acquainted with. If I am to judge by the advertisements I read in newspapers, by the helpful articles I read in magazines, and by the acres of equipment I see in hard-ware-store windows, the "do-it-yourself" command is nearly a national specific. Across America men seem not only willing but eager to install their own plumbing, wire their own kitch-ens, bevel their own bookshelves, assemble their own hi-fi sets, tile their own lavatories, stain their own porch furniture, steel-trim their own linoleum counters, and, when all else is done, hook their own rugs. Indeed, manufacturers of formerly ready-made objects have estimated the situation so shrewdly that they no longer go to the expense of assembling their tables, benches, cribs, and Christmas rocking horses at the factory but pass them on to the purchasers in shards, certain that every man has the time, the tools, and the desire to put these things together.

It is also clear to me that the "do-it-yourself" movement is unrelated to any urge toward economy. It is not the refuge of the impoverished man who must make with his hands what he cannot afford to pay others to make for him. An impoverished man could not afford the tools, for one thing. Add to the cost of the tools the cost of mistakes, plus a decent accounting of the man's time in terms of his earning power, and the final object will prove, in nine cases out of ten, more expensive than its professionally-made counterpart.

There are, I must conclude, other men with leisure-hour problems. The problems may vary, in kind and intensity: liquor is not the only solace for an intolerably empty day or the only menace to be met by an intensified labor. But whatever peculiar coloring the individual difficulty takes on, a single cathartic seems effective in our time: work. I find, too, that the flight from leisure to labor is not confined to the longish weekend we were once so proud of.

Great critical sport has been made, in recent years, of the "business lunch." On New York's Madison Avenue and in Chicago's Loop, in Scranton's Hotel Casey or in any town's equivalent of the old Kiwanis Club, executives of greater or lesser rank are known to meet over Martinis, ryes, or beers, chef's salad or *Bratwurst*, to nurture, and then to consolidate, deals. Because such conferences constitute a continuation of the working day, the costs of liquor, food, cigars, and other *divertissements* are charged to the expense accounts of the participating companies: each firm is expected to pay for work done in its interest. The United States Government, through its Bureau of Internal Revenue, has recognized the validity of the situation. These meetings represent, of course, the twentieth-century dream of the longish, relaxed lunch period, or what is left of that dream. There are those who smile slyly and intimate that, no matter what explanations are given on the expense-account vouchers, the business lunch is devoted to something less than business, that it is a rationalized break from the sales charts and a chance to down a few drinks that will keep the rest of the afternoon from becoming too strenuous. I am not sure that I share this cynicism. I have been in business offices on a number of occasions when an executive's lunch date was unexpectedly called off. On none of these occasions did the executive first sigh with regret and then hopefully cast about for a friendly soul to replace his lost guest and keep him casual company in a restaurant for the next hour or two. In each instance the executive ordered up a sandwich from a nearby delicatessen and ate it absently while he went on working.

The selection of leisure-time friends and party guests on a calculated basis has come in for its share of kidding, too. In 1958 a national magazine ran a cartoon that was intelligible both as humor and as realistic social criticism to almost everyone: an upper-middle-class woman was saying brightly to several of her peers, "We're going to enlarge our circle of friends to include some people we like."

We are also wryly familiar with the party assembled in such a way as to make certain that its costs may legitimately be entered as professional expenses, against taxes. One bright-eyed guest arriving late at a thoroughly successful party I recently attended whisked off her wrap, glanced at the fifteen or twenty familiar faces turned cheerfully in her direction, and caroled winningly, "Oh, the annual deductible!" The fact that the thought of party-giving tends to fill the twentieth-century hostess with apprehension and that the party itself, so far from relaxing her, builds up a tension that requires a week's recuperation thereafter is equally plain. Three days after the successful party I have just mentioned the man of the house was rushed to the hospital for an emergency appendectomy. His wife, our Sunday hostess, called a friend on the telephone, her voice filled with grievous distress. "In one week," she cried, "the party—and now this!"

Generally, the tendency to confine one's friendships to business acquaintances and to make up guest lists for parties on the basis of professional obligation and possible professional advancement is regarded as one of the more unattractive and self-seeking strains in the contemporary American psyche. This is status-seeking, we are told, when it is not appalling snobbery. Once again, I suspect that we are not being quite fair to a conscientious and hard-pressed society. It is an entirely legitimate practice to select one's friends on the basis of a community of interests. What is odd, to me, is that twentieth-century man seems able to find, and to share, a community of interests only among the working community. If he wants to go bowling, he does not call to his eldest son to join him on the spur of the moment or go off alone in some confidence that he will find a congenial partner at the alleys; he joins the interoffice bowling league. If he rather likes a Friday evening of living-room conversation, he does not look among his neighbors for the best conversationalists; he looks for the best conversationalists among his professional colleagues.

I think that there is a certain innocence in the pattern. The man who behaves in this way is not necessarily a crudely calculating man or a greedy one. He is very likely aware that on Friday night he is entitled to some pleasure, that he has an incontrovertible right to make himself comfortable. And he is comfortable only when he is talking shop.

I find an innocence in his wife as well. The cartoon caption I have quoted is funny and pertinent. It is also wistful. Whether the cartoonist meant to put it there or not, there is something overwrought in that chattering matron's eye. She has been so long dominated by the twentieth-century pressure to entertain such people as may be useful to her husband that she cannot help but take the situation in her matter-of-fact stride, cannot help referring to it as though nature itself had ordained the pattern. At the same time she is foolishly aware that it is possible to like some people better than others, no matter what work they may do. Caught between the unquestioned rules of the game and an irresponsible fondness for certain faces she has noticed in passing, she is absurd—and, in her frantic, hypertense way, faintly touching. It is touching, too, to think that her giddy plan will probably not be realized, or realized only under pain of embarrassment. A woman's yearning for casual friendships may survive the requirements of her husband's job or her husband's temperament; the man in question may very well agree to the plan. But there is the problem of the other wives she has in mind and their requirements. The social expectation of the twentieth century is that an invitation will bring with it the insurance of meeting "someone interesting," a phrase which has come to mean someone whose work is interesting and, if possible, intelligibly related to one's own. Phyllis McGinley, in her poem "A Word to Hostesses," issues a small warning about the upper-class dinner party:

Celebrities are lonely when
They congregate with lesser men.
Among less lambent men they sit,
Bereft of style, deprived of wit,
A little chilly to the touch,
And do not sparkle very much.

The solution to the difficulty is simple enough:

Hostesses, then, when you are able
To lure Celebrity to table,
It is discreet to bear in mind
He needs the comfort of his kind.
Fetch other names. Fetch three or four. . . .

The practice of casting a casual evening as carefully as one would a Broadway play is by no means confined to the world of celebrities who have been celebrated in newsprint. "Names" or no, the names of the guests are an indispensable, if discreetly communicated, adjunct to any invitation: any hostess telephoning her acquaintances to arrange a gathering knows that the question "Who's going to be there?" hovers unspoken but insistent at the other end of the wire. I have heard, and felt a pang for, more than one woman apologizing for her proffered hospitality. "It's just going to be us," the hasty explanation ran, "so if you've got anything you'd rather do . . ." The company of the host and hostess is rarely considered an attraction, even by the host and hostess.

A word about the twentieth-century woman on whom I've been eavesdropping. She would seem to have accepted something more than her husband's compulsion to build companionship for himself, and for her, out of his business directory. She has come to share his compulsive need of a useful end in view, whatever the nature of the activity. If he does not go bowling without the comforting feeling that he is contributing to interoffice amity, she no longer plays bridge without the assurance that the afternoon's proceeds are to be contributed to charity, to the Playground Fund or the Library Fund or the Drive Against Muscular Dystrophy. Though she is at last free enough of her kitchen to settle comfortably in her living room for a few lost hours with a Frances Parkinson Keyes novel or the recorded poetry of Edna St. Vincent Millay, she is rarely to be found in the living room. She may be going from door to door with a cardboard box in her hand, collecting for the March of Dimes. She may be at her children's school, debating the wisdom of released time for religious instruction or listening to a lecturing psychologist. She may be at the Mother's Exchange, repairing castoff clothing for needier families than her own. She may be at the Municipal Building in her community, speaking her mind about traffic regulations or a projected change in bus schedules; she may be cooking for the Campfire Girls or crusading against Communism or campaigning for decent literature or whitewashing the basement. The buzz of her husband's power saw seems to drive her as well, though neither to fatigue her nor to satisfy her in quite the same degree. When she has completed the social tasks assigned to her by her husband, and has momentarily finished with the tasks she has assigned to herself, she is often to be found writing to one or another counselor in the women's magazines. We have all become accustomed to the lament that is here given voice: "I do not have enough to do; I do not respect the place I occupy in the world."

For both husband and wife the need of a defined objective is omnipresent: the sort of objective that is essential to work but presumably hostile to free play. The goal does not have to be a specifically mercenary one: once more, greed would not seem to be the sole or even the primary cause of so much striving. It is still perfectly possible for a twentieth-century couple to set off on a jaunt in the family car without having in mind the economic motive of stopping at a garden market where money may be saved on vegetables. The leisure-time trip is not necessarily expected to produce a tangible result. But the leisure-time trip has, in my experience, come under a curious though increasingly familiar psychological pressure: it is expected to achieve *something*, if only an arbitrary destination. The man who asks you to join him in a day's outing no longer suggests that you get into the car and see where the wheels go, poking at random into unexplored roadways. He picks a point on the map which may have no other charms than that it is a point on the map; he picks it because it is at a sufficient distance away to require him to maintain a certain relatively high speed; and, having decided upon a predetermined speed toward a predetermined goal, he is free to work steadily at the task. He may become angry at more casual drivers; he may sweat out the risk of passing other cars on curves; he may arrive at his destination with no real desire to do anything but get back into the car and forge his way home. But he will have invited you on a trip and taken one himself; he will have mileage on his speedometer to show for it.

Greed is no more behind the leisure tensions this man has endured than it was behind his decision to refashion the attic or behind his wife's somehow unsatisfying campaign to send clothing to Korea. An emotion closer to guilt seems to impel him to fill the idle hours he has been granted with tasks calculated to justify his idleness.

In speaking of the men and women I have watched I do not mean to suggest that I am detached from them or in any way wiser than they are. I live in the twentieth century and I find that, like it or not, the twentieth century lives in me. I have become aware, for instance, of a marked change in my reading habits over the years, a change that began unconsciously but is now extremely difficult to undo. I am, by temperament, a reader: I have read books in automobiles, on elevated trains, in restaurants, in theater lobbies, and on street corners while waiting for buses. The sight and the smell of books huddled cover to cover on a library shelf has always warmed and contented me; by the time I left high school I could not leave a public library without the maximum number of books that could be borrowed, eight, under my arms. My reading was by no means discriminating: William Dean Howells, E. V. Lucas, and Sax Rohmer might well appear in the same bundle. I simply read books because someone had printed them.

I still read, in nearly every spare moment; I earn my living as a theatrical reviewer, and press agents are apt to eye me sourly on opening nights as I go down the aisle with a book in my hand, presumably prepared for the worst and armed against it; and I have, now and then, tucked away a few pages before the lights went down or during longish intermissions. But I must face up to the fact that the essential character of my reading has changed. This is not a matter of decreased volume: few people are able to maintain the avid, incontinent pace of their twenties. Nor would I pretend that it is a matter of improved taste: I can be caught, by those who are quick enough, reading Erle Stanley Gardner. The difference is this: I no longer read to read.

Four years ago, after a trip to Greece which destroyed every preconception I had ever had of that country, I found myself wanting, for the first time in my life, to read Thucydides. I wanted to understand what it was that I hadn't understood about Greece. The desire was conscious and persistent, and for three years I did nothing about it. Not long ago I became briefly engaged in a research project, for which I was being paid, on the decline of Greek democracy. I was at last free to read *History of the Peloponnesian War*. Permission had been granted.

For quite a long time I have been wanting to read the rest of Robert Louis Stevenson. There are twenty-six volumes of Stevenson, bought long ago in a bargain basement, on my shelves, and their rather shabby red backs looked inviting. I recently became involved in a commercial television project which planned to include portions of Stevenson's work in a series. This was my cue to take Stevenson down from the shelf, the excuse, the *ego te absolvo* I had been waiting for. If it had not been given me, I should still not have read *The Beach of Falesa* or even *Markheim*.

Once I had begun to notice how my pleasure was invariably postponed until my work required it, I also paid attention to the quality of that pleasure and to my conduct while pursuing it. I was, I soon realized, racing to get through, though there was no absolute deadline over me. I was making frequent marginal notes, rather more than I should ever need for a report. I was assuaging a powerful feeling that I was cheating in reading Stevenson at all by insisting on the urgency and necessity of the task. I was indulging myself in something for which there was neither time nor rational justification, and I was able to endure my truancy only by keeping firmly in mind its value as profitable labor. When a friend sees me with a book in my hand and reaches to read the title as friends often do, I always feel an urge to explain to him how I happen to be reading this particular book. I have caught myself laughing off a copy of *Northanger Abbey* as apologetically as the hostess who has nothing but her own company to offer. I am acquainted with only one commuter who reads Shakespeare on the way to Wall Street; and he speaks of his habit so often and so exuberantly that I know he feels a fool.

We are all of us compelled to read for profit, party for contacts, lunch for contracts, bowl for unity, drive for mileage, gamble for charity, go out for the evening for the greater glory of the municipality, and stay home for the weekend to rebuild the house. Minutes, hours, and days have been spared us. The prospect of filling them with the pleasures for which they were spared us has somehow come to seem meaningless, meaningless enough to drive some of us to drink and some of us to doctors and all of us to the satisfactions of an insatiate industry.

In a contrary and perhaps rather cruel way the twentieth century has relieved us of labor without at the same time relieving us of the conviction that only labor is meaningful.

Although we assume ourselves to be a people possessed of unusual opportunities for leisure, we are actually occupied in more and more work. Although we assume our children to be coddled and play-mad, they are actually more interested in work than we are. The situation is strange and, in some ways, frightening.

I do not think that my friend with the power saw is about to revert to his drinking. He is likely to remain sober, and industrious, until the day he dies. But I shall not be surprised if that day comes sooner than he has a right to expect. He is engaged in the therapy that kills.

It is customary to explain the hypertensions and the heart attacks that bedevil the contemporary American male by pointing to the abnormal pace and the abnormal work pressures of twentieth-century life as though that pace and those work pressures had been established by someone other than the man himself. We imagine some blind, mindless, mechanized force in whose grip we all are, and whose thrust we are unable to resist. But what force should this be in a society that has provided more time for relaxation than any other? Isn't it odd that a century which should, by all rights, be the most leisurely in all history is also known to be, and condemned for being, the fastest? Who has set this pace, if not the fellow who has insisted upon maintaining its tempo during all the hours when his office doors are locked?

Work-minded as we have become, we are not yet wholly unaware of a world that exists, or was meant to exist, apart from work. We have, for instance, a memory of pleasure; fragments of idle and delighted hours freely squandered when we were younger come back now and then to haunt us, and when Robert Paul Smith writes a brief evocation of childhood called *Where Did You Go? Out. What Did You Do? Nothing* an ounce of nostalgia stirs in all of us. We are vaguely aware that an uncorrupted pleasure awaits us somewhere, if we can only learn to forgive ourselves for taking it; we sense that the taking is both possible and desirable. We even suppress a sigh as we reach for our hammer and nails by telling ourselves that the work we do today is done in the interests of a pleasure postponed: when we have finished the terrace and the barbecue pit we shall have the unalloyed delight of a carefree cookout. The cookout, too, will be corrupted when it comes by being made the occasion of shoptalk with colleagues, but no matter; a promise remains half alive and we may sooner or later find some way of realizing it.

It is probable that our very awareness of the existence of pleasures that we are either postponing or denying ourselves adds to the tensions induced by unrelieved labor. We feel guilty when we take our pleasure, because there is so much work we might do. We feel guilty when we work so hard, because our lives may depend upon pausing for pleasure. The two guilts are incompatible, and we suffer further from the head of steam their mutual abrasiveness builds up. Still, there is always hope of resolving the dilemma; the life line may be badly snarled, but it has not been permanently cut.

What disturbs me most about our admirable children is that the life line, the thread of release, the promise of a pleasure that is not in itself labor, seems never to have existed for them. They are not only accomplished in their command of what is useful but are also content with it. They will not have my memory of a foolish and useless and all-consuming passion; they do not want it. They will, I must conclude, grow to manhood without a nagging acquaintance with a possible alternative to their pursuits; they have not been interested in making such an acquaintance. They will have single, rather than divided, minds, and the unquestioning simplicity of their lives may release them from feelings of guilt. But, given the sudden descent of a dark night of the soul, they will have no place to go.

It is almost as though the twentieth century had been engaged in a long struggle to produce a new kind of man—a man whose sole concern should be his useful work—and, in our children, had successfully accomplished the mutation.

Though they do not know it yet, I know that my children will one day come to a paralyzing moment in which everything they have loved is robbed of its flesh, a moment in which the circle of light that has long surrounded an object flickers sickeningly and its dimensions collapse like a retractable tin cup. For one of them a column of figures will straggle down a page in mocking unintelligibility, defiant. For another geology will turn to so much carefully sifted dust.

What will the robin do then, poor thing?

2

✼
✼✼
✼

A Philosophy and Its Aftermath

John Stuart Mill,
  By a mighty effort of will,
Overcame his natural bonhomie
    And wrote 'Principles of Political
      Economy.'

—EDMUND CLERIHEW BENTLEY

I᠎T MAY SEEM as though I have been basing my rather sweeping statements about an entire society on a handful of people I happen to know. My lot, you may think, has thrown me among an odd assortment of suburban malcontents and high-strung professionals who are driven to their occasional hard drinking and incessant hard labor by ambition, by a financial treadmill they have foolishly got themselves on, or simply by those rhythmic metropolitan pressures that stem, psychologically, from what a novelist has symbolically called "The Big Clock."

I was asking myself if this mightn't be the case when I picked up a copy of *The New York Times* and noticed a casual report tucked low on the page:

"Emotional stress, usually associated with job responsibility, is the chief cause for heart disease in young adults, Dr. Henry I. Russek of Staten Island, N.Y., contends.

"But leisure-time activities are also nerve-racking, the physician noted in an article to be published here tomorrow in *The Journal of the American Medical Association.* . . .

"The young executive class has no monopoly on tension-induced heart disease, Dr. Russek indicated.

"He said that his findings, based on the study of 200 persons, had shown that the malady occurred in 'all socio-economic strata.'

"He said that the most characteristic trait of the young coronary patient was restlessness during leisure hours and a sense of guilt during periods when he should have been relaxed."

I am not alone, then, in feeling guilty when I read a book I don't have to read. My friends in one socio-economic stratum seem to have friends in other socio-economic strata who feel just as jumpy and just as dissatisfied the moment the harness is removed from their backs.

"Guilt" is a strange word to have become associated with the experience of pleasure. It suggests, to begin with, that we have a deep conviction of time wasted, of life wasted, of worth-while opportunities missed, whenever we indulge ourselves in a mild flirtation with leisure. There are valuable things we might be doing if we were not goldbricking just now; those valuable things might prove enormously useful to society, to our families, to our own souls; in goldbricking itself there is no value. We are either laborers in the vineyard or we are slackers in the shade.

The conviction goes deeper. When we turn down the chance to turn an idle hour to profit, we are not merely failing in a social obligation but are also failing in a moral one. What we are doing is not only boorish and unco-operative. It is wrong.

An ancient Puritanism returned to haunt us? Hardly. All of the other tensions engendered by Puritanism have long since been sprung, deliberately and with some abandon; why should the fear of pleasure alone have lasted? An even older distrust, older than the adage "An idle mind is the devil's workshop," old enough to remember medieval injunctions against the snares and delights of this world and to remember and share that faint distaste that has always attached, in the public mind, to the Greco-Roman philosophy known as Epicureanism? Not likely, either. One after another historical release has come along to dissipate the force of these earlier pressures: the Renaissance, the Restoration, the giddy 1920s, if you wish. Though every restraint that makes its mark upon history leaves a residue, that residue is rarely vigorous enough to hold an entire society in its grip. This is something new, and it is something universal.

It is a philosophy, an article of faith, and one to which we have given assent at a fairly recent date. It cannot be so casual a thing as a nervous reflex, a sudden jump in the blood pressure of the body politic due to the temporary and unexpected speeding-up of our lives. Unforeseen circumstances do affect societies; they have affected our own. The machines we meant to drive drive us. The automatic elevators that were meant to make things so much easier for us in our sleek new office buildings make things harder; we are always fearful that the doors are going to close before we get in or out, we are terrified that we are going to be trapped without human companionship between floors, we miss the old operator because it was comforting to think that the old operator would know how to take care of us. Airplanes get us to Europe long before we want to be in Europe, assembly lines threaten to leave us miles behind and frantic (Chaplin touched both our funny bones and a sore spot when the mindless belt raced on alone in *Modern Times*), and intercom systems can startle us half to death everywhere but in the privacy of our bathrooms. We are pushed. But while being pushed does breed in us a habit of walking faster, it should not in the normal course of things lead us to like being pushed. If we were wholly sane, and had a spark of manliness left in us, we should resent being pushed, rebel against being pushed; and if rebellion were not really possible during working hours in the mechanized twentieth century, then we should, at the very least, leap to our leisure with a wild cry of relief, with singing and dancing and shouting in the streets, with the exhilaration of escape from everything intolerable. We should certainly not beg to be pushed again after hours or spend our afterhours pushing ourselves for the exercise. If we were granted a holiday from detestable pressures, however brief that holiday might be, we should feel entitled to it, grateful for it— not guilty about it.

Pangs of guilt imply patterns of belief. No one feels furtive and shamefaced because he is being unfairly hounded; he feels furtive and shamefaced because he has himself, in his deepest being, violated a law he holds to be true. The law that the twentieth century holds to be true may be stated this way:

Only useful activity is valuable, meaningful, moral. Activity that is not clearly, concretely useful to oneself or to others is worthless, meaningless, immoral.

This is a plain code, easy to understand, easy to apply. It has a strong ring of virtue about it. It leads to solid citizenship, to responsible family life, to personal dignity. It is, in its way, quite Spartan. But how has so Spartan a notion managed to fasten itself so fiercely upon an age that really hoped to make machines do all the useful work while man enjoyed his freedom? Where did the surprising, contrary, rigid notion come from?

It came, as all philosophies do, from a philosopher. The particular sentence in which a particular philosopher crystallized it was this:

"Repeated reflection and inquiry have led me to the somewhat novel opinion, that *value depends entirely upon utility.*"

It is unlikely that more than a few of the millions upon millions of honest men and women who ordain their lives to conform to this thought have ever read the sentence in which the thought was finally, firmly articulated. Indeed, I challenge you to buy the book, published during the last third of the nineteenth century, in which the statement appeared: it has taken two booksellers ten months to find a copy of the original edition for me. If I mentioned the name of the man who wrote it, as I shall do later, it would be recognized only by a handful of specialists. Yet a sentence that has already passed into history has passed effective sentence upon us.

That such a thing should happen is by no means unusual. Ideas that are powerful enough to dictate the conduct of whole generations must indeed come from powerful minds. But they are not often announced in single broadcasts, with the philosopher taking polite little bows at the end of the program and warming himself with the plaudits of the press next morning. They are more likely to enter the blood and marrow of a people as spirochetes do—unnamed, invisible—quite a long while after a lonely thinker has set them loose in the silence of his study.

If, as Victor Hugo said, "no army can withstand the strength of an idea whose time has come," it takes time for the time of an idea to come. Thinkers work, as a rule, in isolation, gathering up the threads of present history—the new accidents of invention, the new impulses of feeling—and weaving them into coherent patterns that may be named and used. While they are busy sorting out all of the circumstances that may give birth to a new idea, they are little known. The butcher may know Karl Marx because he hasn't paid his bill; but the policeman on the corner will not ask him questions about dialectical materialism, or even wonder who he is, as he bustles by. If a philosopher's painfully formulated concepts are in any way arresting, they—and he—will first become known to other philosophers. Professional colleagues will then engage him in debate. If the debate is lively, and if the concept seems to be gaining adherents, other men will catch the word on the wing, men who are not themselves original thinkers but who have a talent for explaining, elaborating, and popularizing materials that were first conceived on a difficult intellectual level. Popularization begets popularization: more and more translators appear, speaking increasingly in the common tongue; the stone dropped in the pond sends out wider and wider wavelets; what began in a library will at last become a problem for the corner policeman.

In this process, various things may happen. For one thing, it is likely that the concept will lose precision. For the strict terminology of the practicing philosopher a series of easy approximations is offered, substitute catch phrases that convey the essential notion roughly, without hairsplitting and without subtlety of inflection. If this does some damage to what the thinker had in mind, it has the curious compensating value of strengthening his influence: his syllogism may now be transformed into a slogan. In the end, a proposition that few men could have analyzed becomes for millions of men a perfectly intelligible battle cry.

And the battle cry may or may not have the name of its author attached to it. It is clear to us, for instance, that whole continents behave as they do today because a man named Karl Marx had a thought and wrote a book; it is not difficult for us to understand that Marx's private and lonely act helped to produce—through the successive stages of popularization, indoctrination, and practical application—the Communist, stubbornly believing though he may never have read *Das Kapital*, who moves through the streets of Kiev today. The name Marx and the image of an international movement are quickly coupled in our minds.

If Karl Marx is constantly credited with a social phenomenon that concerns us all in the twentieth century, it is, perhaps, because he had two publicizing forces working for him. One was the fact that his massive idea appeared in a single massive book and that his massive effect depended relatively little upon the refining debate or the added contributions of colleagues. The less imposing but equally pervasive concept with which I am concerned in this chapter, the concept that makes our teeth chatter whenever we are forced to spend five minutes alone in idleness and that causes us to send our children out tricking and treating on Halloween with UNICEF collection cups in their hands, did not come from a single, emphatic source: it was the work of many men, of a philosophical "school," with each thinker contributing to the swell of a tidal wave but no one of them making it his very own.

The other reason we are so swift to identify Marx is that Marx's idea was, in its essence, an explosive one. It ended in what it demanded—a revolution. Now explosions are interesting to us as earthquakes are interesting and as soil erosion is not. We are less fascinated by, and therefore less apt to observe, evolutionary processes that make their way not by violent eruptions but by the slow, steady spread of a dye through one social layer after another. The name of the man who has lighted a fuse fastens itself upon our minds; the name of a man who has merely spilled a stain is often lost before the stain can reach us.

In short, we notice what happens by holocaust but not what happens by gradually increasing habit. Yet a quiet habit of thought that has come to its term is every bit as powerful as a concept enforced by gunfire.

The philosophy that won the twentieth century without seeming to have fired a single shot was called "utilitarianism" (the term is familiar enough to us, but its moral imperatives might shock us if we took the trouble to define them), and its relevance to our inquiry may be most rapidly summarized by recalling the youthful nervous breakdown of John Stuart Mill.

Mill, who occupies a middle position in the development of nineteenth-century British thought, was the son of an earnest and single-minded utilitarian philosopher. His father, James, was not only an ardent defender of the century's fresh line of thought but also a close friend and colleague of the man who had formulated it, Jeremy Bentham.

Bentham had begun by erecting a bold new system on which "the standard of right and wrong" might be based and through which "the chain of causes and effects" might be understood. It may be one of the monumental ironies of history that Bentham should have founded his system on the principle of pleasure.

Pleasure, he said, was the sole motivating force that drove men into all of their activities. The pursuit of pleasure and, what is the same thing, the avoidance of pain "govern us in all we do, in all we say, in all we think." A moral act is one which gives us, or someone else, pleasure; an immoral act is one which gives us, or someone else, pain.

Clear enough. But how are we to know whether we are giving or receiving pleasure? How can we be sure that we are leading upright lives? Bentham had a quick, unequivocal answer. The amount of pleasure any action or object possesses may be reckoned by its *utility*, by its usefulness, and by no other norm. Utility, in Bentham's definition, is "that principle which approves or disapproves of every action whatsoever" in proportion as it seems to "augment or diminish the happiness of the party *whose interest is in question*" (italics mine). Or if it is a desirable object rather than a desirable action we are considering, then utility is that property in the object "whereby it tends to produce benefit, advantage, pleasure, good, or happiness (all this in the present case comes to the same thing)." Bentham later added the words *profit*, *convenience*, and *emolument* to his list of synonyms for the word *pleasure*, so that pleasure and profit come to mean one and the same thing. This identification of happiness with utility, of pleasure with profit, is absolute. "Systems which attempt to question it," Bentham wrote, "deal in sounds instead of sense, in caprice instead of reason, in darkness instead of light."

Some apprehensive men did begin to question the airtight equation almost immediately. These men admitted swiftly that they could see the pleasure, and the simultaneous utility value, in possessing certain tangible things. Bentham had asked: "An article of property, an estate in land, for instance, is valuable, on what account?" He had answered: "On account of the pleasures of all kinds which it enables a man to produce, and . . . the pains of all kinds which it enables him to avert." There was no difficulty here, or in Bentham's mentioning "the pleasure of acquiring . . . a sum of money."

But what, these men said, of disinterested friendship, of friendship continued out of unconsidered liking and without the practical motive of hoping to turn the friendship to some benefit or advantage? If he had been a less strict man, Bentham might always have replied that the very return of the friendship itself could be considered a benefit or advantage, even if the advantage could not be precisely measured. But Bentham was a strict man. He had himself devised a series of tests for measuring pleasure precisely: the tests of a pleasure's *intensity*, its *duration*, its *certainty* or *uncertainty*, among others. And no straightforward thinker, believing in the utilitarian ethic, could pretend that the intensity of a disinterested friendship could be weighed as gold might be weighed, that its duration could be forecast as the life of a thoroughbred horse might be forecast, that its certainty consisted in very much more than the ambiguity of a smile. Bentham inflexibly, and with a marked interior consistency, went on to quote with approval a new maxim of this new age: "few acquaintances, fewer friends, no familiarities."

Inflexible, too, was his colleague James Mill. Mill now turned his attention to the education of his small son, an education which has since become famous for its range and for the rigidity of its utilitarian grounding. No time was to be wasted on childhood pleasures. At the age of three John Stuart Mill began the study of mathematics and Greek. By the age of eight he had read some of Plato and masses of history: not only Hume and Gibbon but thirty volumes of the *Annual Register* and Mosheim's *Ecclesiastical History*. Between eight and thirteen he continued to concentrate on history but added logic, Euclid, algebra, and political economy to his schedule of study. His father demanded not only that he read but that he rethink for himself each proposition. At thirteen he was grappling with Aristotle and Aquinas in their original tongues.

At twenty-one the boy broke down, victim of a dejection which robbed life not only of its pleasures but also of its purpose. "My heart sank within me," he later remembered; "the whole foundation on which my life was constructed fell down. . . . I seemed to have nothing left to live for."

Prophetic of our time as his collapse may seem, I do not really wish to use it as a symbol with which to flog an entire philosophy: any child must have broken down under such pressure from such a father. But John Stuart Mill himself came to regard it as a valid criticism of utilitarianism as it was then developed. When, after several years' battle with the melancholia that overwhelmed him, he gradually found his energies restored, he also found his horizons widened: "I, for the first time, gave its proper place, among the prime necessities of human well-being, to the internal culture of the individual. I ceased to attach almost exclusive importance to the ordering of outward circumstances, and the training of the human being for speculation and for action."

He now saw, he reported in his autobiography, "that the habit of analysis has a tendency to wear away the feelings . . . when no other mental habit is cultivated," and "the maintenance of a due balance among the faculties" became for him a matter of urgent importance. Unexpectedly, it was poetry that had most helped him recover his joy in life:

"What made Wordsworth's poems a medicine for my state

of mind, was that they expressed, not mere outward beauty, but states of feeling, and of thought coloured by feeling, under the excitement of beauty. . . . In them I seemed to draw from a source of inward joy, of sympathetic and imaginative pleasure, which could be shared in by all human beings. . . . I needed to be made to feel that there was real, permanent happiness in tranquil contemplation. Wordsworth taught me this. . . . The result was that I gradually, but completely, emerged from my habitual depression, and was never again subject to it."

But the dual experience—of depression and rejuvenation—posed a sobering problem for a mind trained to utilitarianism. Mill faced the problem: had a philosophy built upon pleasure succeeded, through some mad mental gymnastic, in excommunicating certain pleasures? Was it further possible that the pleasures most rigorously excluded from the system were in fact the very highest pleasures?

Alerted to the dangers that might overtake mankind in general, Mill set about rectifying what he took to be a misunderstanding, an error of emphasis. As he moved on to his own brilliant life's work as a political philosopher, he did not surrender the fundamental principles that his father, and his time, had taught him. He seems never to have considered challenging the essential equation that "usefulness equals happiness." He remained a utilitarian philosopher to the end of his days.

But he returned again and again to the problem of the pleasures he feared might wither away. Why *should* utilitarianism be thought to exclude so much that had helped and delighted him?

He knew that many men thought it did exclude these things. "It is often affirmed," he wrote, "that utilitarianism renders men cold and unsympathizing; that it chills their moral feelings toward individuals; that it makes them regard only the dry and hard consideration of the consequences of actions. . . ."

And he felt that this "misconception" might be due, in part, to that inevitable corruption of terms which takes place whenever a principle is being popularized:

". . . the common herd, including the herd of writers, not only in newspapers, and periodicals, but in books of weight and pretension, are perpetually falling into this shallow mistake. Having caught up the word 'utilitarian,' while knowing nothing whatever about it but its sound, they habitually express by it the rejection, or the neglect, of pleasure in some of its forms: of beauty, of ornament, or of amusement. . . . And this perverted use is the only one in which the word is popularly known, and the one from which the new generation are acquiring their sole notion of its meaning."

The common man was making the common mistake of employing a precise philosophical term in the "merely colloquial sense in which utility is opposed to pleasure." But if this opposition—this ironic divorce between pleasure and a philosophy presumably founded upon pleasure—was actually rooting itself in the public mind, if all sorts of people had come to the conclusion that the attractions of friendship and of beauty were somehow banished from the strict utilitarian canon, must not the philosophers themselves have paved the way for so total a misunderstanding? Mill's predecessors had talked a great deal about money, about emolument, about the durability of real property. Bentham had even scoffed at the notion that pleasure might have anything to do with "the fine feelings of the soul"; pleasure was the practical motive that drove a man into practical action for his own gain.

Mill proposed that pleasure might be more generously defined. Without yielding any of Bentham's principles, he sought to stretch their application. Happiness might indeed depend upon use; but it should be possible to enlarge everyman's understanding of what was useful.

"A cultivated mind," he wrote, "finds sources of inexhaustible interest in all that surrounds it; in the objects of nature, the achievements of art, the imaginations of poetry, the incidents of history, the ways of mankind, past and present, and their prospects in the future."

It cannot be doubted that Mill, out of his private experience, had come to love literature and landscapes as much as he loved Euclid and justice. He may have been ready to love them more. As a utilitarian philosopher, however, he was under an obligation to logic: the obligation to prove that each of these things conferred a benefit as solid and as certain as Bentham's "sum of money."

He tried to meet the obligation. "The art of music is good," he said, meaning that listening to music was a morally good act in which man might honorably indulge himself, "for the reason, among others, that it produces pleasure." Taking this for granted, he asked the next necessary question: Could the pleasure which music might give us be objectively measured, so that we should know it was real and not a sickly, wasteful illusion?

Mill was not such a fool as to suppose that the delights of music could be measured by Bentham's standards. One of the truths that had tormented him, during his time of depression, was that "the pleasure of music . . . fades with familiarity," and he was not going to announce now that an hour spent listening to Bach could be shown to be as *certain* a pleasure and as *durable* a pleasure as owning two dozen shares of British railway stock. In the hour spent immobile with Bach, after all, a man might easily have built himself a solid oak chair which would likely last longer than his memory of the music; and he could point to the chair, long afterward, as proof of the pleasure it had given him.

Mill needed, for his purposes, another set of standards. He desperately wanted, in addition, a set of standards that would rank the pleasures of music *higher* than the pleasures to be squeezed from shares of railway stock or durable oak chairs.

He now developed an argument that satisfied him but gained few adherents among his contemporaries.

Insisting that it was "quite compatible with the principle of utility to recognize the fact, that some *kinds* of pleasure are more desirable and more valuable than others," he went on to say that we could always tell which of two pleasures was the higher by the number and kind of men who preferred it. Look for men of experience and note their choices. "If one of the two [pleasures] is, by those who are competently acquainted with both, placed so far above the other that they prefer it . . . we are justified in ascribing to the preferred enjoyment a superiority in quality." Because a great many thinking men think music better than mortgages, utilitarianism must hold music in high esteem.

The argument was an unlucky one because its proof was insubstantial. Instead of the objective measurement to which an acre of land might be submitted, we were offered subjective opinion. The position was unscientific: no laboratory could test it for honest weight. It was unphilosophical: the rigors of reason and the rules of evidence vanished before a vague reliance upon a vague authority. It was unbusinesslike: music could put up no real collateral for the time it wanted to mortgage, and the names offered as credit references were those of possibly insolvent dreamers. We were, in fact, now only a few words short of that television commercial which urges us to buy a product because "doctors everywhere" endorse it; and the kind of argument that is greeted with cynicism in the most ordinary living room was not the kind of argument calculated to persuade Mill's severely rational colleagues. The age was, increasingly, an age determined to reject all evidence that was not "scientific" evidence. In such an age, few men were going to accept Mill's "proof." Few did. Bentham's standards were sounder for the obvious reason that the profits they guaranteed were profits that could be seen, weighed, banked; and music could not survive them.

Mill came at his crusade in another way. Putting aside for a moment his confidence in what the best men have always held to be best, and still refusing to try to measure music as though it were so many yards of muslin, he made note of the fact that utilitarian writers were too much inclined to place the value of things "in their circumstantial advantages rather than in their intrinsic nature."

He had now turned over a hornet's nest, casual as his remark may seem. He had ventured to suggest that there were two forms of pleasure: the pleasure that might be taken out of a thing and the pleasure that might be taken in it.

This is no light play on words; it is vitally important. For Bentham all pleasure had been circumstantial. That is to say, a man's happiness did not depend upon the nature of the act he was performing or upon the nature of the object he was dealing with, but upon the incidental profit which *followed* from his performing the act or dealing with the object. A circumstance, by definition, is something that accompanies, or follows from, another thing.

Let us say that I inherit a house. The house itself, in utilitarian terms, is neither good nor bad; it cannot in its nature—in its shape, its size, its color—give me either pain or pleasure. The house is neutral. My pleasure, if I am able to get any, will come from what I do with the house that works to my advantage; it will come in the form of shelter, or prestige, or the profit from a sale. My pain, similarly, will stem from any secondary disadvantages the house may saddle me with; if my possession of it embarrasses me, socially or financially, then the house will have had, for me, unhappy consequences. Bentham is concerned only with consequences, not with any intrinsic quality the house may or may not possess (what matter that it is beautiful if I lose money on it?); and he is further concerned, as he stresses, only with *material* consequences. The conditions that produce pain and pleasure are all *external* conditions.

Bentham had been aware that there were such things as internal acts and that these acts did not always have consequences. A man might hold a thought, or a memory, or a fragment of melody in his mind and never do anything practical or profitable with it. Such acts, ruled Bentham, contributed nothing to human happiness. They did not provide a sufficient practical motive to drive the man dreaming over them into activity productive of material consequences. Unless the man with a tune in his head became a teacher of music, or a critic of music, or a publisher of music, he could not be called happy because he had not turned the tune to his concrete, demonstrable advantage. With acts that "rest in the understanding merely," concluded Bentham, "we have not here any concern."

Mill, who admired a great many acts that rested in the understanding merely, now proposed that all such acts, and all the attractive objects that tended to produce them, be regarded, simply and plainly and without further proof, as good in themselves. He proposed that these be described as *intrinsically* good —good in their shapes and colors, their sounds and textures, good simply because they existed—regardless of what extrinsic advantages they might or might not be persuaded to yield.

Mill was an admirable man urging a lost cause. The cause was lost because utilitarianism itself, when it was consistently applied, demanded proof positive and proof tangible of the pleasurable benefits conferred. "What is the use of it?" was Bentham's inflexible test question for determining the happiness quotient of any object or act. If no other test question was allowed, no experience that failed to meet it could be admitted. Further, use had to be documented, demonstrated beyond doubt.

That is why the next important philosopher to come along was quick to close the escape hatch Mill had been working so valiantly to construct. Mill had struggled to restore to a constricting society certain vanishing delights; William Stanley Jevons, made of sterner stuff, rejected them out of hand.

It is almost possible to hear, even at this distance, the ring of contempt with which Jevons disposed of Mill's contention that some objects and experiences were good in themselves.

"A student of Economy," he wrote in 1871, "has no hope of ever being clear and correct in his ideas of the science if he thinks of value as . . . anything which lies in a thing or object. . . . Persons are thus led to speak of such a nonentity as *intrinsic value*."

All value is extrinsic, outside things. Mill's intrinsically good world is an idle illusion. "Utility, though a quality of things, is *no inherent quality*." Neither pleasure nor profit resides in the actual house, the actual landscape, the object held lingeringly in the hand or the melody held lovingly in the mind. All pleasure and profit derive from the mathematical equations we are able to establish through the useful manipulation of our actions and objects. Utility is that "abstract quality whereby an object serves our purposes, and becomes entitled to rank as a commodity."

With Jevons' intransigence, the doorway to all of those experiences that do not rank as exchangeable commodities is finally sealed off. Speaking of a game of cricket, Jevons remarked that "if it be undertaken solely for the sake of the enjoyment attaching to it, we need scarcely take it under our notice. . . . we need not occupy our attention by cases which demand no calculus." The theory of utilitarianism is "entirely based on a calculus of pleasure and pain" and may best be described as "the mechanics of human interest."

As a twentieth-century man born to this philosophical heritage, 1 am offered a certain range of calculable pleasures. The range is quite wide. Nearly everything I do and nearly everything I own can, with some effort and some craft, be forced to yield a commodity value, provided that I am willing to live my life and manage my belongings with that uncompromising end in view. Commodity values exist in some depth, and I am morally free to seize all of them.

There is, for example, a small clay mask hanging on the wall of the room in which I work. It is one of thousands or perhaps hundreds of thousands made in ancient Greece to be placed, symbolically, in actors' graves. This one was taken from the grave of an actor who had died sometime in the third century B.C. Speaking as a utilitarian, and trying to be "clear and correct" about the matter, I must not say that my mask has any value in itself, simply as an object.

I am permitted, however, to attach many kinds of circumstantial value to it. If I choose to sell it for twenty-five dollars, and if I am able to find a buyer who is willing to pay me that much for it, I shall have succeeded in giving it a precise extrinsic value in terms of money. If I should find it useful in illustrating a book, I can assign it a circumstantial value in proportion to its importance in the scheme of the book; and if the book should sell enough copies, I might even be able to estimate its value, once again though infinitesimally, in money.

If it were only somewhat rarer I might be able to donate it to a museum—even as it is, one or another theatrical library might want it—and, by stipulating that my name be displayed near it as donor, I might make it earn me the profit of some small prestige. I can also keep it and, when we have visitors, carefully guide the attention of my guests to a curio I picked up while visiting Athens: if the extrinsic value of my mask is steadily becoming more difficult to compute, it remains an extrinsic value nonetheless—it is worth something to my ego to be able to place-drop in this way.

Circumstantial value may be subtler still. I may never show the object at all. I may keep it about me, and look at it now and then, because it is a theater mask, because it is Greek, and because I am interested in the Greek theater. I may retain it as an illuminating link to something I love. Now, for all the affection that seems to be slipping in here, I am still speaking of circumstantial value. I value the object not for what it is but for something it is not. It is not the Greek theater; it is a clay mask. I admire it, and I cling to it, out of enthusiasm for something that existed quite apart from it and that would have existed just as truly if the mask had never been made. The value that I give it lies in the circumstance of its relation to another thing to which I am already committed. My interest in it, then, is a self-interest, not a generous and disinterested recognition of such intrinsic properties as it might, in the mind of someone like Mill, have been thought to possess. The heart I bring to it is a secondhand heart.

I have deliberately refrained from describing the mask. The fact that one particular craftsman made one particular mask in one particular way has no bearing on its worth to me, except insofar as he made it attractive enough for me to sell or characteristic enough for a historian to use in explaining another reality that is dead and gone. Of what use is the precise curve of the slavering mouth, the thyroid bulge of two nearly-crossed eyes, the clot of the hair? What is it worth to me to see how these familiar, frenzied lines in poor old Silenus' face happen, perhaps just this once, to meet and tangle and flame like a burning bush? The peculiarities that make this mask *this mask*, and no other, both defy description and are not worth describing.

For in attending to them we should be talking of intrinsic value, of properties or accidents that are unique, independent, circumstantially unrelated to the self-interested activities of men. In its most intimate nature, secret and isolated from all the useful things that can be done with it, the mask—as Jevons tells me—is valueless. The private roughness of the clay in the hand, the strange shallowness of the impress upon it, the forward tilt of the matted locks that seem almost to turn into horns and to half hide the eyeballs beneath them—these are all, in themselves and apart from whatever future benefit may be practically extracted from them, nonentities.

Jevons was the man who made the unqualified pronouncement that *"value depends entirely upon utility,"* and though some men still professed shock at so absolute an assertion, and though Jevons is thought to have considered modifying its phrasing, the phrase continued to fly, banner-bright, at the head of his *Theory of Political Economy.* The phrase became, as it were, the last word, the conclusive word in a philosophical debate that had preoccupied one century and was about to occupy, in an almost military sense, the next.

Jevons had won; the utilitarian theory of value, in its strictest and most uncompromising sense, had won. "Value," as everyone knows whether he has consulted a dictionary or not, refers to worth, moral or monetary; it signifies whatever men hold to be estimable, important, worth doing or having. What twentieth-century man holds to be important and worth-while is usefulness, the profit that may be extracted from an experience or a possession. This is no crude justification he has made for his own greedy conduct. It is an ethic that has been handed to him, imposed upon him, in the guise of "clarity," "correctness," "reason," and "light"—and as an infallible guide in the pursuit of "pleasure." It is the truth in which he believes—not simply an economic truth, calculated to fill his home and his bank account with treasures, but a moral truth, calculated to fill his heart with a high sense of rectitude. When he does not put his every waking hour to useful pursuits, he is, socially, a poor citizen. When he wastes his time on acts that "rest in the understanding merely," he is, morally, guilty.

It is true that the utilitarian philosophy, writing its signature with a great final flourish in the last thirty years of the nineteenth century, was developed during a period in history that could not help feeling congenial to it. The period of its inception, debate, and resolution was also a period of flowering factories, rising exports, and ever-expanding rewards for mercantile enterprise. It is not surprising that a predominantly industrial age should have accepted, with very little murmuring, the sober announcement that the goods of this world constituted the good of this world and that felicity lay in the multiplication of commodities. Men and women working in such an age did not really have to wrestle with the notion as a philosophical concept; they could feel it in their bones.

But whatever they felt was honorably felt. The identification of the worth-while with the practically profitable was no mere matter of selfish, sensuous desire; indeed, sensuousness had all but vanished from the universe. It was a matter of conscience: stern, righteous, right-thinking. By the time the twentieth century had begun to realize that its productive machinery might also produce leisure, its conscience had been formed in a manner calculated to make leisure meaningless. The century could insist upon leisure as a profit of its labors. But it then had to find a profit in leisure itself.

It had arrived at a contradiction, an impasse, a tension between irreconcilable drives. It had nowhere to turn. Moral sanction had been withdrawn from all those indulgences that might have relieved the pressure. Worse still, the habits of delightful recreation had been lost. It is terribly difficult to give one's attention to an experience that is supposed to provide pleasure if the pleasure it is supposed to provide can be neither remembered nor quite imagined. One hundred years of progressive self-denial does more than damage the appetite; it alters the living tissue.

F. S. C. Northrup, in *The Meeting of East and West*, has summarized our hundred-year obeisance to the utilitarian premise by pointing out that " the modern British empirical philosophers and economists did actually neglect the aesthetic and emotional values" which might have been observed and savored in the otherwise useful world about them and that they did tend to turn all of the materials of this world "into mere counters

. . . for understanding and computing the course of prices in the market place.

"Thus," concludes Northrup, "the equally important aesthetic values . . . were lost, and the modern Western world fell into the very serious fallacy, to which the Marxians as well as the Anglo-Americans are heirs, of tending to identify the whole of human value with nothing but restrictedly utilitarian economic value."

A friend who dropped in to see me a few nights ago expressed two fears in the course of the conversation. One was that, if he did not slow down, he would have a heart attack. The other was that, if he did not hurry up, he would not be able to accomplish enough that was useful before he had his heart attack.

As vaudevillian Joe Cook used to say, "Does anyone in the house have a strait jacket?"

☼   *He is the Poet . . . unfit for any-*
thing except love, friendship and
ardor—a failure, therefore, in our
utilitarian age which pushes out onto
the fringe everything that is unpro-
ductive, that does not pay dividends.
A useless mouth to feed!

         —MICHEL DE GHELDERODE

The loss of the habit of "unprofitable" pleasure was gradual during the latter half of the nineteenth century, causing in some men a vague unease, in some artists a blind and flailing rebellion, in some institutions an awkward and baffled search for a fresh identity.

Bewilderment is the note struck everywhere. It is first heard, in rather a mild form, in a now well-known passage from Darwin's *Recollections*, written for his children. Recalling that music had once given him "intense pleasure, so that my back-bone would sometimes shiver," the celebrated naturalist went on to this somewhat disturbed confession:

"I have said that in one respect my mind has changed during the last twenty or thirty years. Up to the age of thirty, or beyond it, poetry of many kinds, such as the works of Milton, Gray, Byron, Wordsworth, Coleridge, and Shelley, gave me great pleasure, and even as a schoolboy I took intense delight in Shakespeare, especially in the historical plays. I have also said that formerly pictures gave me considerable, and music very great delight. But now for many years I cannot endure to read a line of poetry; I have tried lately to read Shakespeare, and found it so intolerably dull that it nauseated me. I have also almost lost my taste for pictures or music. Music generally sets me thinking too energetically on what I have been at work on, instead of giving me pleasure. I retain some taste for fine scenery, but it does not cause me the exquisite delight which it formerly did. . . .

"This curious and lamentable loss of the higher aesthetic tastes is all the odder, as books on history, biographies, and travels (independently of any scientific facts which they may contain), and essays on all sorts of subjects interest me as much as ever they did. My mind seems to have become a kind of machine for grinding general laws out of large collections of facts, but why this should have caused the atrophy of that part of the brain alone, on which the higher tastes depend, I cannot conceive. A man with a mind more highly organized or better constituted than mine, would not, I suppose, have thus suffered; and if I had to live my life again, I would have made a rule to read some poetry and listen to some music at least once every week; for perhaps the parts of my brain now atrophied would thus have been kept active through use. The loss of these tastes is a loss of happiness, and may possibly be injurious to the intellect, and more probably to the moral character, by enfeebling the emotional part of our nature."

It is charming to find Darwin suggesting that the decline in taste and the loss in happiness which he so laments need never have overtaken a better brain; and it is almost foolish to ask what was happening to less agile minds if this was happening to his. It is, however, possible to explain Darwin's surrender of his delight in Milton and Shakespeare, if not his confusion over the matter, on quite ordinary grounds: the man was a practicing scientist, and practicing scientists are apt to be the first—the fact is natural and unexceptionable—to lose interest in the mere playfulness of unscientifically-formed images.

If Darwin's decreasing fondness for music and increasing dependence upon historical and biographical fact puzzled him, it is probably because he felt that his being a scientist was not the whole explanation of the change taking place in him; he may have suspected that other men, like and unlike him, were feeling and noticing the mutation.

They were. It is astonishing to us to be told today that a hundred years before Darwin wrote, in the very reasonable eighteenth century, the most hardheaded of businessmen sometimes spent happy evenings at home translating Horace from the Latin or fashioning poetry of their own. On other evenings they might come together to exchange verses or play chamber music.

I do not want to exaggerate the ease with which a "retired stockbroker" like Anthony Chamier could accommodate himself to the company of such men as Oliver Goldsmith and Joshua Reynolds, or the unself-consciousness with which a prosperous brewer like Henry Thrale could invite to his house and, with his wife, manage to entertain the principal artists and intellectuals of his age. The eighteenth century was still an age of sharp cleavages: between the aristocrat and the tradesman, between the tradesman and the pauper. But it had not yet come to a rupture between the professional man and the practicing poet. When Dr. Johnson marched off to The Club—only later identified, in a more limited way, as The Literary Club—he meant to spend an evening in conversation not only with the scribblers whose working problems he shared but also with an assortment of clergymen, doctors, lawyers, and statesmen. These men, in turn, meant to spend the evening with Johnson and Goldsmith, Garrick and Reynolds; they were even prepared to be patient while Johnson dictated to them, and not on matters of syntax but on matters of statesmanship. To arrive at something comparable in our own time, we should have to imagine that William Faulkner, W. H. Auden, Aaron Copland, Fredric March, Willem de Kooning, Lyndon Johnson, Robert Oppenheimer, Thomas Dewey, Reinhold Niebuhr, Dr. Dana Atchley, and one of the vice-presidents of Merrill Lynch, Pierce, Fenner and Smith, perhaps with Leonard Lyons as their Boswell, were to meet regularly, drink heartily, and at all times give their greatest deference to the voices of Auden and Faulkner.

As I say, it is a temptation to idealize what went on over coffee, tea, or spirits in eighteenth-century London; it is also a temptation to make our own time seem more underprivileged than it is. Both temptations should be resisted, somewhat. Nevertheless, and for all that was crude and caste-ridden about it, the eighteenth century had not yet begun to think of the poet or painter as a person apart, or the things he produced as the province of specialists only. The painter was a man, a familiar about town, engaged in an entirely respectable occupation; and what the poet had published yesterday was as much a subject for discussion and debate as what Burke had read into the Parliamentary record yesterday. Politicians did not think painting beyond them; painters did not think politics beneath them. A degree of intercourse between men engaged in useful pursuits and men engaged in the production of fine objects was accepted as, at the very least, not unnatural; some mutual interest, relaxed and genial in spirit, could be assumed.

Indeed, if one voice tended to carry more weight than another, it might be the literary voice. A very old tradition had leaned in this direction, and its rightness had not yet been seriously questioned. From the time of Aristotle it had been felt that the useful arts were somewhat inferior to the fine arts and that men who dealt with practical matters, however wonderfully skilled they might be, possessed less in the way of "wisdom" than creative artists. Aristotle had explained the distinction quite simply. He began by pointing out that at the dawn of history the practical craftsman "who invented any art whatever" had been "naturally admired by men, not only because there was something useful in the inventions, but because he was thought wise and superior to the rest.

"But," he went on to say, "as more arts were invented, and some were directed to the necessities of life, others to recreation, the inventors of the latter [the arts of recreation] were naturally always regarded as wiser than the inventors of the former, because their branches of knowledge did not aim at utility." Utility was a necessary aim, but a lower one; the men who aimed at producing something no one needed but everyone loved may not have been cleverer men or shrewder men or more indispensable men, but they were wiser men. That the eighteenth century had not yet surrendered this ancient impression is evident from the fact that Samuel Johnson was free to bully some of the ablest practical minds of his generation. Put bullying to one side. It is evident from the mere fact that he was able to break bread with them.

Johnson found himself irritated when the dialogue between Parliamentarian and physician and poet was interrupted or curtailed by a busy man. Christopher Hollis, in his *Dr. Johnson*, tells us that the compiler of the first English dictionary met only one "forerunner of the modern busy man" in his lifetime. It is interesting, parenthetically, to note that this busy man was neither a brewer nor a stockbroker but a missionary-reformer. "John Wesley's conversation," Johnson said grumpily, "is good, but he is never at leisure. He is always obliged to go at a certain hour. This is very disagreeable to a man who loves to fold his legs and have out his talk as I do."

Johnson did not find Wesley disagreeable because Wesley was neither a poet nor a lexicographer. He did not find him disagreeable because their religious convictions clashed. He found him disagreeable because he was in a hurry, because he could not sit still long enough to make companionship possible, because he was eternally preoccupied with the urgencies of his work. Johnson himself blended well with all manner of men, many of whom were well below him in intellectual stature; the blend was in part accomplished by a folding of legs.

If Charles Darwin, a hundred years later, had known such a circle, he might have prevented the "atrophy" of his tastes by means of a little poetry or music "at least once a week" experienced in congenial company. But the circle had been, or was being, closed.

It was being closed, as we know, by a word. Until now, men in general had supposed that there were two kinds of arts: the useful arts and the fine arts. The useful arts, which may also be called sciences, embraced all of those skills or crafts by which men were governed or supported in the struggle for survival. Politics was such an art; so was cabinetmaking. The fine arts, on the other hand, tended to come into being only after survival was assured. They were a reward for stability, a gratification of the soul after all of the urgent work had been done; they were decorative and pleasurable and somehow satisfying to a side of man's nature that could not assert itself until the whole man had achieved repose. Neither branch of the arts excluded the other. One was necessary, the other delightful.

The distinction had not ended with Aristotle. Thomas Aquinas had drawn lines between what he called the "liberal arts" and the "mechanical arts," and he did not choose to refute the contention that "the liberal arts excel the mechanical arts." Three centuries later Francis Bacon was accepting the same terminology casually, and well into Dr. Johnson's own time the philosopher Immanuel Kant was still speaking of a "mechanical" art or science on the one hand and, "should the feeling of pleasure be what it has immediately in view," a "fine" art on the other.

The terminology varies slightly from age to age. The arts that satisfy a practical human need may be "mechanical" or "useful" or even "servile." The arts that look principally to delectation may be "fine" or "liberal" or, astonishingly, "free." (A fine art is free in the sense that it is not chained to utilitarian requirements: whereas a chairmaker is not free to make a beautiful chair on which no one can sit, a poet is at liberty to follow his inspiration and to create a poem quite unlike anyone else's preconceived notion of what a poem ought to be.)

Along with variations in terminology go variations in grouping. One man will think an art what another man considers a science, and an orphan like History may be shuttled back and forth forever. But the incidental divergences and disagreements had not, before the nineteenth century, destroyed a rough, common-sense understanding that there were two rather different things to be considered and to be separately honored: the crafts that served and the arts that enchanted. Indeed, the distinction was such an ordinary and obvious one, as Martin Turnell has remarked in *The Art of French Fiction*, that in earlier ages either a writer must have argued that the aim of literature was simply to please or he "might have had difficulty in prescribing an aim at all."

In the late nineteenth century, the balance, and the affection, between these two things was being destroyed because one term in the equation had insisted upon usurping the position of both. Of what significance was a distinction between the fine and the useful arts if only the useful could be called significant? If all value depended upon use, what place in the circle was left for the fine, the liberal, the free?

Given the philosophy that was then conquering the age, these questions were unanswerable, or answerable only with a heavyhearted "None," and the circle in which men of divergent pursuits had respectfully met now dissolved. It was a time in which men were turning their backs on one another, parting company firmly upon a matter of principle.

Those who were engaged in "useful" occupations found themselves more secure than they had ever been, elevated to a new position of distinction in the public mind. These were the truly productive men, the creators of wealth and the contributors to the commonweal, the solid citizens whose activities were demonstrably "worth while." If they could take pride in their clear priority in the fresh scale of values, they must also be prepared to pay the price of that pride: they must dissociate themselves firmly from men of unprofitable habits. It could be embarrassing for a responsible citizen to be found in the company of men of mere letters, or "aesthetes" as they were to be called when the separation of the workers from the drones had been accomplished. An industrialist might become quickly suspect if it were bruited about that he wasted his evenings over Latin; and the day was coming when a politician would find it helpful to boast that he had no patience with "eggheads" and to acknowledge confidently that he read nothing but paperback Westerns. The twentieth century was not very old before it found itself baffled by the inexplicable conduct of a man like Paul Claudel, now and then an ambassador, now and then a writer of verse; it could only wonder in which trade he had failed, and if he had not, because of his divided mind, necessarily failed in both.

When the productive men of the nineteenth century picked up their bowler hats and abandoned The Club forever, the writers and painters they left behind them had literally nowhere to go. The value of what *they* produced had been denied. The admittedly charming but hopelessly casual objects they offered for something other than sale were, in the philosophical terms of the time, nonentities, giving rise to acts that rested "in the understanding merely." Neither moral nor social justification could be granted them; from a wholly "useful" world the objects must be excluded as irrelevant and their makers outlawed as dilettantes.

The poet and his brethren now began their long, lonely journey to the outer edges of society, to the intellectual fringe and a new Bohemia, to the only company permitted them, the company of the clique. If Alexander Pope had all but tyrannized early eighteenth-century society, and tyrannized it with his verse, not more than three American poets in the midtwentieth century were to find themselves able to earn their keep by the art they practiced. The divorce, when it came, was not even friendly; the parties behaved as though they never wanted to see one another again. The utilitarians took the house and the aesthetes wandered off with the children.

It is surprising, by the way, that the universities should not have continued to make room for the liberal arts. The universities are, of course, their traditional home; and they have traditionally stood apart from the concerns of the commercial world and the emphasis upon commodity value. It may be thought that the universities did hold the line against the utilitarian ethic: no student goes to school today without taking courses in English and American literature, and the lettering on the façades of a good many campus buildings still reads "College of Arts and Sciences," with the arts listed first.

The evidence, like so much of the evidence upon which we base our contradictory and exhausting beliefs, is illusory. I do not mean to make anything in particular of the loss of Latin as a discipline; Latin is by now so thoroughly lost that any mention of it must seem old hat and die-hard. But we have spoken of the fact that as late as the eighteenth century some men continued to take a limited pleasure in it, and its fate in the "liberal arts" curriculum may be taken as symptomatic.

Latin is a dead language, though for a good many centuries after its formal death it did yield, in a curious way, a continuing profit to lawyers, doctors, and philosophers, as it still does to some theologians. The very fact that it was dead, that it was no longer subject to change, made it a peculiarly effective tool for achieving precision where precision was desperately wanted and where the shifting and blurring of meaning that constantly characterize any living language proved to be something of a disadvantage.

By the eighteenth century, however, the common tongues of most countries had achieved a stability sufficient for most such purposes—it will be remembered that Johnson himself compiled the first English dictionary—and Latin was losing its last claim upon the attention of the professional man. There was now only one reason for dabbling in it at all: the fact that one liked to, that one enjoyed listening to Ovid or Catullus, that one found something appealing in Latin even when one could take nothing practical from Latin.

But such a spontaneous and disinterested act of love was, in the eye and ethic of the nineteenth century, meaningless. As a consequence, the academic community found it less and less possible to justify the time and energy consumed by so unprofitable a discipline, and decade after decade saw its standing and its practice whittled away.

Latin teachers sparred a bit as the times closed in. Casting about for some likely defense of a pursuit to which they were committed, they hit upon the only argument likely to persuade twentieth-century man: they protested that Latin was useful, that, for instance, a knowledge of the language helped the ordinary student to grasp many English roots. But they were fighting the battle on enemy territory and in disguise: they were campaigning for Latin not as a liberal art but as a mechanical science. Utilitarians are not stupid; they saw through the pretext, exposed the profit as superficial, and the retreat of the Latinists continues to this day.

Literature has been luckier, not because of any greater liberality on the part of the universities, but because it succeeded in perfecting a better disguise. Through the procedures of textual criticism developed by the modern German mind, literature found a way of passing itself off as science. English courses, especially at the mature level, took up calipers, microscopes, and adding machines. Masterpieces were examined in their original printings, for printer's errors; texts were collated; pagination was questioned and recurring images were counted. The degree to which a student was thought to possess the work in hand came to depend upon the critics quoted, the references documented, the flurry of footnotes with which he crowded the text off the page. The aspect of literature that came to be studied at all was the aspect that could be subjected to scientific measurement and scientific proof—the aspect that was not, in itself, literary or imaginative but was factual and historical. A seminar in "bibliography and methods" became the basic graduate course. That this sort of investigation has had its practical uses cannot be doubted: through it works can be dated, authors identified, forgeries exposed, and certain mechanical features of technique analyzed. That it has bred in the student, or in the society to which he graduates, any passionate and enduring concern for the elusive interior life of the texts he has disemboweled may well be questioned. I have gone over a good many master's theses in my time; but I cannot remember ever coming upon one that suggested that its author had fallen in love. The fact of the matter is that the buildings on our campuses are now really "Colleges of Sciences and Sciences," and it is interesting to notice that wherever the arts do manage to survive as arts they are staffed by faculties filled with such profound feelings of embarrassed inferiority that they hasten to describe their subjects as the "Communications Arts," giving the program the metallic overtones of a scientific commitment and implying strongly that they are less concerned with poetry and drama than with decibels and wave lengths.

The practicing artists behaved better in the time of their excommunication than the professors did. They did not behave perfectly: no outlaw can. As they marched into the social wilderness to which a utilitarian world had condemned them, they permitted many of the things to happen to them that must happen to all outlaws. They became first introspective and then introverted; cut off from their fellows as they were, they became secretive and sometimes neurotic. It should surprise no one that vast areas of contemporary art employ a private language, insist upon subjectivity, deliberately refuse to communicate. The man to whom no one speaks is the man most likely to fall sick.

What is remarkable about the art that had been dismissed as "fine," and hence useless, and hence valueless, is the energy and courage with which it determined to reassert itself, in one way or another. Two ways were, in fact, tried. The first was a matter of simple assault, and the man who carried the colors with the greatest arrogance was Oscar Wilde.

Neither Wilde nor his late-nineteenth-century clansmen chose to question any of the premises on which utilitarianism rested. They accepted them all, defiantly. Had the new philosophy failed to find any "use" in fine arts? Very well. "All art is quite useless," declared Wilde. Had Bentham made the moral nature of an act entirely dependent upon its usefulness? Amen, crowed Mr. Wilde, "all art is immoral." Had poets been banished to outer darkness because they had "nothing to say" to busy and productive men? Splendid. If a poet "had something to say he would probably say it, and the result would be tedious." Let the poet say nothing and the rest of us do nothing, except, perhaps, listen to the pretty nothings the poet pronounces. "Let me say to you now that to do nothing at all is the most difficult thing in the world, the most difficult and the most intellectual." Besides, "industry is the root of all ugliness."

But what of society? Could it survive on such terms as these? Certainly not, admitted Wilde. Society is a rather grubby little organization that "demands, and no doubt rightly demands, of each of its citizens that he should contribute some form of productive labour to the common weal, and toil and travail that the day's work may be done." The difficulty is that no good will come of all this labor, or of society either, for that matter. "We live in the age of the overworked, and the under-educated; the age in which people are so industrious that they become absolutely stupid. And, harsh though it may sound, I cannot help saying that such people deserve their doom. The sure way of knowing nothing about life is to try to make oneself useful."

What Wilde is doing here is accepting the utilitarian understanding of the needs of society and then dismissing society itself as beneath contempt. In the urgency of his determination to reaffirm the glories of art, he has not tried to reacquaint society and art but has simply declared art to be above society, as "aesthetics are higher than ethics." But in placing art above society he has only continued to do what the utilitarians had done: keep art apart from society. We are moving now into the realm of what eventually came to be called "art for art's sake," art which does not pretend to possess any kind of value for mankind at large but is content to reveal "her own perfection" in the solitude of the closet or at most in the presence of those few choice souls who "are at once too cultured and too critical, too intellectually subtle and too curious of exquisite pleasures" to be concerned with life in the raw. Such art, Wilde acknowledged, "rejects the burden of the human spirit, and gains more from a new medium or a fresh material than she does from any enthusiasm for art, or from any lofty passion, or from any great awakening of the human consciousness."

The fireworks were jolly while they lasted, and it is still great fun to read the blithe and sometimes blistering dismissal of "the burden of the human spirit" that fills Wilde's essays "The Critic as Artist" and "The Decay of Lying." But these flashes of bravado are rockets fired by the damned as they cheerfully go down with the ship. They accept the divorce of the general run of men from the materials that might have pleased them, they condemn ordinary mortals to their no doubt necessary lot with the suggestion that they deserve no better, and they elevate the delightful objects they themselves so passionately admire to a position in the stratosphere that is distant, cool, and indescribably lonely. Wilde and Whistler and Pater —"pale, embarrassed, exquisite Pater!" Henry James called him—could look with horror upon the gray utilitarian scene and boldly proclaim their willingness to live where they had been placed: outside it. But they would not conceive the possibility that the deprived and the dispossessed might again be brought together.

This is fine art rampant and confessedly irrelevant. The position is admirable in its energy and regrettable in its resignation. Art has, in a single haughty breath, given the challenge and given up.

But we have mentioned only one of the responses art found itself capable of making in a frustrating situation. If some artists had decided to give up, others thought it might be best to give in. The second energetic claim made by those who had been outlawed from a "useful" society was that their work, too, was useful.

Thus began the effort to reinstate art in the good opinion of society by showing that it could be made to turn a social profit. The novel, for instance, need not confine itself to giving pleasure or even consider the giving of pleasure a matter of much concern: it could become a reporter of the contemporary scene, a political analyst, a spur to action. Zola now suggested that in the past the men of an undeveloped science had made the mistake of working as the poets did, out of guesswork and intuition; it was time, he said, for the poets to learn to work as the new scientists were doing, by piling fact upon fact until a statistically certain and hence useful truth could be arrived at. "The aim of the novel is not simply to describe," Zola said; "it must also correct." The "socially significant" novel had been born; its usefulness had given it its value.

Ibsen worked the same miracle for the theater. A play, too, could change the world, could assist in the political emancipation of women, in the rewriting of the marriage laws, in the rooting out of industrial corruption. There were quickly Ibsenites in England. Justice was examined, and its failures exposed, by John Galsworthy; one of the earliest studies of anti-Semitism came from the same playwright's hand. Bernard Shaw, confident that "in all my plays my economic studies have played as important a part as a knowledge of anatomy does in the works of Michelangelo," was just as certain that in a very short time audiences would be begging to be "tormented, vivisected, lectured, sermonized." People were becoming aware that these things were good for them, good in Bentham's moral sense, good in the sense that audiences could take something worth-while home with them. After all, they had taken a clear emolument home with them from performances of *A Doll's House;* they had been able to extract a practical profit from a practical play on the subject of the awakening of women. "The play solves that problem just as it is being solved in real life," Shaw said. Even Shakespeare might have bestowed upon mankind a far greater benefit if he had "begun where he left off."

This last thrust is both entertaining and illuminating, and I should like to quote a bit more of it from *The Quintessence of Ibsenism.* "Suppose," Shaw suggests, that Shakespeare "had been born at a time when, as the result of a long propaganda of health and temperance, sack had come to be called alcohol, alcohol had come to be called poison, corpulence had come to be regarded as either a disease or a breach of good manners, and a conviction had spread throughout society that the practise of consuming 'a half-pennyworth of bread to an intolerable deal of sack' was the cause of so much misery, crime, and racial degeneration that whole States prohibited the sale of potable spirits altogether, and even moderate drinking was more and more regarded as a regrettable weakness! Suppose . . . women . . . felt nothing but disgust and anger at the conduct and habits of Falstaff and Sir Toby Belch! Instead of Henry IV and The Merry Wives of Windsor, we should have had something like Zola's L'Assommoir."

Zola's *L'Assommoir* is a novel of a tenement block dominated by a distillery and of the distillery's oppressive and finally destructive effect upon the hopes, minds, and lives of all who exist within its reach. Now Shaw, for all his inability to resist the wink that would wipe from his face the pose of sobriety, truly thought the editorial comment of *L'Assommoir* more valuable to society than the no-comment "jollities" of Shakespeare and that if "the first performance of The Taming of the Shrew had led to a modern Feminist demonstration in

the theatre" we might have sooner, and most profitably, exchanged "the jest of Katharine and Petruchio" for the "earnest
of Nora and Torvald Helmer."

Shaw made a further comparison. To someone like Ibsen,
"every human being is a sacrifice," whereas to someone like
Dickens, "he is a farce." Taking delight in the farce of the
human condition is a wasteful occupation; taking thought for
the man who is sacrificed to a social evil, or for the man who
sacrifices himself to a social need, is, just as clearly, a profitable
one. The latter helps us to reform the evil, or, at the very least,
to understand the need. The playwright committed to revela-
tion and reform thus becomes a moral force in the best utilitarian sense, and his work acquires the commodity value of a
tract that produces results extrinsic to itself. The mind does
not rest in the work; it leaves the work ready to swing into
social action.

In the guise of a good utilitarian, Shaw went on to write
some delightfully irrelevant comedies: if it was sometimes hard
to find the precise social profit in the plays themselves, Shaw
could always insert the profit by pointing a moral in the pref-
aces he wrote for them. Shaw's conduct was, in the end,
wickedly deceptive: he produced some fine art while resolutely announcing that fine art was obsolete.

The men who followed him, deep into the twentieth century, followed their creeds more slavishly. In France Eugène
Brieux lectured, from his profitable dramatic platform, on such
matters as divorce, the birth rate, and venereal disease. "Had
I lived in the seventeenth century I would have been a
preacher," he said, "but now I write plays." In Russia Leo
Tolstoi, having produced two novels ranking among the unquestioned masterpieces of the form, turned on his own work
with a deep sense of guilt, decided that "art is not a pleasure,
a solace, or an amusement," and devoted the remainder of his
life and literary activity to moral reform. In Germany, once

World War I had played itself out, a band of dedicated young men hurled plays that looked and felt like crowbars at the heads of the industrialists, the politicians, the militarists. Ernst Toller, best known of the group, spoke bitterly of past ages that had failed to give birth to the "social drama," those "days when society indulgently tolerated the artist as a sort of luxury unrelated to the real business of living." For Toller the real business of living, and the real business of drama, was the elimination of all that unnecessary suffering which arises from the presence of an inadequate social system.

In America the drama of "social significance" lagged for a while, then flowered swiftly in the disturbed 1930s. Clifford Odets made his reputation with a play urging union men to strike, Lillian Hellman scored one of her greatest successes with a play urging American participation in World War II, Robert Sherwood advocated pacifism in *Idiot's Delight* and participation in *There Shall Be No Night*, and lesser men and women devoted themselves to the problems of racial discrimination and economic injustice. The Federal Theater arrived, during this time, at a form called The Living Newspaper, dramatized journalism concerned with such issues as public ownership of utilities and public responsibility for the effects of unsanitary housing. Before the thirties were out, the play that was not socially significant was dismissed as having no significance; the audience that could not be lured to the theatrical lecture platform was shrilly dismissed as "escapist." One had a moral obligation, a clear duty, in the theater and out of it. The duty in both places was the same: to work toward social justice.

Though a considerable distaste for the "message" play has developed in the postdepression, and particularly in the post-war, years, the American stage has found no alternate significance with which to replace a useful social significance. It has floundered, casting vainly about for values that might be con-

sidered important by a public conditioned to use; it has continued to bolster its otherwise irresponsible entertainments,
including its musical comedies, by inserting incidental gestures
toward social utility ("You've got to be taught to hate and
fear," sings the juvenile in *South Pacific*); moving nervously
away from politics, it has still sought to justify its existence in
the twentieth century by borrowing from the casebook of the
sociologist, investigating the perils of abortion and the inci-
dence of homosexuality at considerable length.

And the youngest and most vigorous of British theater critics, Kenneth Tynan, has recently undertaken a campaign to
return us to the political arena, not simply to the play which
has politics for a theme, but to the play which has politics for
a purpose. Having learned "from men like Bertolt Brecht and
Arthur Miller . . . that all drama was, in the widest sense of
a wide word, political," Mr. Tynan now believes that the
theater is "a branch of sociology as well as a means of self-
expression."

Indeed, if there is one name in the theatrical-literary firma-
ment that stirs excited conversation among younger critics and
directors today, it is that of Brecht, the German-born, Rus-
sian-oriented inventor of a technique called "alienation" and
a dramatic style described as "epic." "In this scientific age,"
biographer Martin Esslin explains, "Brecht wanted his audience to experience some of the exaltation felt by the scientist
who has uncovered one of the mysteries of the universe." In
order to accomplish this, "from the time of his final conversion
to Marxism in the late twenties he endeavored to make his
writing a scientific activity, a series of controlled experiments
devoted to the elucidation of social relations and to the trans-
formation of society, by producing strictly calculated, socially
useful responses in the audience. . . . the audience is to be confronted with a body of evidence from which it is to draw its
conclusions in a critical, highly lucid state of mind."

"All the plays of Brecht's maturity," adds H. F. Garten in *Modern German Drama*, are "parables designed to illustrate [Marxist] doctrine. The subordination of artistic values to political objects implied the conscious renunciation of those poetic qualities which distinguished his earlier, pre-Marxist writings. . . . whenever his innate poetic power broke through it did so almost in spite of himself." Brecht's purpose remained, in Esslin's words, the production of "socially useful emotions such as indignation at injustice, hatred of oppressors, or an active desire for the overthrow of the existing social order." The age, then, of the propagandizing that Shaw thought would have improved Shakespeare is by no means over.

It is probably not over in the other arts, either, though it is some time since painting professed to find its worthiest end in the muscular political symbolism of a Diego Rivera, and just as long since Bartolomeo Vanzetti's "Last Speech to the Court" was thought to belong in an anthology of poetry side by side with William Rose Benét's "Jesse James." Difficult as it is to detect an ideological deviation in a musical phrase, the Russians continue to do so: symphonies composed by men of genius are rewritten to bring them into closer conformity with the latest political "reality," and, lest it be thought that Americans indulge in no such foolishness, the American government refuses to export certain home-made musicals on the grounds that the "value" judgments they contain, so useful as correctives at home, may be put to prejudicial political use abroad. In general, art has successfully acquired a reputation for social utility, whether one looks with favor or disfavor upon a particular result of its labors.

I have wished to indicate a considerable admiration for the energy with which art and artists responded to a fiat that tended to exclude them from the living, breathing, working community. With the triumph of an ethic that held all value to depend upon use, it had become imperative for every human activity to display its unequivocal usefulness. Oscar Wilde's rebellion, attractive as it was in many ways, could not and would not do this for art: accepting and even glorying in the division between society on the one hand and sensibility on the other, it made the breach greater, the public poorer, and art more precious in the suspect sense of that term.

The "social" novelists, dramatists, poets, and painters did negotiate a kind of surrender, did agree to conform to the new single standard. But their compromise accomplished something. It readmitted the artist, even if on a somewhat servile basis, to the community; it kept some of the forms, and some of the techniques, of art within reach of the busy and conscientious modern man; if it did not precisely renew an old friendship, it nevertheless maintained a nodding, and sometimes argumentative, acquaintance. Survival at some level was assured because art had proclaimed its utility and promised practical assistance in the urgent work of the moment: it would forego its old emphasis upon pleasure and help to analyze, to debate, and to solve such problems as continued to bedevil an imperfect, though profitably engaged, world.

Art had, as a consequence, kept a roof over its head. But for the man who rather liked certain of the arts, or wanted to like them, a fresh problem had arisen. Whenever he found time to come to the arts, he was coming from his work and to his leisure. But whenever he picked up such a book, or listened to such a play, or looked at such a painting, he found himself back at his work.

3

A Danger and Its Calling Card

> . . . was I made for this, to lay me down, and make much of myself in a warm bed?
>
> —MARCUS AURELIUS

Instead of berating the man who works all of the time, we should pause to salute him. He is devoting himself without interruption to an activity that has always been possessed of great dignity. "In the morning," wrote Marcus Aurelius, "when thou risest unwillingly let this thought be present—I am rising to the work of a human being."

The human being who is profitably busy can respect himself: in addition to what he is doing for the welfare of his immediate family, he is giving his own private nudge to the national economy and he may even, in certain circumstances, be contributing to the increase of knowledge that is so imperative if the economy is to grow and the nation to survive. He may, in one sense, be enjoying himself as he makes these creative movements. If he is not enjoying himself freely, as Huck Finn might have enjoyed himself now and then on the raft, and if he is conscious of being constricted by his time-tables and weighed down by his tools, he can take a considerable satisfaction in the size of his accomplishment. Even when the accomplishment does not seem altogether stable, or the satisfaction deeply personal, there is an impersonal glory to be derived from serving—in Bentham's phrase—the greatest good of the greatest number. For one human being to devote his days and his nights to the hoped-for happiness of all other human beings is by no means despicable.

Furthermore, the time in which we live seems to offer no alternative. History races ahead of us just now: continents are unexpectedly roused from their sleep, the earth's population suddenly promises to run wild, the moon has been touched and not by us, a rival political system is in the ascendancy, the very globe on which we work may be rocked from its orbit. This is not, we sensibly feel, the moment for idleness. Small matter that some of us have quite enough to eat for the moment and are even worrying about eating too much; without instant, constant, and massive labor at all practical and theoretical levels each bite we eat may be the last we are granted.

Plato spoke for us. "What will be the manner of life," he asked in the seventh book of his *Laws*, "among men who may be supposed to have their food and clothing provided for them in moderation, and who have entrusted the practice of the [crafts] to others, and whose husbandry . . . brings them a return sufficient for men living temperately? . . . To men whose lives are thus ordered, is there no work remaining to be done which is necessary and fitting, but shall each one of them live fattening like a beast?

"Such a life is neither just nor honourable," he answered, "nor can he who lives it fail of meeting his due; and the due reward of the idle fatted beast is that he should be torn in pieces by some other valiant beast whose fatness is worn down by brave deeds and toil."

We do have a clear and intelligent fear that "some other valiant beast" may, even as we fret, be working harder and more efficiently than we are; only by doubling our labor can we hope to catch up. "Night and day are not long enough," Plato warned us, for the necessary work of nourishing the body and educating the soul, "and therefore to this end all freemen ought to arrange the way in which they will spend their time during the whole course of the day, from morning till evening and from evening till the morning of the next sunrise." Toil around the clock is called for; we cannot even be sure that so much single-mindedness, and so much dedication, will turn the trick.

Our total absorption in work, then, is justified on several counts: work is worthy of a man, it is satisfying to a man, it is the unavoidable duty of a man in times like these. There may be only one thing to be said against our generous willingness to undertake the labors of Hercules and Sisyphus together without rest or regret; there is always the danger that unrelaxed pressure on a tool may break the tool, in which case the work will not get done.

We need not concern ourselves long with the most obvious aspect of this danger: the chance that the man at the wheel will crumple, losing control of his muscular power, his nervous responses, and the wheel. We know that such catastrophes do occur and that no death-wish need be involved. I once talked for a few minutes, on the steps of a sanitarium, with a man who had been a bookkeeper: he was pleasant, he seemed calm and coherent, and he explained that one morning the column of figures he was accustomed to working with had simply meant nothing to him; though he was normal enough in every other way, the significance of numbers had fled from him.

This silent and invisible rebellion sometimes becomes noisy and visible. The newspapers will always let us know when the president of a railroad has blown out his brains or a high government official has hurled himself through a window, just as the gossips will keep us informed of the prominent playwright's latest visit to a mental institution. "Crack-up" is a slang term that has made itself quickly and intelligibly at home in the twentieth-century vocabulary.

But the backlash that is forceful enough to lead to self-destruction or even partial incapacity is relatively rare. The human intellect is incredibly resilient, even stronger and more resilient than the physical constitution that houses it. We have had, and will have again, prodigies of industry whose fibers never fray. We have had damaged constitutions whose disabilities seemed to liberate, rather than imprison, the minds they played host to. We have had spectacular evidence of the human animal's recuperative powers: after all, John Stuart Mill was once more in possession of his energies after a mere two years, and perhaps wiser for the experience. Unlike machines, men can be repaired from within. And when they cannot be satisfactorily repaired, they can be replaced: society is prodigal at throwing up reserves, and nature itself is not instantly dismayed at the lemming-like loss of vast numbers who have overtaxed their private resources. For a very long time, there are more where the last battalions came from. Men break down, and the experience is privately, sometimes publicly, painful; but the likelihood that a great many men will break down at a moment of great crisis is encouragingly remote.

The most obvious danger is not necessarily the greatest. The abrupt disintegration of a few, for instance, would not be half so alarming as the progressive disillusion of the many, as a steady loss of faith in the hearts of men standing firmly at their tasks. Damage done to the constitution is not so irreparable as damage done to the will; nervous exhaustion is not so serious as the exhaustion of personality.

Is there any sign that the perpetual pursuit of a very real profit may produce such a secondary, and insidious, infection? I think so. The contemporary evidence seems to suggest that something other than an occasional crack-up threatens us, that we are more widely menaced by a near-universal ennui, an ennui rooted in a contradiction. Even as we hurl ourselves feverishly into more and more work, we are quietly aware of a stirring nausea, of a faintly sickening distaste for the work we must do, the world we must do it in, and the selves we must live with while we are doing it. But before we can ask why this should be so, we had better see what the evidence is.

The twentieth century has gone about its chores with a clear conception of where value lies. Value lies in the extraction of use or profit from the available world, whether it is the world of farm produce or familiar faces, of interlocking directorates or plays to be seen. The century has given all of its time and all of its energy to this work, the constant and apparently limitless accretion of value. Now, in the 1960s, as it studies its own image in whatever mirrors it can lay hand upon, it sees no values at all.

Let me give you a few examples from the mirror I know best, which is the mirror of the theater, though it should be plain enough in a moment that the other means we have of looking at ourselves also show us the same drained mask. The arts are good mirrors, because they must be. No matter how urgently the artist may wish to pierce the contemporary surface and draw us with him toward a reality so profound that it is universal and timeless, he is obliged to begin by saying "How do you do?" The journey commences in an act of recognition, a handshake; artist and auditor must have the same cut of clothes, know how to get to the same restaurants, read with the same bifocals. The meeting takes place in a common clubroom, where all of the members hold the very same views, having been born in the same years, served through the same wars, married the same wives, and told the same jokes. The artist who presented himself as a total stranger, or issued his invitation in totally unintelligible terms, would have no hope of gathering passengers for his conducted tour. He is himself a man of his time and has certain sunspots to show for it; he introduces himself by showing them—by displaying the marks he and his companions in time share—in order, a little later, to try to show something more.

This may seem a strange thing to say in an age which has covered the walls of its most progressive museums with what appear to be severed intestines, run-over rubber dolls, abandoned jelly beans, and voids into which ink has been spilled; but it is the very point to which I have been so slowly coming. When we look at these paintings and say that we loathe them, as we so often do, we are not really deceived. These surfaces are not unintelligible, or even unfamiliar. They look like us, as we are secretly convinced we are. That is why we loathe them.

Those Stuart Davis streets from which depth has vanished, or in which an anti-perspective threatens to curl forward into our faces, are our streets, make no mistake about it. There was first shock, then humor, then a dismissive silence a few years ago when an exhibition of contemporary sculpture, gathered from all over the world, was held in New York City. As though the shapes had all come from the mind of a single man, they were uniformly bowed, cowed, curved to the womb. The surfaces were not baffling, though they might have been to a Greek in the springtime of Pericles or even to the very young Picasso.

I said I would speak of twentieth-century man's image of himself as the theater now shows it back to him. Here is the Swiss dramatist Friedrich Duerrenmatt's carefully polished reflection of the values modern men live by:

Into a small contemporary community comes a former resident of the community, a woman who was long ago "wronged" by a local official, who is thirsting to revenge herself on that now respectable and rather commonplace fellow, and who is at last possessed of the power to do it. The power is, in this instance, money. The woman is prepared to stimulate the faltering economy of the village on one condition: that its residents jointly murder their friend, the official.

The residents, quite naturally, make an initial show of pious revulsion. What, kill dear, familiar, fumbling old Anton simply to sell a little more bread, build a few more factories? And kill him in cold blood, as though he were an impersonal factor in a necessary equation? They will not do it—not, at least, until they have thought it over for a few minutes. Having given the matter their considered attention, they gather in the town hall and stomp Anton to death with their boots.

The Grand Guignol aspects of Duerrenmatt's *The Visit* are not important, except as they add theatrical shock to a point that is already shocking enough. Nor do we need to be told at this late date that the love of money is the root of all evil. What identifies the Duerrenmatt theme as an original and contemporary one is that it is ready to describe the love of money as the root of all virtue or, rather, as the only virtue intelligible enough to move modern man into worth-while action. Commodity value is at once understood, everywhere. Such values as might have been set in the scale against it—personal loyalty, human affection, respect for life as a value in itself—are not quite real, certainly not real enough to warrant their interfering with what is so plainly the common good.

The Visit has been successfully performed on the Continent, in England, on Broadway, and across America. Some theatergoers, of course, have not liked it. I have not yet met, however, anyone anxious to tell me that he did not believe it. The only forthright defiance of the image I have encountered came from an executive of a large manufacturing company which had been asked to sponsor the play for television; this clearheaded gentleman declined the opportunity on the grounds that the objective of his company, and hence the objective of any television show it might sponsor, was to make money. He did not say that he did not understand the play; on the contrary, he was convinced that a good many people would understand it and perhaps feel momentarily disinclined to rush to the market place. Elsewhere, when faces have been averted from M. Duerrenmatt's insistent implications, they seem to have been averted not in anger or challenge but in mild distaste, a distaste composed partly of the uneasy fear that these things are probably so and partly of uncertainty about how they might ever be altered. On what grounds does one defend a value that produces no clear emolument or that runs counter to a clear emolument?

England's famous "angry young men" are most articulate, and they are prepared to show us in scathing and often exhilarating terms where value is not. In such a lively specimen of the school as John Osborne's *Look Back in Anger*, even more successful in New York than in London, restless candy-store proprietor Jimmy Porter specifies the social forms that have provoked his contempt: the state has failed him, education has failed him, literature has failed him, and friendship can move out any time it likes. But Jimmy Porter never specifies the social form he thinks might satisfy him. He cannot imagine one. Value of any sort eludes him. If he is unable to believe in old values, he is unable to conceive new ones. He is not a weakling; he is a virile young man fairly bursting with energy. But his energy has nowhere to go but to his tongue, and the adderlike strike of his tongue is directionless: it does not leap to demolish ancient loves in order to clear living space for a new and brighter love just coming over the horizon; the horizon is empty. This is virility in a vacuum, expending itself as venom. And it is not so much the sins of the fathers, as the sense of the vacuum, that makes Jimmy so angry.

In Jean Genêt's *The Balcony* three nondescript men hire prostitutes to provide them with values they do not, and can never really, possess. One hires a girl to dress him in bishop's robes and to conduct herself as a penitent. One asks his companion of the moment to pose as a thief so that he may pass sentence upon her from beneath a judicial wig. The third, of military bent and in need of a horse, persuades his brothel hireling to canter and to whinny. When a revolution overtakes the unnamed city and all of the former authorities have been swiftly executed, it is no trick at all to persuade these costumed nonentities to assume ecclesiastical, judicial, and military command or to persuade the populace that the succession is perfectly meaningful. Value in the modern world, according to M. Genêt, resides not in the man who wears the robe or in the institution that has designed the robe as its symbol but in the negotiable robe itself. Value is extrinsic, abstract, marketable, and a fraud.

If it is difficult to find potent value in human relationships, in familiar social forms, or in the apparatus of duly constituted authority—in the heart of man or in the hundred houses he has built for himself—may there not still be some redeeming or restorative value waiting to nourish him in the house he did not build himself, in the universe he was born to?

Samuel Beckett doubts it. Didi and Gogo, two likable vagabonds, sit in purposeless patience beside a nearly barren tree during the standstill time of *Waiting for Godot*. They speak, of course, as they wait for someone, or something, that never comes:

". . . things have changed here since yesterday."

"Everything oozes."

"Look at the tree."

"It's never the same pus from one second to the next."

"The tree, look at the tree."

"Was it not there yesterday?"

"Yes of course it was there. Do you not remember? We nearly hanged ourselves from it. But you wouldn't. Do you not remember? . . ."

"And all that was yesterday, you say?"

"Yes of course it was yesterday."

"And here where we are now?"

"Where else did you think? Do you not recognize the place?"

"Recognize! What is there to recognize? All my lousy life

I've crawled about in the mud! And you talk to me about scenery! Look at this muckheap! I've never stirred from it!"

"Calm yourself, calm yourself."

"You and your landscapes! Tell me about the worms!"

In another Beckett play, *Endgame*, while a paralyzed man sits at center stage staining himself with his urine because his catheter has not been brought to him, and while two of his already discarded forebears repose rather too symbolically in twin ash cans, the last servant left in the world climbs a ladder to a very high window to look out. He uses a telescope and reports what he sees. What he sees in the universe beyond this festering cesspool is "Zero . . . zero . . . zero."

Very well. Contemporary man finds himself, his social activities, and his home beneath the stars lacking in value. Isn't he still possessed of a compass that will enable him to continue the search? Hasn't he the powers of reason to guide him?

According to Eugene Ionesco, reason itself is a trick man plays on himself. In a play called *The Bald Soprano* the doorbell rings several times. Each time Mrs. Smith goes to answer it there is no one there. Mrs. Smith arrives at a rational conclusion, based upon her experience: "When one hears the doorbell ring it is because there is never anyone there." A little later, when the doorbell rings again, *Mr*. Smith answers it. He discovers a Fire Chief on his doorstep. He now arrives at his own equally logical deduction: "Each time the doorbell rings there is always someone there." Each conclusion is proper for the person who has arrived at it, and each cancels the other out.

Ionesco's plays are built upon successive cancellations. The Smiths have a friend named Bobby Watson. He is married to a woman named Bobby Watson. "Since they both had the same name, you could never tell one from the other when you saw them together." But (Mrs.) Bobby Watson is precisely described. "She has regular features and yet one cannot say that she is pretty. She is too big and stout. Her features are not regular but still one can say that she is very pretty. She is a little too small and too thin." Now that (Mr.) Bobby Watson is dead, it is fortunate that the couple had no children. A disturbing question haunts their friends, however: Who is to take care of the children?

The question in Ionesco's "anti-dramas" is never "What is true?" but "How is anyone ever to know what is true when his equipment for discerning the truth is in itself essentially absurd?"

Something more than the reasoning process is called into question. The very tools that the reasoning process makes use of are suspect. Words, for instance, are so hopelessly without meaning that they may be run together like colors on a palette without any real loss of significance. Since they were ambiguous to begin with, a further blurring is going to do them no damage:

"Mice have lice, lice haven't mice."
"Don't ruche my brooch!"
"Don't smooch the brooch!"
"Groom the goose, don't goose the groom."
"The goose grooms."
"Groom your tooth."

As words are mocked in this passage from *The Bald Soprano*, so even the lowly letter that helps to make up the word is denied its identity in Ionesco's *The Lesson*:

"I had a friend . . . who suffered from a rather serious defect in his pronunciation: he could not pronounce the letter *f*. Instead of *f*, he said *f*. Thus, instead of 'Birds of a feather flock together,' he said: 'Birds of a feather flock together.' He pronounced filly instead of filly, Firmin instead of Firmin, French bean instead of French bean, go frig yourself instead of go frig yourself, farrago instead of farrago, fee fi fo fum instead of fee fi fo fum. . . ."

With reason reeling, words dissolving, and even ƒ proclaiming that it is at once ƒ and not ƒ, gibberish is near. It is, in fact, at hand. Toward the end of the first act of *Waiting for Godot* a speech ends: "unfinished the skull the skull in Connemara in spite of the tennis the skull alas the stones Cunard tennis . . . the stones . . . so calm. . . . Cunard . . . unfinished. . . ." And when, in Ionesco's *The Chairs*, the savior who is to bring the message of life to one and all does finally arrive, his message is this: "He, mme, mm, mm. Ju, gou, hou, hou. Heu, heu, gu gou, gueue."

The collapse of value is now complete, so complete that it will no longer be possible to spell the word "v-a-l-u-e," let alone pretend that this particular combination of irrelevantly grouped letters is a coherent sign for any experience of life. If the value of the universe is "zero," the term "zero" is also valueless.

Is this an extravagant vision for talented men to be holding up to us as though it accurately mirrored the state of our minds and hearts? Is this doubt *our* doubt, this fear *our* fear?

The grotesque image is, for the moment, exaggerated. We still answer the doorbell with some confidence that someone has rung it. We still mail letters feeling relatively certain that the postman will not read "Illianda" or even "Indiana" for "Illinois." Our expectations are cheerier than that: P. G. Wodehouse reports that he flings properly stamped and addressed envelopes out of his fourth-floor-apartment window in the hope that an honest man with a generous heart will pick them up and mail them for him, and his hope has never yet been disappointed.

In selecting the examples I have given above, I have moved

away from the relatively optimistic, relatively benign, face of Broadway—though four of the five playwrights quoted have in fact been seen on Broadway—to the traditionally darker visage of the experimental, and very often coterie, stage. But before we dare dismiss the hobgoblin despairs of Genêt and Ionesco as though they were little more than iconoclastic fantasies coined by irresponsible cynics, we had best look around us a bit.

Looking about, we quickly discover that this "experimental" theater, so often housed in cellars and patronized by cultists, is not so much avant-garde as a good twenty years behind the times. When Emily Genauer, art critic for *The New York Herald Tribune*, visited a Broadway performance of *Waiting for Godot* and came away dismayed, her dismay was aimed not at anything obscure in Mr. Beckett's play but at its rather tardy imitativeness; in Miss Genauer's view Mr. Beckett had barely caught up with the Dadaist canvases of the early 1920s.

The theater is, by nature, a laggard institution. Because it does not speak in private to a single intelligence but is obliged to communicate at once to all levels of intelligence gathered at random in a public meeting place, it is slow to acknowledge what is most lately in the wind, eager to cling to commonplaces that are familiar to everyone. The commercial theater of Broadway shares this circulatory sluggishness with its off-Broadway brother and adds a further retard of its own: its massive economic burdens make it very careful to continue to appeal to the expense-account trade while it is tentatively soaking up fresh insights. This snail's rate is not always a disadvantage: by the time Broadway has found a way to translate what the avant-garde has been saying into terms acceptable to a buyer from Des Moines, it may also have pared from the statement much that was merely show-offish about it, may have refined it and discovered its relevance to a broader, older, continuing tradition.

No one who has seen the plays of Eugene O'Neill or Tennessee Williams needs to be told that the old order continues while the new takes shape. O'Neill used the vigorous melodrama that had kept an earlier generation awake as a kind of guarantee of theatrical good faith; into its ancient pattern of rousing excitements he steadily wove something that was not rousing at all, a thread of hopeless disillusion, an assurance that all illusions were lies. Williams has made so many concessions to "blockbuster" effects that he is not content to let others criticize him for his audience-baiting; instead, he is quick to criticize himself. His concern for keeping his plays running, however, has not kept his plays from saying what they mean: contemporary society is riddled with "mendacity"; most men live lies; the man who would seek a value that is not already corrupted must leave society and even the earth he walks on, taking wing into the heavens like some mythical bird. Even Broadway has noticed the sickening insubstantiality of the universe beneath our feet.

Still, the theater's pain over the loss of value is only now coming to the fever pitch that painting and poetry and music recorded, like mirrors in a sickroom, so very long ago. How long ago was it that music listened to the heartbeat of twentieth-century man and heard dissonance? When was it that dimension vanished from canvases and faces flattened out, as though—if I may misappropriate a phrase of Margaret Kennedy's—modern men and women were suddenly aware of "a chaos of buses running over them for no reason at all"? When were the following lines written?

> *We are the hollow men*
> *We are the stuffed men*
> *Leaning together*
> *Headpiece filled with straw. Alas!*
> *Our dried voices, when*
> *We whisper together*

Are quiet and meaningless
As wind in dry grass
Or rats' feet over broken glass
In our dry cellar. . . .

They were written in 1925, and by the most influential poet of our time. T. S. Eliot had, in fact, handed us the phrase by which we know our way home, "The Waste Land," three years earlier.

The macabre excerpts I have given from a handful of plays, then, do not constitute a very advanced, or even an especially jaundiced, view of our case. They are not outrageous innovations at the beginning of a form; they are closer to echoes near the end of one. When that ten o'clock scholar, the theater, has got round to hearing the news, the news is likely to be yesterday's, and common gossip.

It should be stressed, before going on, that the impotent people and empty places that have come to constitute the cast of characters and the *mise en scène* of so much contemporary art are not simply the ugly end-products of a bad art. All of the arts have indeed been damaged in some degree by their isolation; they have nervous tics, and occasional hallucinations, to show for it. Much bad art is produced, as always. But art is helpless in its good habits: it cannot resist the impulse to show back to the world the spiritual face the world actually possesses. It has no other materials to work with but the reality that is there to be seen. We are all of us perfectly free to say that we dislike much modern art; but we are not instantly free to fault the artist, as though he had been faking. Faking a universe is a hard thing to do; the artist is much too dependent upon us for his inspiration. As Rene Huyghe has remarked in his *Ideas and Images in World Art*, "Psychology is well aware that the imagination never creates *ex nihilo*." From the cut of our clothes to the slant of our souls we are sitting to have our portraits done. They may be well done.

Harold Rosenberg has made this clear in *The Tradition of*

the New. It is often the practice, Mr. Rosenberg observes, to attempt to comfort those laymen who are honestly distressed in the presence of contemporary painting by assuring them that, as is sometimes the case, the work in question is "vacuous and deranged." It is simply not pertinent to offer such solace, he continues, "without giving those laymen a hint of their own abstractness and inner isolation."

But it is not necessary, I find, to appeal to the professional critic of painting for such home truths. I recently listened to the seriously impatient protestations of an attractive, well-balanced, happily married young mother, strident across a dinner table. That a visit to a gallery had put her on edge was perfectly plain. But the edge had been sharpened to a far finer point by hearing the very paintings she had recoiled from dismissed out of hand by others at the table. "Of course I don't like them!" she stressed with some heat. "But why do you talk the way you do about them? That's the way things *are!*"

The situation is exceedingly odd. We have given up what used to be our pleasures in exchange for a set of assured values, only to discover that the values have vanished in the course of the transaction and that our old pleasures—when we glance back at them—merely confirm the void.

Our former friends do not, of course, mean to mock us. If anything, they would probably like to save us, which may be why they press so hard. Is there anything to be learned from the mirror on the wall?

☼   *I lost touch. I lost such touch.*

—Arnold Weinstein

The commonest word applied to contemporary art is "abstract." Why should this be so? How is it that artists in every medium have agreed, virtually to a man, that the proper manner of mirroring the modern mind and the modern world is in terms of lines, planes, shapes, and even conversational exchanges from which everything concrete and—as we say—lifelike has been removed?

Given our beliefs, we should have expected nothing else. For we have long since subscribed to a habit of thought, and a pattern of living based on that habit of thought, which holds that only what is abstract is worth-while. We shall have to quote Jevons again. Jevons, steadily maintaining that all value depended upon utility, further defined utility as "the abstract quality whereby an object serves our purposes."

What does this mean? Put as simply as possible, and remembering our earlier inquiries, it means that the value we are permitted to attach to an object does not come from, or reside in, the object. The concrete, solid, "lifelike" object, as it exists in nature, is, by definition, worthless. No question of value arises at all until the object has been bartered for something else and so been made one-half of a mathematical equation. And it is only in the equation—in the abstract formula—that value of any kind is to be found.

Thus an ounce of gold is not valuable to us because it is hard, glittering, pretty, or even rare. Indeed, the ounce of gold, as such, never acquires any value for us at all. "If a ton of pig-iron exchanges in a market for an ounce of standard gold, neither the iron is value, nor the gold; nor is there value in the iron nor in the gold."

Where we discover value, suddenly and happily, is in the transaction whereby x amounts of gold may be traded for y amounts of some other desirable material. But we are now in danger of honoring the transaction itself too much. It is not the actual exchange of objects, the passing from hand to hand of solid things, that holds value in suspension and bestows it upon the things exchanged. The gold does not grow rich in the act of being handed over. The new thing I possess has no more natural worth in it than what I have surrendered; the physical manipulation in the middle of the market place has no special magic about it. Value is in neither the objects traded nor the act of trading. It is in the wholly abstract, perfectly bloodless and perfectly goldless concept that $x = y$. The precise location of every kind of worth is in the disembodied ratio and in the disembodied ratio alone. To cite Jevons once more, and then have done with him, "the word Value, so far as it can be correctly used, merely expresses *the circumstance of its exchanging in a certain ratio for some other substance.*"

Is it really surprising that the walls of our galleries and the walls of our homes should be covered with ratios? We have, out of sincere conviction, made a way of life for ourselves, and a way of looking at ourselves and the world around us, in which nothing is meaningful to us except the single proposition that $x = y$. That our faith in the validity of the proposition should have enabled us to get our work done, and to get it done with extraordinary efficiency, was to be expected. The effectiveness of our work always has depended upon such formulas and always will. Making x dollars equal y hours of labor or x acres equal y bushels of corn is a practical necessity.

But what happens as we walk away from our work with our heads still filled with the conviction that *all* value depends upon making x equal y? The friend I meet in a bar for a quick one before going home is named Harry Jones. Harry himself is both unique and concrete, so distinctly an individual that I may like him or dislike him upon purely personal grounds, so solidly there that I can slap him on the back or punch him in the nose. In my inherited scheme of things, however, value lies neither in uniqueness nor in concreteness, and before I can have anything to do with Harry—and not feel guilty—I must discover an equation into which he fits. I begin, almost unconsciously, by making Harry Jones x. I wonder what he is worth, to me, and to the useful life I must lead. My wonder becomes an equal sign, agitating toward a possible y. Until I can find a y for Harry, until I can place him in a significant ratio, I may be wasting my time saying "hello" to him.

If Harry Jones is a member of a firm with which I may soon be doing business, and if he is influential enough in his firm to help me get the business done, then, of course, I have found y. Or perhaps Harry belongs to the Century Club and I would like to: y again. If Harry Jones, x, can be made to equal the possibility of a new contract, y, or my admission into the Century Club, also y, then I have found a value not in Harry Jones or in my personal response to Harry Jones but in the abstract ratio in which I have succeeded in placing Harry Jones. I have done the one necessary and good thing I can do; and I must locate my happiness in it. Happiness, in Bentham's terms, is what I did it for.

It is now possible to explain, on irrefutably logical grounds, the compulsive and preoccupied life I have been leading. I go to lunch, and lunch is x. I spend a weekend with friends; the weekend is x. I attend a play, which is also x. Until I have discovered a y for each of these things, my conscience is uneasy. I am not profitably, or responsibly, engaged.

I am inventive, however, and I can most likely discover y. If I should happen to like puttering about with garden flowers, in themselves a meaningless x, I may be able to persuade myself that the prestige my garden gives me in the neighborhood, or the increased resale value my landscaping gives to my property, amounts to y. Now I can continue puttering. If I am fond of travel, or need a vacation, I can always go somewhere where y is; by doing a little homework along the way I shall even be able to deduct the sport from my income tax, compounding y deliciously. If I have always had an affection for the theater, I can console myself by using it to work off a social obligation (y^1), chat knowingly about it in circles likely to be impressed (y^2), or "increase my awareness," thanks to a co-operative playwright, of the principal political, economic, and sociological issues of the day (y^3). How wonderful if I can bag three birds with one stone! I am clever.

When I am not clever enough, and cannot quite establish the equation I am looking for, I can always abandon x altogether. X may live next door to me, or in the apartment directly across the hall, but if I cannot find a y in him, I am free to ignore him. It is, strictly speaking, my moral obligation to do so.

The successful man in the twentieth century—and by successful I mean happy, integrated, and productive—is, or should be, the man who has manufactured for himself the largest possible number of effective ratios and who has pared from his life any lingering attachment to nonexistent "values" which refuse to enter into practical equations. Success consists in the power to see circumstantial relationships abstractly and to derive pride and pleasure and contentment *from the abstractions*.

Twentieth-century man does not, of course, always realize how abstractly he is behaving, any more than he fully remembers the logical processes that brought his patterns of behavior into being. Often he does not entirely succeed in being moral in Benthamite terms; his code breaks down, his heart lights up, and he gives in to kindliness. And sometimes he is lucky: affection and abstraction coincide. But on the whole he has become extraordinarily skilled at the fashioning of ratios and has learned to measure his happiness by them. He knows what country club he should belong to and why; what newspaper he should read and why; what school he should send his children to and why. He knows what church he should go to and where he should sit; and lately, as those prophets who are appalled by a new "conformity" have pointed out, he knows what he should think and when.

At the same time, and in spite of the fact that so much propriety and so much success should give him a substantial sense of well-being, he is unexpectedly dissatisfied. Even at the highest professional level, Kenneth Keniston has suggested in *The American Scholar*, there is a marked unease as "work becomes increasingly distant, partial and abstract." And at every level men are aware of "a dumb unrest, a vague sense that something is wrong, an unwillingness to put up with a life that seems in some undefined way less than we might demand."

Whence this feeling of "dumb unrest" that besets all of us? It comes from the fact that we are not only committed to *working* with the kind of abstraction into which gold and pig iron may be fitted. We are also trying to rest in an abstraction, which is impossible.

This needs talking about. Perhaps the best way to begin is to look once more at Harry Jones and to notice—unless we are simply subject to a trick of the light—that the closer we come to placing Harry Jones in an equation, the harder it is to see Harry. I begin, almost on the instant of our acquaintance, to superimpose upon Harry's face an invisible, suspended x and to superimpose on the x a shimmering question mark, just as, arriving at a party where many of the guests are unfamiliar to me, I do not give my whole attention to the first stranger I meet for a long enough time to be satisfied that we are congenial. I exchange evasive pleasantries, hesitating to commit myself upon any subject that is truly important to me, for a period that may be designated as minimum-polite. I then swiftly detach myself from this unresolved x, and this as yet unseen personality, until I can brush shoulders, in a sufficiently isolated corner, with someone I already know. "Who is he?" I ask him, inclining my head slightly in the direction of the stranger. My question, which is promptly understood, does not mean what is his name (I have been given that), what is he like (a matter that is irrelevant in a ratio), or where does he live (though this information may begin to place him in abstract space); it means what is his significance to the group at large or to me? In short, what is his y? The moment I have been given his y, and supposing it is a *y* that I can make use of, the face that has already been blurred by an *x* and a question mark is stamped across once more with a dazzlingly clear, but equally depersonalizing, *y*. The entire equation now dances in the air just this side of his countenance, a series of neon flashes, live and persistent, conveying an intelligible message. As I drift toward him again, I know what I am doing and how to go about doing it. I must first offer him an acceptable *y* for my own suspended *x*, whereupon a flicker of his eyelash will tell me that he has seen not me but my "value." Safely joined in the wonderland of the worthwhile, we can relax and journey together into that absolutely neutral territory, the world that *x* and *y* make, in which we shall hereafter live and have our communal being. We may come to do many things together, to "know" each other for years; what we will really have known, at the end of it all, is the equation that stood between us. We have not only shaken hands on an abstraction; we have each shaken hands with one.

We shall have great difficulty in ever changing the nature of our relationship. I may develop, after a while, half a suspicion that in my bones I detest this man. But his virtue, for me, is in his *y*, and I shall suppress my suspicion and cling to him. Conversely, I may, along the way, come to feel that I would have liked him even if I had never been told "who" he was. Most of us still do find affection stirring in our hearts in quite irresponsible ways. But I have been taught to be on guard against such weaknesses. I have been taught that the merit, the moral texture, of my continuing to associate with him depends entirely upon his *y* value and that it would be a sign of capriciousness in me, a descent into sentimentality, if I were to give way to secondary, softer considerations. After all, my pleasure in this man's company may, if it is permitted to turn into a personal matter rather than an abstract commitment, cause me to lose clear sight of the equation that brought us into tentative balance, may even lead me into holding onto the man after the equation has begun to disintegrate. In this case, I shall find myself defending lost causes, justifying fifth wheels, arguing for the expendable. As an apologist for deadwood—either professionally or socially—I may damage my firm, my neighborhood, my family, myself. It is essential, in the clear light of the utilitarian day, that I never permit the superimposed abstraction to dissolve, giving me an unconsidered view of my companion's face. That face need not be wholly blanked out, but it must be veiled by its value if I am to spend my few hours on earth in happy and profitable intercourse.

In the long run, my companion and I should have to have the misfortune of being cast on a desert island, where *x* and *y* have not yet been born, to know whether or not we know one another.

Abstractions detach. That is their function. The human animal's capacity for forming and manipulating abstractions is, of course, one of its most singular and powerful gifts. Reflection is possible because abstract concepts can be held in the mind quite apart from the coarse and gravity-burdened objects they are meant to signify. Communication is possible because we have found ways of translating abstract concepts into abstract counters, called words, which once more free us of the necessity of lugging the physical universe about with us on our backs so as to be able to point to the pieces of it we want others to see. Trade and industry and science are possible because the abstraction of numbers permits us to manage volumes so minute that they cannot be seen and volumes so vast that they cannot be marked out on foot: it is good to be able to sell four thousand horses without bringing the horses into the office. Thanks to a thought in his head, a word on his lips, and a numeral scratched on a piece of paper—abstractions all—man has conquered the earth and is thinking of moving elsewhere. He does not need to stub his toe on a rock every day in order to buy it, sell it, or explain its chemical complexity.

That this power is a miracle for which none of us can ever be sufficiently grateful is plain. What is less plain, and easily forgotten, is the dismaying tendency of every human power, especially when it is employed in isolation from all other powers, to turn upon itself. A thousand poets have paid handsome compliments to man's capacity for mating not mechanically but with affection; possibly nine hundred and ninety-nine of them have also pointed out how perilously love hovers over its own negation. (Mary McCarthy has remarked that "the attempt to evolve a perfect product of any kind tends, by some law of limit, to conjure up its contrary: the demand for perfect love, for example, elicits perfect hate.") Man's instinct for socializing, for gathering productively into groups, leads, all too often, to the violent destruction of everything produced. (I remember my sudden depression, during a visit to Agamemnon's crumbled citadel at Mycenae, on realizing that there had been very few Greeks in Agamemnon's Greece, that bands of them had clustered together on a very few hilltops spaced miles and miles apart, and that, instead of traveling to a common meeting place from time to time in order to rejoice in one another's company, each band had made the long trip only to knock from the remote hilltop the other's citadel.)

Does man's astonishing capacity for controlling reality through the use of abstractions also lead, in some similarly perverse fashion, to his losing his grip on reality? Yes, it does, almost in the nature of things. An abstraction, by definition, has nothing of its source matter in it. That is to say, there is no actual stone in the word "stone," there are not five of anything in the numeral "5," there is no sound in the quarter note ♩, there is neither earth nor asphalt on a map. The virtue of the power of abstraction is that it enables us to deal with all of these things in their absence.

But it must always be remembered that they are absent. An abstraction is a kind of divorce; to form one I must, as Webster reminds me, "withdraw, separate, take away." In arriving at the useful abstraction "rose" or "chrysanthemum" or "marigold," I must first get rid of all the concrete properties of any actual rose or chrysanthemum or marigold. I cannot stuff a living stalk or a living leaf into my head, nor do I want to. What I want to get into my head is an immaterial idea that will serve me even though I never see a rose or a chrysanthemum or a marigold again. But as I "take away" this immaterial idea, I leave behind me the natural bloom: I abandon, in this process, the reality of color and odor, of a dimensional stem that dips in the wind or nods to the sun, of a felt texture that may be either prickly or silken to the touch. By "mental separation from particular instances or material objects," I crowd my brain with abstract substitutes for once visible and tangible things. My new tool exists "apart from" nature, as nature was first presented to me, and is "not concrete." I hold a variety of species, not a flourishing green garden, in my mind.

Because I have disengaged the idea of a rose from any rose that can be fondled or pleasurably sniffed, a gap between these two things has begun to appear. My idea of a rose is an idea and not a rose. Isn't this gap somewhat healed by the fact that I am able to talk to my friends about roses, that we have agreed upon a word that bridges *my* immaterial idea of a rose and *their* immaterial ideas of roses and so makes the rose come alive again as we reach out to communicate? No, as a matter of fact, the translation of a private idea into a public word only widens the gap between the concrete and the abstract.

For a word is not only an abstraction in itself but an artifice besides. The word has no more aroma than my idea does, no more silkiness, no more greenness or redness; and in attempting to reduce an evanescent notion held in the mind to some spelled-out formula on which we can all agree, it has had to become wholly arbitrary. The word "rose" looks even less like a rose than does the ghostly notion, derived partly from memory, that

I hold in my mind. The peculiar arrangement of four arbitrary letters in an arbitrary sequence—"r-o-s-e"—has nothing natural, nothing absolute, about it. It is an empty sign which we have permitted to stand, by common consent, for an already disembodied idea. Any other arrangement of letters, provided we were to agree upon them, would do as well: the Italian for "daisy" is *margherita*, and *loup* is the French for "wolf." To one kind of withdrawal from the natural world we have added another, and the second is far less flexible and far more stubborn than the first because it is so bluntly and so rigidly set down and so firmly fixed in the common consciousness. If Gertrude Stein could become shrill in her effort to remind us that "a rose is a rose is a rose," that there lurked behind the granite word a fragrance that could still be visited, we were unable to grasp what the poor dear was saying because we seemed to be staring, on the page, at nothing more than a meaninglessly repeated, bone-dry symbol. The repetition of the word did not bring more of the garden rose to our eye; it brought less. That is the habit of words.

There is no strong link between the names we give to things and the things for which they are named. We imagine, occasionally, that in such a device as onomatopoeia we have succeeded in establishing a bond: the word at least sounds like the object it means to describe. When we speak of the "ripple" of a brook, aren't we being brought closer to the brook? Doesn't "gurgle" keep us in touch with the heard properties of a liquid? Not very much. We are able to use "cripple" without hearing the lap of waves, and "burgle" suggests nothing in the way of a waterfall.

The fact of the matter is that the thread that stretches between the things of this earth and the arbitrary constructions we have invented in order to talk about them is so perilously slender that it is in constant danger of snapping.

Most of us have felt it snap momentarily. We have been

reading a book and, suddenly and for no known reason, have seen a word disintegrate on the page before us. For a fraction of a second we are looking at a jumble of letters that suggests nothing at all, that is, on the instant, so inexplicable that we cannot imagine what meaning we had ever attached to the un-prepossessing muddle of arbitrary shapes. The word, so famil-iar, has lost its face and is—for not much longer than it takes to blink one's eyes—shockingly irrelevant. It neither belongs to anything actual nor constitutes anything actual in its own right.

This sensation of disintegration, detachment, irrelevance does not, as a rule, last very long. We do blink our eyes, and the connection does come back. It must, however, be *brought* back, with an effort that is made at lightning speed but is none-theless a real effort. Being wholly arbitrary, the connection cannot reassert itself. We must, however rapidly, try to pull the scattered letters back into a bundle, link the bundle to a remembered concept, and link the concept to a fragment of the natural world. That is a considerable activity, and we can surely be excused if a fleeting sense of panic stirs somewhere in the middle of it, a terror that—this time—we may not be able to achieve the fusion.

We normally succeed in achieving it—though my acquaint-ance who had permanently lost touch with the significance of numbers had not so succeeded—and we are properly not given to undue worry when we are confronted with such evidence of the chasm between the actual and the abstract. The experience is an infrequent one. And it has until recently been customary for most of us to lead lives in which there is a sufficient amount of interplay between the thing and the word, between the object and the artifice, to sustain their fragile relationship. If I live on an avenue of trees, it is unlikely that I shall ever have much trouble with "tree": the trunk and the branches and the filter of light through the leaves all help keep the concept healthy. The concept, in turn, helps me to know what I mean by this living mass of pulpy tissue and to say what I mean to my friends. It is easy to keep a thought in my head so long as the thing, in its richness, is often before my eyes.

If the sickening little lesion that sometimes catches me by surprise when I am reading has any value as a warning, it is as a warning that all abstractions need occasional refreshment by their referents, that they are intermittently dependent upon new nourishment. I must feed them, now and then, if they are not to lose weight. I am in no danger—indeed, I am immensely enriched—if I can hold in delicate harmony the thicknesses of life and the supple insubstantialities of language. Danger pops up only when such interplay ceases or is thrown seriously out of balance.

Are we out of balance now? If so, why? I have been taking, more or less consistently, the end of the eighteenth century and the beginning of the nineteenth as a point of departure for this inquiry into our malaise, and it may seem that I have been arbitrary in selecting so limited a portion of the historical landscape as the scene of the crime. It may well be asked if nothing went wrong before that. Are all of our distresses so recently born? I would not wish to pretend so, and Mr. Keniston is undoubtedly wise in reminding us that "our widespread doubt as to whether there are *any* values which can be legitimately and passionately held . . . begins with the breakdown of medieval certainty, progresses through centuries of increasing rational skepticism . . . and culminates in the cynicism and sense of ideological defeat that have followed our two world wars." To know the whole soul of a man, one must know the whole history of the man.

Still, the selection of this one moment in time may not be entirely arbitrary. There are such things as turning points. A discussion of the problems of pleasure may well begin with the formation of the philosophy that defined pleasure for us. And there is another reason for circling the date.

One titanic event, closely related to the philosophy that accompanied it, did take place at the end of the eighteenth and the beginning of the nineteenth century, and it was calculated to urge us, unless we were briskly on guard and ready with a remedy, toward a serious imbalance between the abstract and the concrete. Odd as the statement must seem to all of us at first hearing, it was at just this moment in history that we came to the end of the Neolithic age.

The statement is Henri Breuil's, quoted with approval by Pierre Teilhard de Chardin in his exhilarating study of the evolutionary processes, *The Phenomenon of Man.* Père Teilhard goes on to explain. However remote and primitive the connotations of the term "neolithic" seem to us, the adjective simply describes that stage in the development of human society during which man sustained himself by local husbandry. Life was centered, during this age, on the building of family dwellings, the cultivation of wheat and other grains, the raising of sheep and cattle, the production of such tools as were necessary to a rural economy, and the maintenance in general of a group self-sufficiency. "Advanced as it was in many ways two centuries ago," Teilhard observes, "our civilization was still based fundamentally on the soil and its partition." The family and the "arable field," the personal and the concrete, constituted the immediate environment of most men. "Property" was not a series of leases in a vault but a section of earth underfoot and a stockpile in the barn. The wealth of a community, or even of a nation, was contained for the most part within its readily defined boundaries and was under the control of men living within those boundaries.

Old as the neolithic pattern of living is, we did not "cast off its last moorings," in Breuil's phrase, until the onset of the nineteenth century. Then, with the electrifying rise of industry and the swift "dynamization" of money, virtually every man's environment changed. Property "evaporated into something fluid and impersonal," became so mobile that the very wealth of nations today "has almost nothing in common with their frontiers." Local government became a matter of small consequence, meaningful only as it functioned in routine and humble co-operation with a complex network of political commitments leaping city, state, and finally national boundaries. Each individual's private experience was altered to fit.

The man whose hands had mended a silo and assisted at a calving found himself using those same hands to twist a piston into place on a factory assembly line. We have heard a great deal about this transition as a speeding-up process; we have heard rather less about it as a detaching process. The single, repetitive piston this man now saw and handled was neither a natural object nor a whole one: it existed at several removes from the shaped mechanical body of which it would become a part and at several more from the earth that body would eventually subdue.

The peddler who had formerly bargained with a farmer and then chatted with housewives as they stood round his cart testing vegetables with experienced fingers retreated first behind a cash register and then—most recently—behind glass-and-steel partitions equipped with chutes through which merchandise might flow; the housewives were left to peer through the partitions, or investigate vast shelves of tinned goods, by themselves. The bill collector, already an intermediary, who had called on neighborhood families to settle accounts in person found himself seated in a cubicle, confronted with a ledger, surrounded by filing cabinets, handling everything by mail. In time even the names of his debtors vanished, to be replaced by identifying holes punched in IBM cards. Every bit of this expedited the work of the world.

But the man engaged in doing the stamping, the punching, the "processing" was no longer anywhere near the real things he was buying, selling, or even helping to create. He was, to use a term that has become popular in television production, in "limbo"—that is to say, nowhere in particular. He was suspended in an efficient void, and his vision could feed only on the generally rectangular lines and flat planes of graphs and mimeographs, of inks and indexes, of cylinders and certain digits that guaranteed him social security. Unimpeded by the need to wrench a carrot out of the ground or a dollar out of a known personality, commerce flowed through his hands and his head with the ease that is the special property of the disembodied.

This ease—and the detachment and impersonality that go with it—increased as the size of the manipulation grew larger. We are still both shocked and vaguely thrilled, I think, to read that someone has purchased the Empire State Building without any actual cash having changed hands. We shiver with a small grin at the unreality of it all, aware that the layers of insubstantiality are being ever compounded. We had always known, for instance, that the phrase "actual cash" was something of a misnomer: "cash" isn't actual; it is a substitute for various real things—oil wells, tin mines, ranches—that the buyer hasn't bothered to bring along. But when for this initial substitution still another substitution is made, when cash itself vanishes in favor of a formalized shuffle of unseen assets in the whisk of a signature, the mind reels very slightly and then congratulates itself on its accomplishment.

We have mastered matter quite nicely, left tons of impedimenta behind. At the same time, we are slightly shaken. How does the new owner of the Empire State Building feel as he strides into its corridors on Monday morning? Does he feel on solid ground, in personal possession, clothed by steel and concrete that have become part of himself? And how does he feel when, a little later, the papers are shuffled again and he has lost it all? Does he now feel as he did when he lost his cap on the

first day of school, or has he simply brushed wings with a form
in a dream? It would be interesting to know.

Idle speculation aside, the progression from a wrestling match
with the obstructively real to an easy canter with property that
is "fluid and impersonal" constitutes, for mankind, a perfectly
clear gain. It is not in itself a movement to be decried on
nostalgic grounds. Quite apart from the fact that evolution
cannot reverse itself, man's sudden liberation from local boundaries and his exciting discovery that he can perform most of his
necessary operations with a very few pieces of onionskin paper
are in themselves signs of his unshackling. He is freer than he
was before, certainly freer of physical burdens, specifically
freer to increase the life of the mind.

Why, then, do I want to suggest that this irreversible and
also desirable push forward became one of the causes of our
present imbalance, our evident misery? Precisely because, as we
made increasing use of the flexible abstraction, we were forced
to leave most of the referents, most of the real things, far, far
behind. And because we took insufficient precaution to pre-
serve them, as needed refreshment, in some other form.

The fault is not in our gains but in our forgetfulness. Until
the end of the eighteenth century the proportions between the
concrete things of this world and the abstract terms used as
substitutes for them were, of necessity, more or less regular.
Men touched the objects they knew by name as they shod
horses or shucked corn; leaders spoke to their followers and
solicited their votes face to face in the meeting house. With
the transfer of human activity from pea patch to push button
and from town hall to the vast bureaucratic honeycomb we all
know, the old, habitual coupling of natural substance and
arbitrary symbol came to an abrupt end. The weather continued to affect the price of wheat, but most men no longer
felt the weather; instead, they felt only its effect as registered
for them in abstracts on their desks. Men continued to feel

emotionally about their elected representatives, but the representatives knew the emotions only as percentages in a poll. The natural substance no longer obtruded itself; the symbol could be used without experience of its source.

But we need never have concluded that, from this time forward, the abstract and the concrete were utterly forbidden to reinforce one another. The shift merely meant that reinforcement would never again be casual, unthinking, automatic. In the future, we should simply have to see to it for ourselves, if we wanted to keep our abstractions from blowing up in our faces, that at least a nodding acquaintance was maintained with the dimensional universe we had learned to bypass and on which both the validity and the vitality of our abstractions depended. The concrete was no longer insistently, even troublesomely, at hand; we should have to go look for it, from time to time, if we wished to draw strength from it.

This new need was sensed, however indirectly, by the men who founded our own government toward the close of the eighteenth century. As it happens, America has embraced, and become dominated by, the utilitarian ethic and all of its consequences more fully than any other nation. There are obvious reasons for this. One is that America chanced to come to birth at the very moment the new philosophy was coming to birth: a fresh ethic and a fresh continent could grow up together. The fresh continent, with its vast resources, became the perfect laboratory for the swift application of the principles of use, profit, and the pursuit of a happiness that could be measured by these things. It was also free to take the maximum advantage of a new post-neolithic fluidity: even as it was cultivating farmland, it was throwing up railways calculated to leap over homestead boundaries. No other nation invented so many devices tending to banish the personal and the concrete, substituting a filament for flame and a voice on the wire for a face-to-face encounter. Further, and because it was a fresh continent, it placed no obstacles in the way of its singular progress: it possessed no ancient traditions, no cherished folkways, no stubbornnesses of belief to resist, retard, or in any way modify the onrush of a new enthusiasm. Europe, with a longer memory and a more complex philosophical tradition, even now moves slowly by comparison, attempting to adapt what it cannot bring itself to abandon.

The American founding fathers were highly conscious of the vast transition that was taking place. They were themselves engaged in a blurring of thirteen local boundaries so that a larger, more "fluid and impersonal" concept of government might succeed to power for the benefit of all. They were also, in some ways, apprehensive of pitfalls in the exciting new path the world was taking. They were careful, for instance, to limit the tenure of office in all branches of the newly centralized government. Though the real work of government would now be done in a somewhat disembodied place without a political identity of its own, no man engaged in that work was to be permitted to detach himself from the community he represented indefinitely. The original Articles of Confederation had speci-fied that "no person shall be capable of being a delegate for more than three years in any term of six years," and, though Hamilton later made the strongest possible case for longer terms of office, when the Constitution was ratified it gave each Congressman two years and each Senator six, with the shape of the Senate itself shifting regularly during the six. These men might indeed succeed themselves, but not without making a fresh personal appeal to the residents of the territories they represented; even Hamilton was forced to concede that "it is a misfortune incident to republican government . . . that those who administer it may forget their obligations to their con-stituents." After a controlled time in the legislature, each man was to march back home and take another look—submitting himself meanwhile to the ordeal of being looked at—lest the lands and the locals for whom he spoke should become entire abstractions to him.

It was necessary, as these constitution builders saw, to "keep in touch." If it was no longer advisable to waste one's energies and limit one's productiveness by tangling daily and directly with the worms and the weeds at the "grass roots," it was nevertheless wise to remind oneself—however forcibly and under whatever negatively phrased rules—that the worms and the weeds and the roots were there. It was wise to do more than renew one's awareness; if one did not wish to wither on the unfed vine, affection had best be renewed, too.

It is now nearly two hundred years since these small, rather legalistic, suggestions were made to us, cautions in a single area against forgetting the tangible core deep within our mushrooming, ever more abstractly-managed, complexities. Where do we stand today, in this same area? During the 1960 Presidential campaign, *The New York Times* pointed out that the old-fashioned whistle-stop technique of rousing voters from the rear platforms of trains had at last vanished and that "in its place, candidates have substituted the plane campaign, hurtling at speeds ranging from 250 to 600 miles an hour across the continent with occasional touchdowns to address local workers at the airport.

"The result," this report continues, "has been an increasing detachment, not only from the countryside but also from the people." But even as this detachment was taking its toll, a greater one was in the making. Now "television debates have threatened to overshadow the plane campaign. In these, with everyone but technicians shut out of the studio, the break in human contact between candidate and people is complete."

Where do we stand, not simply in the political arena, but generally? We began this chapter by suggesting that the arts must always, in some way, return to us our own faces. The faces our contemporary arts return to us possess, at the very least, two clear characteristics. One is the determination to see all things abstractly. The other is an inclination to despair.

Between the time that we banished from the ordinary courses of our lives a direct involvement with the concrete things of this earth and the time that our plays and paintings decided to reflect our conviction that these things no longer existed on the earth in any relevant way, we were apparently faced with a chore that we failed to perform. It would seem that we were confronted with a new need, in our new age, to seek out—deliberately and experimentally—the delightfully solid substances on which our evanescent concepts depended. If we were no longer going to work with the refreshingly concrete, we should at least have to learn to play with it. But we did not, even though our infants in their cribs kept demonstrating to us daily how delightful solid substances could be as they played, for hours on end, with empty talcum-powder cans. We made no effort at putting the world back together again, so that it should please us in its oneness rather than distress us by its fragmentation. We did not try to heal the breach because we were forbidden to do so.

We were forbidden to do so by the philosophy that in part took its impetus from, and in part reinforced, our new and ever-increasing dependence upon abstraction. The thinkers who grew up and grew potent during the first hundred years of the post-neolithic age were not content with teaching us how to extract the maximum use from the millions of new equations open to us. They were determined that we should locate *all* value in these exciting and swiftly proliferating ratios and that we should dismiss the tangibles of this world as nonentities.

Thus at the very moment when I ought to have been reaching out my hand to keep the real world from slipping away from me altogether, the command came to let go. I was sternly warned that I should find neither profit nor happiness, neither sustenance nor rest, in any concrete object—animal, mineral, vegetable, or, for that matter, human. Value was not in things; it appeared exclusively in those abstract equations that were already beginning to overwhelm me and that I was beginning to find tasteless as a steady diet. Value itself was one of those equations. How should I hope to find it elsewhere?

Worse still, my problem was compounded by a paradox. I remained, unfortunately, an earthbound creature. I had not yet succeeded in wholly detaching myself from flesh and other valueless matter. Since I was not yet pure spirit and could not walk through walls or converse by extrasensory perception, I was forced to continue to deal, somehow, with a concrete world that had grown worthless. As I rose from my calculations at the end of my workday, I had to put on a real coat with an actual surface texture. I had to speak to people whose personalities dared differ, I had to put my feet on solid ground if I wanted to get home, I had to water the azaleas if I wanted them to brighten my property in the spring. I had to touch my wife and pretend to play with my children. I was not free, after all. I still had to do all of the things in which I had once placed my happiness, even though I was now assured that no happiness was in them. I was obliged, it would seem, to live a lie.

I was taught how to do it. Instead of looking at the road ahead of me and thinking, with E. E. Cummings, that it was "mud-luscious" and "puddle-wonderful," instead of stopping to chat with Harry Jones because, I couldn't tell why, I had always sort of liked Harry, instead of poking at the azaleas because their color, in the spring, invariably made me catch my breath, I was to take the necessary precaution of inscribing across each of these things the x and the $?$ and the $=$ and the y that would make them abstractions and, hence, valuable too. Concrete things were really mirages, mere illusions of value. It is always best to clear one's head of mirages. By invoking the sign of the ratio, which is the guarantor of moral health and private happiness, I could make them all but disappear. I have done so.

Having done it, I find myself living in a world in which my abstractions seem to elude me more and more, as though there were nothing substantial behind them. I have accepted abstract value as the only value, and now—perversely—it does not seem much of a value. When I turn to concrete things, as I must occasionally do, I find myself unable to face them with a whole heart. I am forbidden to regard them as worth-while in themselves, so that they already seem ashes before I have reached out to touch them. Unable to find rest in the abstractions I manipulate, and commanded not to seek it in the tangible world about me, I feel displaced, unrefreshed, dizzy over a void. Neither of the two faces the universe may put on—the abstract or the concrete—gives me pleasure. I am alienated.

4

✿
✿
✿

What Is Left and What Is Needed

May I join you in the doghouse, Rover?
I wish to retire till the party's over.

—OGDEN NASH

I AM obviously guilty of painting the picture too abstractly, too theoretically, myself. In spite of the detachment. that has overtaken our work, and in spite of those philosophical pressures that bid us find our happiness within our work and within its very detachment, we are neither so work-ridden nor so despoiled of small comforts as I have pretended. In the autumn of our discontent, we continue to play bridge, go to movies, read novels, dress for dinner-dances, and decorate trees for Christmas. We have secreted small stores of pleasure in our inside pockets, and we draw upon them more or less regularly.

If I cite, at this point, still another medical bulletin plucked from the front page of *The New York Times*, it is less with the idea of putting one more log on the fire of my argument than with suggesting that we are still capable of laughter. Grisly as the following just-after-Christmas bulletin is, I think you may find it funny:

"Relief from the pressure of having to be happy during the holidays is beginning to brighten the lives of many persons who react violently against Christmas, according to a current medical journal.

"Hives, overeating, crying jags, dishonesty, sexual deviation and just plain orneriness are said to be some of the 'Christmas reactions' that those people develop around Thanksgiving and carry on until after the first of the year.

"Underlying those difficulties are the rituals or 'rules' of Christmas, four Utah physicians and psychiatric social workers wrote in the December issue of *American Practitioner and Digest of Treatment.*

"Those rules, they said, require that everyone celebrate, renew family ties, exchange gifts, put up holiday decorations, have a special Christmas dinner, and—above all—be happy . . .

"One case involved an obese woman and her sulky, skinny husband. When Christmas approached, they wrote, she would indulge herself by eating faster and faster, and he released his pent-up aggressions by getting madder and madder.

"In another case, a man who became severely depressed every Christmas decided to give himself a treat and let go his exhibitionistic-voyeuristic impulses. He joined a nudist colony and now celebrates the holiday with a seasonal trek to the camp."

Now it would be easy to engage in sober speculation about the findings of our four Utah physicians. One might take the tack that Christmas, with its inescapable religious implications, is being celebrated by hundreds of thousands of people who are indifferent to, or even hostile toward, those religious implications and that the tensions built up in the process must sooner or later explode. Or one might, just as soberly, suggest that the family festivities—the coming together of so many otherwise neglected, and possibly despised, relatives—constitutes a clinging to ancient tribal patterns in an age when the tribe is no longer workable or desirable as a basic social unit. There is a fertile field for the social scientists here.

But I suspect the report is likelier to amuse than alarm you. It is amusing, to begin with, because it is in one real sense true:

it is virtually impossible to get through the holidays as we know them without intermittent irritation and ultimate exhaustion, and it commonly requires several weeks of recuperation for a contemporary householder to get back on the straight-and-narrow path of unjoyous living. The report is also amusing, and therefore less than alarming, because it seems excessive: if it is just true enough to stir recognition and so nudge our funny bones, it is not so true that we feel compelled to abandon our practices instantly lest the very next time we go through the motions of gaiety we find ourselves coming apart at the seams. We are still able, most of us, to perform a ritual at a fairly even temperature.

We are able to endure the forms of a holiday without either making a wholehearted commitment to them or questioning them so severely that we become bound in conscience to reject them. We do not appear to have much appetite for creating new holidays. It is quite a while since anyone proclaimed a feast and lived to see it lodge itself in the popular imagination; most such proclamations now come from the advertising agencies and are treated with the contempt they deserve. But we are ready to bestow a kind of minimum benediction, a bemused tolerance, on the old ones. The Fourth of July does continue to be observed, even if it can no longer quite make itself heard. It doesn't have the color or the crackle it had when I was seven —and don't tell me my being forty-seven has anything to do with this, the firecrackers were simply taken out of my hands— but I know that it still exists when, along about eight-thirty in the evening, I am asked to drive the family over to an amusement park for a short, conventional display. I am aware that Columbus Day comes once a year, because I notice that the children haven't gone to school. I discover Labor Day, too, as I arrive at the bank doors to find them closed.

We honor such occasions apparently out of politeness. We have not yet abandoned every sign of a gala. A man may fuss and fume at the realization that the evening is going to be "black tie," and he may stare in bafflement at the absurd studs he is so uselessly expected to inter in his shirt, but he does put on the shirt and the tie and the red-lapeled jacket. I have seen people wearing paper hats during Captains' Dinners on shipboard.

I have also talked to the Captain. I was standing at the rail one evening, looking at the Atlantic, when the Captain himself appeared beside me, folded his arms, and helped me look. It was the custom, on this particular evening and on this particular ship, for the passengers to create elaborate hats of their own— I knew that one passenger had created his out of a toilet seat, because I'd passed him in the corridor coming up—and for prizes to be awarded to the most imaginative inventions. It was still early, however, and the Captain and I had time for a casual, pleasant chat about currents and dolphins and good restaurants in Venice. After a while he heaved a great, unexpected sigh, righted himself by pushing heavily against the railing, and excused himself. "Now I'm going to have to go down and inspect those damn hats," he said.

The point is that he went. He inspected the hats, he awarded the prizes, the passengers applauded and ordered more drinks, and conviviality reigned until early the next morning, without anyone on shipboard supposing for a moment that the whole thing wasn't an eerie and inexplicable relic of some earlier society's childish notion of a good time. Not a soul aboard could have invented this occasion for himself or would have wished to. But ten days at sea is quite a long time, the nights must be spent somehow, and one had best be brave, pretend to be giddy, and play the game.

We tend to make, I would say, a deal with the patterns of happiness. We indulge *them*, rather than ourselves. We tolerate them lightly, perhaps for fear of being thought spoilsports (after all, someone else may enjoy this sort of thing—but is that possible?). We give them elbow-room, but just elbow-room. Let these vestigial remnants of someone else's irrepressible foolishness survive in some small corner of our otherwise knowing and responsible lives. Why not? They are harmless enough so long as we don't give our hearts to them. We don't, of course, truly believe in such forms of pleasure: they seem to us only forms and not really pleasure. But they can be kept about the house as occasional pets if we are careful never to give them, at any one moment, our full attention, our helpless surrender.

The practice of permitting certain old friends (rather the worse for wear) to remain as casual house guests—novels on the table, playing cards in the drawer, artificial holly in the attic where it can be retrieved in early December—does mean that certain symbols of pleasure, and even opportunities for pleasure, remain at hand in an age that cannot conscientiously find a value for them. The fact that they continue to be available but cannot be assigned a value has helped create, I think, two of the phenomena of our time.

One of these is the prevalence of *kitsch*. We have all heard, and often lent our voices to, the cry that has gone up in the second half of the twentieth century lamenting the omnipresence of the second-rate. And we know what we mean by *kitsch:* brightly-colored magazines that are all eye-catching pictures and easy-to-read captions; digests of digests; films as synthetic as the celluloid they are printed on; television that has been described as "chewing-gum for the eye"; music that fakes a sentiment buried with Franz Lehár or fakes a folk-song beat in the guise of creating something contemporary, indigenous, and appealing to teen-agers. We sometimes conceive that we live in the land of the blob: blobs of color, hoots of sound, zoom lenses, what the comedians call "grabbers." Surfaces leap at us like babies begging to be picked up; when they are picked up, they have no weight and no conversation, only a smile and a placid drool.

In a way, I find it as easy to forgive *kitsch* as I do a baby for drooling. Given our convictions, how better might the popular arts behave? Our deepest beliefs, in the twentieth century, command us to dismiss the arts, popular or otherwise: they have not had value, they do not have value, they will not have value. Unless they can find some way of jumping into our arms, taking us unawares, stunning us into momentary attention, we shall certainly pass them by.

And they know, even as they jump, that any attention they succeed in claiming will at best be momentary. They do not dare demand our co-operation. We are not prepared, on principle, to give it to them.

What we may be willing to give them is four or five minutes —in rare instances, a half hour—of idle leafing or listening as we wait for a train, stand by for a telephone call, or intermittently check the oven to see if the casserole is done. We are willing to make use of them when we are absolutely unable to do anything else, though on one condition: the condition is that they do not engage us. If they were to engage us, to ensnare our powers of concentration, to entice us into a complexity of thought or of narrative that might absorb us to the exclusion of the world around us, we should, of course, run the risk of not noticing our train, not hearing the telephone, or burning the casserole. More seriously still, we should be at fault morally: we'd have surrendered ourselves to an unprofitable activity.

It is essential, then, for the popular arts in the twentieth century to keep themselves as thin as the matron who is glancing at them. The magazine must be devised—with enormous double spreads that can be grasped in an instant—in such a way that the moistened finger turning the pages will not very often go dry. The condensation must be brisk enough to be clocked in advance, with no threat of overtime. The television show must be written so that the easily distracted viewer, ready on the instant to answer the doorbell or do a chore for his wife,

will be able to pick up the thread of the program without difficulty on his return; nothing essential can have happened in his
absence (and, since some of the viewers will be absent at all
times, nothing essential—or, let's say, nothing that would be
puzzling if missed—can be permitted to happen at any time).
The novel must be one that is neither difficult to pick up nor
difficult to put down: its survival depends upon its being easy
to read and just as easy to drop. Anything twentieth-century
man "couldn't tear himself away from" would, perforce, become a hazard. The popular arts are designed for a world in
motion; the motion is away, toward useful encounters; if they
are to survive, these arts must be careful never to presume,
never to impede the motion. (Shall we speak of something
higher than the popular arts and report the fact that the newest
museum of art in New York City is constructed on an eternal
incline so that no visitor will be tempted to engage himself long
but will be under actual physical pressure to move on?) The
arts, certainly the popular arts, must possess the virtue of
humility, must know how to keep their places. They are tolerable as grace notes so long as they demand nothing for themselves; their very ticket of admission consists in the promise
that they will maintain a quiet and virtuous vacuity.

When I quoted Charles Darwin's account of his progressive
disenchantment with poetry in an earlier chapter, I omitted a
passage which might well be restored now. Having acknowledged his falling out with the works of Wordsworth and
Shakespeare, and with painting and music as well, he allowed
an exception:

"On the other hand, novels, which are works of the imagination, though not of a very high order, have been for years a
wonderful relief and pleasure to me, and I often bless all
novelists. A surprising number have been read aloud to me, and
I like all if moderately good, and if they do not end unhappily
—against which a law ought to be passed. A novel, according

to my taste, does not come into the first class unless it contains some person whom one can thoroughly love, and if a pretty woman all the better."

It is plain that the groundwork for twentieth-century taste is here being laid down not by a thousand housewives or dreamy adolescents but by Charles Darwin. The works of imagination which we find ourselves able to endure are, admittedly, those "not of a very high order." We can endure them best when they end happily, keep their characters lovable, and make the most of pretty women. When, that is to say, they do not surprise us or disturb us or involve us so profoundly that they interfere with our work.

We are in the market—and a very limited market it is—for lazy delight, for incidental delight, for delight that need be only half attended to, for the fruits of the imagination made easy and unobtrusive. We insist that our pleasures be unobtrusive because we have no intention whatever of withdrawing our attention from our proper goals, from the profits to be taken from respectable employment. We do not mean to work for a while and then to play for a while. We mean to work all of the time and let play come to us in passing, like a sandwich that is brought to the desk.

It is a commonplace joke that recording companies have now nearly exhausted a certain kind of album title: we have had Music to Read By, Music to Make Love By, Music to Sleep By, and, as one humorist has had it, Music to Listen to Music By. What is interesting about these titles is that they so candidly describe the position of the popular arts in our time. They admit at the outset that no one is expected to sit down, for heaven's sake, and attend to the music. It is understood that, while the music is playing, everyone within earshot is going to be busy doing something else, and it is merely suggested that, if no one minds, it might be pleasant to have a whisper coming over your shoulder while you go on doing the things you must do.

We have not yet got around to the business of advertising a novel as a Book to Cook By or a television show as a Show to Mend Furniture By. But that is simply an oversight; we have the novels and the shows.

With Darwin's reluctant but nonetheless genial admission, *kitsch* is just around the corner. It is, furthermore, approaching not as a sop to the unlucky illiterate, who is usually thought to be its target, but as the solution to a problem bedeviling intelligent men. Let the artist lower his sights. Let him write no ending that cannot be comfortably anticipated. Let him, suggests a cheerful scientist, bring on the girls. Under these conditions, busy men with fine minds will make a small amount of time for him.

When Darwin reports that he likes all novels so long as they are "moderately good," he no doubt means to say that there are some below this level he cannot quite tolerate. But "moderately good" also becomes an absolute: the standard must neither dip below a modestly acceptable norm nor aspire to rise above it. "Pretty good" is at once the minimum quality we are willing to give eye and ear to—and the maximum.

That is why I find it so difficult, for my own part, to become incensed about *kitsch*. I feel sorry for it—wide-eyed orphan that it is in a world it never made. It is not so much a panderer as a dependent, and it is obliged to behave itself circumspectly.

The second result of our demand that the forms of play never obtrude themselves to the point where they might partially obscure our vision of true value can be seen in our increasing emphasis upon those forms of play that keep our working minds active.

Even though we have abandoned, or pushed far into the background, most of the traditional forms of pleasure, we go right on playing cards. Indeed, we are inclined to be feverish about card games. A passion for gin rummy gives way to a passion for canasta, while the passion for bridge stands confidently by, ready to take over again whenever one of these other enthusiasms dies. We are not long without score pads of one kind or another.

The special virtue of each of these pastimes, and the factor that guarantees their survival in this least playful of ages, is their employment—to a very high degree—of abstract counters and abstract mental processes. If I go into the garden to whack a croquet ball through a wicket, I am forced to deal with the solid properties of certain concrete objects and environmental conditions: a ball with some density to it, a mallet with some weight to it, a wicket possessed of tricky physical dimensions, treacherous grass on an actual slope. My pleasure consists in relating one concrete object to another in such a way that I temporarily master the idiosyncrasies of the physical universe. I will, of course, keep score as I go, but, as I am going, I must touch the mallet, the mallet the ball, the ball another ball, and every ball the grass—all the while that I am apprehensive about the material presence and challenging shape of the wicket.

Playing cards, I must, of course, touch the counters—but not in a way that counts. What matters to me, and what determines my pleasure, is the abstract numerical value attached quite arbitrarily to each slip of nearly undifferentiated pasteboard. I must swiftly calculate the abstract "worth" of each jack and ace that I hold—this worth is so abstract and so little dependent upon the physical shape of the design I am looking at that the ace may count for thirteen points in one game and one point in another and certain other cards, called jokers or trump, may count for anything I wish—while, at the same time, I assign further abstract value to each of the suits in which these abstractions recur. As I play out my cards, I am virtually unconscious of my physical activity or even of the visual detail printed on the counters (how long had you been playing cards before you were told that there were such things as one-eyed jacks—and didn't it come as a surprise?). My hand flies about the board almost unaware of what it is doing, as my eyes remain nearly unseeing, because the calculating machine at the back of my head is working furiously, abstractly estimating the points that may yet be played against me as well as the probable direction from which such plays may come. When I gather in the cards after a trick, the appearance of the cards may be wholly deceptive: that overstuffed and overbearing king may have been taken by a placid and unpretentious trey. The actual game has gone on in my head.

But it is not the fact that the game has gone on in my head that makes it so peculiarly acceptable to contemporary taste. (There is indeed such a thing as genuine play of the mind, and we shall have something to say about that later.) What makes these particular forms popular at a time when few relaxations are popular is their canny, and rather kindly, employment of our habits of work.

That is to say, we are here engaged in doing precisely the same kind of computing and maneuvering that occupies us during our hours of labor. The estimation of the commodity value of whatever I have to work with (what is the value of a parcel of real estate; what is the value of a nine of hearts?), the careful analysis of the shape of the market (should I hold it for another month; should I finesse my lone spade?), the search for a profit through a ratio that is never absolute (what can the purchaser really afford; how many diamonds has the man on my right?) are not so much departures from the methods of my office hours as they are an extension of those methods into the time of my release and into a relatively harmless atmosphere.

There is, of course, a difference between the deal by day and the deal by night. The card game is an abstract contest which can be fought without penalty. The maneuver at the office that is mismanaged may change, and wreak havoc with, a man's life; the overbid that causes him to go "down two" in hearts may bring him nothing more troublesome than a sneer from his wife. If he plays for stakes, he is usually careful to limit his possible losses per point (I once watched two millionaires play fervently for two and one-half hours, after which the victor joyfully collected his winnings of four dollars and twenty-eight cents). If he plays "for keeps," that is to say too tenaciously and perhaps too profitably, he is probably never going to be invited again. The eagerness with which twentieth-century man leaps to a card game soon after dinner—bypassing conversation and scorning charades—stems from the opportunity he is now offered to go right on behaving as he has behaved all day, to continue exercising the only mental reflexes he thinks worth exercising, to remain in the groove as it were —only this time without risk, without fear of serious consequences. Because the consequences are casual, and the penalties so small that he can cheerfully pay up, the slight shift of attention does have some meaning for him as relief or recreation. No sword hangs over his head at the moment; he can work away at his cards in relative comfort.

It should never surprise us, though, to hear that a business arrangement has been worked out over a card table, and without interrupting the game. The mental set required for the two operations is the same; indeed, the precision of the game may find two contestants more on the *qui vive* than either of them might have been at three o'clock on a rainy afternoon downtown. It has always seemed to me proper that firemen should play cards while waiting for the next alarm bell, far better than dozing or reading; when the alarm comes, they are ready. It is easy for an actor to leave the stage after playing a scene, go to his dressing room, while away the time with a solitaire pack, and then return for his next entrance with his mind in perfect trim for the work he must do. In none of these cases has responsiveness been dulled, responsiveness of a working kind. The mind may have shifted its attention, but it has not surrendered its bias. The cogs are in gear; a precise tension is sustained; the tools most needed remain in constant use. Cards were surely invented by someone who had cause to be on the alert.

May I make a small, possibly prejudiced, exception of chess? Chess moves quietly and gently a few squares away from the insistent abstraction of cards. Its pieces are not only dimensional but often different from one another: one can feel a knight in his hand, and know it for a knight, as he cannot the ten of clubs. The enemy is downed not by a count but by a physical presence that whisks him, physically, from the board. The contest is spatial and deeply satisfying; it is fought visibly on a terrain. One does not tally in his head alone the possible threats to his victory; he looks at them on the board, using first his eyesight and then his imagination. Luckier still, the game is complex enough to require quite a long time to play, long enough in some instances to encourage forgetfulness of demands lying in wait on a desk. Chess is also quiet, encouraging silence around it. A degree of surrender is implicit in its ivory bones. One cannot but be sympathetic to Gerald Abrahams' claim, in *The Chess Mind*, that "whereas in many intellectual processes the mind is assisted by conceptual methods—i.e. by abstract ideas—in the mental activity which is Chess such assistance is at a minimum. . . . In Chess the mind comes as near as possible to pure vision, to that spontaneous act of intuition which apprehends and controls processes and relationships without being forced to do so."

But I am cheating, and Mr. Abrahams is surely guilty of a degree of special pleading. All games in which the mind is required to do work of a specifically mathematical nature belong not to the realm of pure pleasure—which may be taken for the moment as that intoxicating state in which the whole man finds himself centered on, and in, a sensation of having just been born and having just been set free and having been born for the freedom he is feeling—but to the realm of diversions. Pleasure

is well-being itself; diversion is a temporary turning-away from
a lack of well-being. Pleasure is time ransomed; diversion is
time passed. Pleasure changes a man; diversion changes what he
is looking at, though not the quality of his looking. Whereas
pleasure actively recharges, diversion keeps the battery running
at an even purr.

When we try to conceive of genuine pleasure, what we
grope for is something more deeply felt and more expansively
filling than the rather neutral and matter-of-fact satisfaction
we take from games of skill which are really "changes of task."
Finishing an evening at cards, we may feel that the tensions of
our lives have been briefly reduced, or at least held at arm's
length, by preoccupation with an interesting pastime; what we
have done, in effect, is soothed ourselves with a harmless "hair
of the dog."

But if we were to envision pleasure proper, pleasure in all
the fullness of its eternally beckoning promise, we should ask
that it achieve something more for us than this: we should
expect it in some way to make us over.

Surely somewhere in this tantalizing universe an experience
awaits us that is richer than canasta or George Harmon Coxe.
Would men keep promising themselves some ultimate "pleasure" when all the work is done, would anyone have bothered
to equate the pursuit of happiness with such important treasures
as life and liberty, if "pleasure" began and ended with the barely
tolerable aridities with which we occupy our free evenings?
An instinct tells us that we were born to something better, a
breeze that touches us unexpectedly as we are locking the
doors at night fills us with a brief, vague distress over the joys
of maturity we once thought were coming to us and never have
come.

The question to be asked at this point in our inquiry is not:
where are such wells of pleasure as these, wells at which we
might drink as deeply as we like? It is this: sensing that such

wells exist, why don't we look for them? Feeling the breeze, and knowing that there is something we have neglected to seize for ourselves, why do we suppress the sudden upsurge that should logically end in a quest, shut the door resolutely, and resign ourselves to the thinnesses of our time killers once more tomorrow night?

We are prisoners of our convictions, hostages of an inertia that permits us to hold two quite contradictory views in balance. We are inclined, on the one hand, to suppose that there must be profoundly pleasing experiences, more exhilarating than those in which we habitually indulge ourselves, which might make us feel bigger with life than we now do; and we feel obliged, on the other hand, to dismiss such possible experiences as unnecessary and even as unreal.

Of *course* there may be sensations of overwhelming delight —if one were to take the trouble to look for them—and the delight might very well prove restorative. But we dare not permit ourselves to grow sentimental about the matter. Sentimentality consists in lavishing more emotion on an object or experience than the object or experience is worth, and our precise scale of values tells us that idle play, sheer delight, and such pleasures as are held in the mind merely are—no matter how satisfying—without essential substance, devoid of worth. *Ergo*, the superior joy we are half imagining might indeed refresh; but, given our creed, we must logically and stoically conclude that the refreshment itself would be valueless. Fun, no doubt. Stimulating, no doubt. But unimportant, unworthy of a man.

The word "recreation" remains in our vocabulary, but we do not think highly of the activity it defines. Children need recreation. Give them a bat and a ball, take them out to the park, send them off on a hike from time to time: growing bodies and immature minds can stand a certain innocent flexing now and then. Deteriorating bodies and weary minds do not require it so much. Of course, *some* men should force themselves into the open air for a few minutes each week: they have not stopped smoking, and their lungs need clearing. Some men may be a bit better off for acquiring an untaxing hobby: the pressures at the office are often very fierce.

There is a "recreation" room in the basement, though it is not used as much as the family thought it would be when the work of paneling it was undertaken. Its principal fixture, and the one that has most nearly justified its cost, is a bar; there is probably a phonograph that has been used for dancing several times; there may well be a ping-pong table which can be moved to the center of the room if no one is going to dance and which has been standing in the center of the room for many months now (it will be used again if someone can find the balls).

"Recreation" is light exercise, taken therapeutically and most often under duress. It is a stamp album, a determined walk with the dog, an amorphous spectral necessity that confronts us whenever we are about to take another life-insurance examination. It is a term used to describe what adolescents are going to be doing in that room downstairs; it is an adult male's minimum gesture, the most he can afford, toward warding off incapacity; it is nothing at all, really, to the woman of the house, not a word she can apply to any activity that concerns her. When we speak of "recreation" we are referring to a brief and casual commitment that is usually physical, that is most often performed both unwillingly and perfunctorily, and that produces, at best, superficial benefits. We are not confused about the meaning of the term.

We are confused only when we read of the absurd claims some thinkers—luckily, most of these are seriously out of date—have made for it. Aristotle has been quoted earlier in these pages as stating, without qualm or qualification, that the men who create for us the necessities of life are less wise, less knowing, less worthy of being held in esteem than the men who create our pleasures. "Recreation" is the term Aristotle uses to identify, and gather together, these pleasures. It would seem to follow that in this philosopher's view recreation is more admirable than work, though why he should have thought so is beyond us. Yet Aristotle is not even concerned to argue the case. The arts of recreation were "naturally" always regarded as superior to the achievements of our labor, he tells us.

We do not pay much attention to ancient saints, even when they were thinkers. "No man can exist without pleasure," remarked St. Thomas Aquinas, who ought—if our understanding of the dour medieval mind is correct—to have been urging us to put away our playthings in favor of prayer. "Life would not be tolerable without poetry," announced St. Teresa of Avila, making it perfectly clear, in a parenthetical remark, that she meant it would not be tolerable even in a convent for contemplatives. St. Augustine thought that whenever a conflict arose between the enjoyable and the useful, the useful had to give way as being, in the ultimate sense, inferior. Many of the soberer thinkers of the past, including those who had by vow denied themselves most earthly pleasures, did not scruple to elevate what they called recreation to a dizzying position in the hierarchy of the worth-while. Indeed, "worth-while" is an inadequate word to describe the value they placed upon pleasure. No man could exist, life would not be tolerable, without such patently superior experiences.

The experiences we, in the twentieth century, tend to lump together as recreational forms—our distracted dalliance with *kitsch*, our bridge games, our dyspeptic Christmases, our sullen visits to the squash courts—do not honestly seem to merit the enthusiasm some minds have bestowed upon the act of play; nor do they afford us anything like the satisfaction we might rightly demand of activities held to be superior to our work. Someone is using a word in a sense that eludes us. However, since we do find our lives increasingly empty these days, it may be worth taking a few minutes to ask whose use of the term is faulty.

Begin with the dictionary—ours, not Aristotle's. Recreation signifies: "*1.* Refreshment in body or mind, as after work, by some form of play, amusement, or relaxation. *2.* Any form of play, amusement, or relaxation used for this purpose, as games, sports, hobbies, reading, walking, etc." Yes, there is the noun as we know it, and there is nothing in it to justify Aristotle. What of the verb, the act that presumably produces the noun? To recreate is "to restore, refresh, create anew; to put fresh life into. . . ."

There is an overtone here. "To create anew" and "to put fresh life into" begin to suggest what a profound pleasure may do and a hobby may not. Is this an echo of an ancient, and now mislaid, hope? If there were actually in the universe a regenerative power that could fill us with fresh life, that could add to our very being still more being, shouldn't we be willing to prize it more highly than the labors that seem to drain our being away? There is a hint, though only a hint, that our foolish diversions and ephemeral amusements belong to an instinctive strain in the human personality that, given its head and nursed to its highest, might place us in the unexpected and exhilarating position of being reborn. Some sort of rebirth is what we are asking for. The word beckons, faintly.

But how can so trivial an activity make good so vast a promise?

☼   *. . . not balances*
         That we achieve but balances that happen,
         As a man and woman meet and love forthwith.
                              —WALLACE STEVENS

Obviously handball will never be enough. We do understand that there is such a thing as physical recreation—indeed, we are inclined to think of all recreation as physical recreation—but we neither underestimate nor overestimate its blessings. We know that our bodies are growing slack as we give orders to the world from our swivel chairs and that half an hour at the gym every once in a while will help to keep them from becoming altogether unsightly. We know that a kink in the shoulder muscles can be relieved by flexing those very muscles and that a backache may yield to a five-o'clock swim. We know that sport is good for us and that we should probably make time for more of it.

We also know, no matter how often we reproach ourselves or how much our wives scold, that we are not going to make more time for it—and for a very sound reason. It is not our bodies that are giving us trouble. Much as we have neglected them, soft and unresponsive as we have permitted them to become, our constitutions are holding up remarkably well. In fact, they are demonstrably more durable than the nature-boy physiques of our pioneer grandfathers, as a glance at the headstones of any hundred-year-old graveyard will testify. Cholesterol and all, we live longer. And we do not really feel notoriously unfit.

The kink we are trying to get rid of is not the one in our shoulders but the one in our hopes. Where we feel a keen dismay, and a gasping need of refreshment, is in our heads—in the minds that shape our convictions and in the convictions that move our wills. It is our powers of belief that are grinding to a halt. The refreshment we need most sorely is not physical but intellectual.

Though we feel this in our bones and reveal it in our restlessness, we have not yet faced it as a fact that might be dealt with. There are two present causes for our inability to act, I think. One of them is a failure of imagination: equating, as we do, nearly all refreshment with physical refreshment and knowing physical refreshment for the limited boon it is, we cannot conceive what specifically intellectual refreshment might be, what it might consist in or how it might be made to work. The other is a failure to keep up with our own history: we have not yet grasped the degree to which we are all becoming intellectuals.

Indeed, we grasp this last point so little that the very statement of it must at first sight seem preposterous. Isn't this the age in which "intellectual" is a pejorative term, the age in which "eggheads" are held in contempt? Haven't we long since lost respect for the well-written sentence, the cogent argument, the philosophically formed principle, and substituted for these things the mushy slogan, the packaged "image," and the comfortable expedient? Perhaps so. But no matter what words we choose to regard as abusive, no matter how frantically we try to relieve the pressure on our minds by pretending to surrender them to Madison Avenue, we are now most of us engaged in working with concepts rather than things, which means that we are working as intellectuals.

If nearly all of my work consists of entering figures in a ledger, I am working as an intellectual. If nearly all of my work consists of arriving at averages and quotas and estimates and profit margins, I am working as an intellectual. If nearly all of my work consists of doing something with words, even though I am using the words to tell lies about soap or merely making stenographic copies of words someone else has dictated to me, I am working as an intellectual. I may not feel like an intellectual, I may humbly and properly make no claim to be one, but I am cornered nevertheless: all that I do depends upon my ability to deal with constructs that have been fashioned, and are now functioning, cerebrally. I am a "brain" worker, not a drawer of water or a hewer of wood.

Few of us are any longer directly concerned with ships and shoes and sealing wax; those are invoices and memos we hold in our hands. When I quoted earlier some of Teilhard's observations on the end of the Neolithic age—the disappearance of a bird in the hand *or* two in the bush and the appearance of that cross-reference filing system in which no bird sings—I did not mention how far the philosopher expects our present movement away from cabbages and toward abstract counters to take us. Teilhard supposes, without regret, that our employment of intricate and infinitely flexible intellectual concepts will not only increase but will increase to the point—a distant point, but one day due—where the activity of man, or of that new creature which man will have become as he continues to advance along the evolutionary scale, will be exclusively an activity of mind. Free of his dirty fingernails, and of the field that made them dirty, man will move in his thought, have his being in the "noosphere"—which is the word Teilhard has invented for this new and as yet unimaginable mode of existence.

Well, we are not there yet. We are not even—it is something of a relief, isn't it?—halfway. But that we are on the way to some such hyperintellectualized state is as plain as the graphs on our office walls and the science-fiction formulas on the tips of our childrens' tongues. Like it or lament it, deny or defy it, we live more and more cerebrally, less and less physically. Each year that passes sees us substituting yet another card that can be punched for what used to be a name and, before that, a face. The multitude of abstractions we spoke of a chapter ago have come to us in this way; that they are going to go on multiplying there can be no doubt, and, as they multiply, our activity must become ever more conceptual. We are intellectuals willy-nilly, and if we don't like the notion or choose to despise "intellectuals" it may be because there is an unresolved tension in our new and unaccustomed place in the scheme of things. We are doing intellectual work without having discovered any satisfactory forms of intellectual play. We are expending a form of energy without knowing how to renew it.

Now it does rather seem as though the play must be brother to the work, as though the human equipment that is involved in the drudgery is the human equipment that needs most to be refreshed. This may, I suppose, seem a plain enough statement as it appears on the page, almost an incontrovertible one. But it is not the position we normally take in practice. Instead of assuming that the man who works with his head must somehow play with his head—even that phrasing sounds absurd—we are inclined to repeat the motherly old saw that urges the sedentary intellectual to get out and play ball. The sedentary intellectual doesn't want to get out and play ball, of course. We know that. He is always being quoted—the remark has been attributed to dozens of bright men—as saying, "When I feel the urge to exercise, I sit down until it goes away." And though we may smile at his impudence we distrust his indolence. The fellow who works with his head should clear his head by doing something with his hands: that is the routine prescription.

But is there an honest man among us who isn't sadly aware that the prescription, when taken, regularly fails? An hour on the sand-lot may indeed clear a broker's head; but the broker knows perfectly well that the clarity doesn't last beyond the hour on the sand-lot, that it vanishes with the first cocktail that is poured in the locker room. The broker hasn't touched the particular nerve that is worn, and the alarm bell rings instantly upon his return to the barricades.

Furthermore, as most of us who degenerate behind desks are painfully aware, the trip to the sand-lot can be somewhat discouraging. Certified public accountants do not normally show to advantage with bats in their hands; teachers make terrible ballplayers. It is the man whose muscular structure has been in use by day who shines on the field of a summer evening; it is he, too, who gets some refreshment out of the sport, since he is unlimbering the equipment that has threatened to knot. Mother's advice to the contrary, physical play is for men whose bodies are both in trim and in danger from their physical labors. What the rest of us are looking for—soon it will be all of us—

is an exercise of mind that will make the mind glory in its capacities as an athlete's body may be said to glory in *its* capacities. We ask to be made happy in our new-found and ever-expanding intellectuality, not depressed and drained by it.

We do, of course, possess certain intellectual diversions, though just as we do not yet think of ourselves as intellectuals we rarely consider that these pastimes are, in fact, intellectual pursuits. The game of bridge we are so ready for is plainly a game played by the intellect; that is one reason why it suits us. The *kitsch* that clutters our coffee tables, even when it is as inferior in quality as the ghostwritten jokebook that has been gleefully labeled a "non-book" by *Time* magazine, is still a thing of words and design demanding a mind to grasp it; the grasp may be feeble, but it is something more than physical. The latest Erle Stanley Gardner mystery novel must, in all honesty, be accepted for what it is: an intellectual structure composed of sentences (however simple), suggestive clues (however misleading), and an ultimate pattern (however contrived). Sentences and patterns cannot be enjoyed without some sort of cerebration. All of these things at least attempt to apply balm to the area that is bruised; they call upon the minds that are overworked to employ themselves sportively. The *divertissement* fits the crime, as it were.

Still, it does not turn us into exultant gods or even exultant men. Few weeks go by that we do not play one game of cards, watch one television show, dip into one detective novel or (for the housewife) its romantic equivalent. The *divertissements* we know do have the virtue of taking our minds off our work and putting them onto other things that don't matter so much. But the soothing distraction we are thus bequeathed does not for a moment make us think that rebirth is just around the corner. The fun may be appropriate, it may in some way employ and ventilate the mental processes that need airing, but it doesn't really catch up with our fatigue, much less transform a fatigue born of intellectual activity into a joyous reveling in intellectual activity. An athlete may be exhilarated by the effortless responsiveness of his body; we have not yet come close to feeling a similar joy, a singing exuberance, in the effortless responsiveness of our minds.

What we are digging for, and presently despairing of, is a play of the mind that will match the labor of the mind—and match it not only in kind, so that it will get at the threads that have begun to snarl, but in scale. We require an intellectual pleasure that will cause us to rejoice in our intellects; and we require an intellectual pleasure that is at least as great as the intellectual burden imposed by our work. With anything less we shall continue to slip downhill.

How great is the burden of our intellectual work, and what, precisely, is its nature? The essential nature of the work is organizational. Intellect, in the most rudimentary definition, is the power to "perceive or understand." It is also, and immediately, the power to perceive possible or necessary "relations" between the things we have come to understand. That is to say, once I have grasped the wetness of rain and once I have grasped the thickness of wood, I can begin to imagine in my head a roof over my head to keep the rain off. I have made an effective relationship between three things: rain, wood, me.

It is important to remember that this primitive exercise in architecture is first performed in the busy quiet of my mind. Out of all the things I have come to know, and out of all the relations I can perceive between them, I form a plan, propose a possible order. Having done so, I put the plan to the test, attempt to impose my projected order on real wood and real rain. If my mind weren't capable of imagining harmonies before the fact, I'd be fumbling around on a hit-or-miss basis forever.

The essence of my intellectual work, then, lies in the effort I must make to conceive a working pattern. I assemble all of the matters that concern me in the factory of my head, sort them and compare them until the pieces fit, and then emerge from my dreaming with an invisible blueprint. "What do you have in mind?" is what the man behind the desk, or the woman across the breakfast table, asks me. Proudly, I explain.

The activity of my intellect in envisioning accurate and stable relationships before the fact has been, beyond question, magnificent. I might well be proud to possess such a tool or at least grateful for having been given it.

But I am in for a shock, a whole series of shocks, and not only because the man behind the desk may turn out to have a mind of his own or because the woman across the breakfast table may have arrived, with less logic but more force, at a possible plan that is different from mine. I have, somehow, not yet brought into balance *all* of the elements that are clamoring to be ordered in my complicated existence. I may very well have worked out my plan for the day; but I have not yet worked my employer, or my wife, into it—and that will take more planning.

Consider, for a moment, the various orders I must struggle to construct every day of my life, one after the other. I am, to begin with, forever at slippery grips with the job that earns my living, wrestling with it hourly in an effort to make it stand still.

It won't stand still. The morning I begin to feel secure, to tell myself that I am entitled to one deep breath, is the morning a blunder of three weeks ago returns to chill my blood, the morning the telephone rings to say that I am wanted in the main office, the morning that someone else is promoted and a suggestion I prided myself on turns out to be damaging and a contract that could not be canceled is canceled and what am I going to do about it? The poet Kenneth Fearing has looked in on me, and made notes:

> *You have forgotten the monthly conference. Your four o'clock appointment waits in the ante-room. The uptown bureau is on the wire again.*

*Most of your correspondence is still unanswered, these bills
have not been paid, and one of your trusted agents has
suddenly resigned.*
*And where are this morning's reports? They must be filed
at once, at once.*

*It is an hour you do not fully understand, a mood you have
had so many times but cannot quite describe,*
*It is a fantastic situation repeated so often it is commonplace
and dull,*
*It is an unlikely plot, a scheme, a conspiracy you helped to
begin but do not, any longer, control at all . . .*

*When they dig you up, in a thousand years, they will find
you in just this pose,*
*One hand upon the buzzer, the other reaching for the phone,
eyes fixed upon the calendar, feet firmly on the office rug.*

Only the feet on the rug are firm, and someone is pulling at
the rug. Any man on his way to the office in the morning is a
man wondering what is going to go wrong today. Any man on
his way home in the evening is a man wondering what has gone
wrong today. Home is another of his problems in order.

He has, from the time he married, been working for stability
there. He has done everything humanly possible to insure it:
he has gathered his family under a roof (the roof needs repair,
taxes are up again, the cat was killed), he has clothed, fed, and
helped educate his children (John has cut himself with a knife
he was forbidden to carry, Mark has no driver's license but has
taken the car out, is there something really neurotic in Sheila's
grinding relationship with her mother?), he has tried to create
a life with his wife that would embrace the children but not be
destroyed by them (why does she leave the punishment to me?,
why doesn't she leave the punishment to me?), he has established a small human community that is constantly threatened
with dissolution—by death, by temperament, by termites. The

foundations seem to have cracked anew each time he sets foot in the door.

His sweat to keep the keel even and the decks dry does not end with the juggling act he performs at the office or the human repair work that awaits him at home. He must also fashion for himself, and then keep from getting out of hand, an orderly social life. He is forced to build, and continually re-prop, not only a small human community but a larger, and somewhat independent, one. He reaches out to construct a neighborly network, a spider's web of friends. It is a web that snaps often. The friends he makes make their own demands; they are not always politely willing to play the parts assigned to them in the structure.

They are offended. They must be seen soon or they will be offended. They bring their own disharmonies to visit: "loved him, hated her." Not all of them mix well together. Separated, they insist upon equal time. They are all necessary, they are all loved, and they are all, taken together, intolerable. Peace made in one corner is resentment bred in another, and it requires no more than an unintended slight, an imagined neglect, a chance glance that may be mistaken for jealousy, to strain and then sever the vast, delicate, patiently-drawn weave.

There are still other structures waiting to be built. A man may very well wish to help arrange, and then find his efficient place in, a political pattern that is strong, flexible, and sensitive, lest one fine day the irresponsibles take over. This will call for some thought and some properly-applied energy, and he will come down to his coffee and newspaper one morning anyway to find that a philosophy he despises has been voted into office. He may feel in himself, a few layers down, a nagging need for spiritual stability and so undertake a possibly painful search for a transcendental order. Along the way, and even at the end of the search, there may be further pain in store for him: it was one of the greatest of saints who gave us the phrase "the dark night of the soul."

But the most defeating task of all remains to be faced. It is the task of creating an order among orders, of relating all of the separate patterns we have separately established to one another in such proper proportion that a master pattern will exist and hold firm. Even success can be a hazard here. Is my professional work going well, so well that if I redouble my efforts just now and work nights for a while I may be able to break through decisively and thereby assure my family of security for a long time to come? The move to break through decisively leaves my family unattended; by the time I turn my attention homeward once again, the emotional lag I have allowed to develop in the living room may have become irreversible—and the security I struggled for meaningless. I can prove so successful in my social life that I never do get to the office in an acceptable condition; and I can be such a spectacularly fine companion for my admiring youngsters that every one of my adult commitments is weakened at the base. Do we see the Williamsons tonight or spend time with the children? Either answer is unsatisfactory, because it leaves one obligation unfulfilled.

Good patterns collide. I may achieve religious stability by making, in good faith and to my intellectual satisfaction, a specific religious commitment. I may find, as many have found, that the commitment is politically damaging. I may arrive at a considered political position and subscribe to it publicly, as I must now do in conscience, only to find that it is professionally damaging. I may lose friends and fail to influence people precisely because of a coherent structure I have managed to erect.

And, alas, these are only the penalties of cohesiveness, of—if you will—achievement. Most of our experience is not of solid structures clashing or of successful structures becoming altogether too successful. It is of actual or threatened failure in one or more of our many simultaneously-built patterns, with the clear implication that at least one of the buttresses of the over-all harmony is now gone and that we may expect, at any moment, the roar of brickwork and the thud of timbers as the tower comes tumbling down. A motion-picture image of my childhood that comes back to me now and then is that of the comedian Harry Langdon, alone in a cyclone in an abandoned town, holding up a swaying building with one hand. Mr. Langdon, in his innocence, at first supposed that he was leaning on the building—as we at first suppose that we are leaning on our jobs or our wives—and not that it was leaning on him. As he casually took his hand away to turn and look up the street for the sight of another soul, the building slowly inclined toward him. Mr. Langdon noticed. But it was not in him, as it has never been in any clown or in any of the rest of us either, to run for his life. His absolute obligation was to put his hand back and keep that mighty building upright, though less and less so all the time. That is the position we are all in with our separate pieces of unstable architecture.

But Mr. Langdon's dilemma would have to be compounded many times before it equaled ours. To reproduce the situation in which we generally find ourselves, we should have to imagine that, while one building was being held up, another was starting to go. And then another. The dash to shore up one leaves the second exposed. As the third starts to buckle, it becomes at long last clear that we have only two hands. The wind is rising.

Of the six or seven orders we are committed to sustaining, which dare we let ride, and for how long? How fast is our foot-work, how much breath have we left? In time, one or another of our obligations overwhelms us. We surrender—with a sigh and with some sense that we have done our best though our best was not good enough—the perfection of the family (well, there's nothing more I can do about Sheila), the affection of some friends (we just don't see them any more, it seemed best not to), the religious commitments we have so carefully arrived at (I thought for a while it might help, but it didn't). With the rottenest timbers cleared away, we are free to concentrate on the ones still standing, and so keep them from coming down, too. But we are conscious now of a partial failure, and we rush back to the fray with damaged wills. Having lost one, are we bound to lose more? All? Is the battle for order really fore-doomed, and are we engaged in nothing more than a strategic retreat, holding off an implacable enemy with the last of our small arms? Was the effort at order always a fool's errand be-cause order itself is an illusion?

I have been using an image that seems to involve our hands more than our heads, and, of course, our hands do come to play a part in some of the work that we do: perhaps in punishing the children, though this is increasingly frowned upon; perhaps in cutting the grass, though power motors are relieving us of the resistance we used to meet; perhaps in passing out leaflets at political rallies, though television is rapidly making the rally un-necessary. Some physical energy is still required as we try to impress upon nature and our fellow men the dazzling visions that our brains have worked out.

But the impulse that has set our wills and our bodies into executive motion, that has plunged them into the practical act of ordering things, has been an intellectual impulse, an intellec-tual conviction. When the order goes awry or seems impossible of execution, it is to the intellect that the boomerang returns. That is where the impulse now falters, the conviction fails. Our minds begin to doubt the mind's own equipment: we have seen the arts doubting, if not denying, the validity of words, the validity of thought, the validity of form and pattern and every sort of order. The mind itself does not quit, or even really tire, as we are well aware when, exhausted, we are trying to get to sleep or, despondent, are trying to blot out our despair. It goes right on coining ideas and relating them to one another. But it is now engaged in an act of self-mockery, spending all of its inventiveness on spurts of denial, making near-hallucinatory connections between images that laugh at themselves and insist upon their unreality; Joyce and Kafka, Pirandello and perhaps Pound knew what was coming. Self-conscious with failure, the mind begins to question the worth of its own consciousness. Busy as ever, it turns in on itself, derides itself, uses the processes of order to proclaim the impossibility of order.

It could be refreshed and brought to something like a rebirth, it would seem, by only one thing: an experience of order. The order would have to be actual, not projected. It would have to be present, not rumored. It would have to be complete, not partial. It would have to be stable, not tentative. It would have to be given, not worked for. But if a man could feel himself moving, effortlessly and unerringly, through the corridors of a house in which each beam and tile, each lintel and sill, had instinctively assumed its palpably just place, in which doors opened without being touched to draw him deeper and deeper into ever more perfect and ever more central recesses, in which he knew, at the last and as he stood at its heart, that every stress of stone and argument of wood and grip of mortar and breath of air had arrived at a pact that would hold them together forever and him in their complacent embrace, in which the whole substantial and unruffled harmony seemed to be smiling at him as though in a mirror and intimating quietly that so much buoyant proportion was only a reflection of something that he, too, possessed, it is possible that his mind would be pleased. He would not only see order and so know it for a fact. He would, for that moment, inhabit it.

It is the struggle toward an unrealized order that drains and disheartens us; only a certainty of order, whether we are participating in it or simply standing humbly before it, can mend the rent in our souls.

It shouldn't take more than a glance to see why our bridge games, pleasant as they may be, aren't quite up to stitching us together again. With all of their virtues—and their virtues are intellectual—they are open contests, guaranteeing us nothing in the way of a perfectly tooled experience. It is always possible, of course, that on some evening when the world is enchanted, the cards obedient, and the players wiser than wise, a perfect game will be played. After it, the players will look at one another in stunned delight, conscious that they have become part of the music of the spheres, sighing with Euclid and Edna St. Vincent Millay. Such an occasion is bound to be rare; the game itself, which proposes to pit players of varying skills against one another in a conflict whose outcome is in part dependent upon chance, promises no such immaculately proportioned shape. I sit down to the table knowing that I may err, that my partner may err, that my opponents may err or play brilliantly without warning; I also know that any one of us may be mindlessly dealt "bad cards." I am guaranteed suspense, perhaps profit, but not harmony.

That is why, as I rise from the table, I am as often as not somewhat irritated. I may be reproving myself for my own stupidity or complaining inwardly about my opponent's much too infallible "card sense." But I rise nettled. The game has not been played with a consonance that could ever be called beautiful. And that is why, too, I am strongly inclined to prolong the agony by joining my fellow players in a "post-mortem." Rehashing the plays that went wrong, re-counting the trumps that were so curiously distributed, making apologies and taking advice, we now work together to construct by hindsight the perfection that might have been and was not.

The casual handiwork of Erle Stanley Gardner comes a little closer to what I am looking for, being a thing of bits and pieces that finally fall into place, leaving me, after my apprehensions, with a comforting pattern. I am also, in this case, promised the pattern. I am assured before I begin to read that every stray shot in the dark, every shapely ankle deliberately displayed, every baffling contradiction Perry Mason uncovers will sooner or later be accounted for, made meaningful in itself and made meaningful as part of a master plan. (It doesn't matter how bizarre the master plan is, so long as everything shakes down to a fit.)

You see, I don't really pick up a prefabricated detective novel for its garish incidental suspense, or at least not for the suspense alone. If the man manufacturing such a novel were merely to lure me along with bloodstained gorillas and goose-flesh escapes without offering me, in the last few chapters, a satisfactory resolution of what seemed a crazy-quilt crime, I should dismiss the novel and its author out of hand as frauds. Indeed, the only detective novels I am likely to despise entirely are those that have "cheated," those that have been intellectually dishonest in the final accounting.

What I am racing toward so breathlessly as I flip the light-weight pages—it is a law of the genre, really, that no man's prose must ever detain me—is the display of hitherto concealed logic that goes off at the end like the snowflake burst of a Fourth of July rocket. The logic may be no more durable than the shoot of fireworks is; but, while it is billowing out into its utterly balanced glory, I am as happy as a child in the bleachers. Order unfolds before me.

The fact that all of this is prefabricated does not disturb me. I insist that it be. I insist that every clue that is laid down be both pertinent and misleading, that my companion, the author, be a cunning sleight-of-hand artist, that he hold in his head from the outset the solution to the jigsaw so that he may tease me along the way by seeming to mislay the pieces. My confidence in the author and my delight in his book depend altogether upon a bargain we have made. I have been willing to pretend to be fooled; he has guaranteed to turn the fooling into a limpid pattern by the time I have finished his fanciful story. I am so enamored of the patterning, in fact, that I do not resist—I even rather like—the transparent adherence to formula that marks chapter after chapter. The blonde who comes in to cross her legs for Perry Mason's benefit comes in on a precise stroke of the clock; Paul Drake shows up faithfully four reading-minutes later; Perry Mason does something reckless on the eighth swing of the metronome; and Hamilton Burger enters the courtroom on what must be the very same page each time. These echoes do not revolt me; they reassure me. I am moving within a pattern toward the disclosure of that pattern, as before.

Of course, I realize I am also in a rut. Perry Mason gives me a certain pleasure, a pleasure which is intellectual because it takes place in my mind and because it concludes in a clear assertion of relationships. But it is a pleasure I find static. That is, it does not grow from year to year; it may not diminish if I keep to a reasonable diet, but I cannot feel its powers—or mine—expanding within me. I am bemused by a kind of ordering; but I am not taken in by it. I cannot really go back to my own problems in order, feeling that what Perry Mason can do I can do, or what Erle Stanley Gardner has contrived I can contrive. I have had an experience of order, of a sort, and it has relaxed me; but it has done nothing to renew me because it is patently irrelevant. Perry Mason is a fake, and Mr. Gardner is at most an agreeable conjuror.

Their order is unreal. It does not correspond, either at way stations or at journey's end, with anything I face. Compliant, efficient, beautiful Della Street is a dear girl; *my* secretary is pregnant and has a cold. Perry Mason is a very strong man for a paper doll; when *I* throw my weight around, I get hit. I never seem to meet any Hamilton Burgers; the opponents I must contend with are unfairly intelligent. I never do get a chance to sit around in the last chapter modestly explaining the secrets of my success. Life is tougher, less co-operative, where I live. I have not been made over because I have not been convinced; Mr. Gardner and I have passed an evening kidding one another.

Suppose, though, I were to pick up a book, or halt at a painting, or attend a play, or lift my head at a strain of music that did seem to have heard of just my pain, to have felt just my frustration, to have known the precise grubbiness and ambiguity and occasional honor and more frequent humiliation that I know—an unexpected reflection, in short, that handed me back the truth; and suppose that this strange echo of my days and my desires seemed to possess not a too easy order artificially imposed upon it but the whispered, squirming hint of an actual order within it, an order that was not a mechanical stamp but a living seed? Would that begin to do anything for me?

We are now, of course, at the threshold of that special, eternally hospitable, world that has been made in man's image by the so-called fine arts. That the fine arts have been willing to mirror the meanest of truths is well known: Oedipus blinds himself, and Medea murders her own children; Anna Karenina ends beneath the wheels of a train, and obsessed Ahab clings to the back of a monster; though Dante's Hell would seem to be full, Michelangelo continues to rain upon it a storm of stunned sinners; galleries can scarcely contain all the bloodied St. Sebastians; the orchestra must be expanded to accommodate Beethoven's cry.

And yet the one insistence that rings through history, the one plain platitude on which angry and arrogant philosophers instantly agree, is that in all of this festering turmoil, this implacable tragedy, this cynical comedy of clinging indecency, we are in the constant presence of order. From Plato to T. S. Eliot the refrain varies little. Plato, never quite certain whether he trusted artists or not, was nevertheless willing to explain that "we are endowed by the Gods with vision and hearing, and harmony was given by the Muses to him that can use them intellectually" in order to "assist the soul's interior revolution, to restore it to order and concord with itself." T. S. Eliot, wanderer of the wasteland, remains certain that "it is ultimately the function of art, in imposing a credible order upon ordinary reality, and thereby eliciting some perception of an order *in* reality, to bring us to a condition of serenity, stillness, and reconciliation. . . ."

Order, harmony, concord, reconciliation. These are not only in art but are also produced in man by art, if we are to believe what we have ceaselessly been told. In a mysterious meeting of minds—the mind of the artist as it is illuminated in his work, the mind of the auditor as it is illuminated *by* the work—a healing energy comes to birth, flowing from the canvas or marble or concentration of sounds to the susceptible auditor in a secret metamorphosis.

The order that washes such waves of strength from a canvas is not, to be sure, a particular order we have asked to have demonstrated; we haven't filed all of our grievances with a mechanical brain and let it return to us a practical, pertinent answer. It is simply order itself, breathing in and out regularly, capable of self-support and asking no work of us, order self-evident, order at peace in its palpable wholeness, order identifying itself not by name but by stance.

We are made aware that order *is*, because there it is before us. It is also relevant, having managed to gather into its embrace as unruly a crew of sinners and as ugly a set of home truths as any of us has ever encountered. And it is, whether one had any hopes for it or not, instantly recreative.

It is strange how often we must prove to ourselves what we know to be so. I have believed for a long time in the directly recreative power of the arts; I would have argued the issue with anyone. Yet when I first climbed the forbidding steps of the Bargello in Florence, it was not with any confidence that I might come away relieved of the fatigue I was feeling. My fatigue was overwhelming. I had clambered about Rome in the weeks before, had stirred every inch of brick dust at Hadrian's destroyed paradise, had descended and ascended the tiers of gardens at Tivoli and the hill-streets of Assisi. I had been rewarded many times, never more than in Florence itself a few days earlier when I had turned away, disconcerted, from the vacuous copy of Michelangelo's David that stands in the central square and had sought out—and been stilled by—the original sculpture in the Galleria Accademia.

But there had been so many days in Rome and Tivoli and now more in Florence and I felt that even ardor could at last bring its own exhaustion. I did not want to mount these stone steps. As I mounted them, sighing, I promised myself that this would be the last gallery. I would protect my gains and go sit, indefinitely.

I was thus unprepared for Donatello. Donatello is not much discussed these days. One hears of dancing stone *putti*, loaned for this or that exhibition; one is familiar, courtesy of post cards, with the official lion of Florence and perhaps with the fact that Donatello carved it; one may well have paused, leafing a book of photographs, over a gouged and almost male Mary Magdalen and looked for the credit line that would say whose work it was. I knew that Donatello was a sculptor, that he stood in some sort of relation to Michelangelo, and little more.

Moving into a showroom undergoing repair, and seeing a huddle of temporarily displaced statuary at its unscaffolded end, I reluctantly threaded my way into the jumble. I now seemed to have stumbled into the confusion of the Last Judgment itself, with St. George and John the Baptist and a David who looked like a juvenile delinquent all milling about seeking their proper categories. One joined this group more than one observed it; it was difficult to observe the thyroid gape of an adolescent Baptist without backing into Marzocco, the lion. But the enforced intimacy won. It would not be resisted, not by weariness, not by apathy. Donatello had gathered so many stresses into so much composure that first the stresses and then the composure became mine without further ado.

I have no wish to write an essay on What Donatello Means to Me. What I am forced to record is the simple thoughtlessness with which I left the Bargello and walked through more days of Florence (where in Santa Croce I came upon a Donatello, a gray sandstone *Annunciation*, that no one had promised me), more days in Ravenna, more and more days of what had threatened to exhaust me but seemed always to replace in excess the energies it used. I never did think of rest again until the very foolishness of Venice caused me to sit down, laugh out loud, and realize how rested I was.

The infusion was not only psychological, it was total, carrying a leaden body along with it blithely. Without meaning or wanting to, one can learn that some kinds of pleasures have almost frightening restorative powers. These powers do not, by the way, confine themselves simply to generating a prolonged love affair with the object that begot them, any more than they become the specific powers we require in the conduct of our work. They are general powers, powers held in suspension as Donatello's St. George holds his virility in suspension, reservoirs of well-being that make all challenges tolerable, even welcome. They may be spent, or husbanded, in almost any way one wishes. They are pools of knowing, of knowing so much more than can ever be said, coursing through the blood stream and finding an outlet in renewed liveliness.

It has always fascinated me to watch people coming out of theaters. When they have not enjoyed themselves, they seem tired, and they want to go home. When they have enjoyed themselves, it is as clear from their muscle tone as it is from their eyes: they are alive, and they are ready for something, whatever that something may be. The difference is as simple, and as literal, as that. A vision of order wakes everyman up.

Argument as to the precise qualities that account for this miracle of insight, this vision that blinks nothing and still resolves everything, is not a thing we are going to settle here.

When the Last Judgment does come, experts will still be debating how Michelangelo managed to anticipate it.

Many terms have been coined to account for the secret formula; all of them no doubt are in some part appropriate. One man will insist, as a friend has insisted to me, that the clue to all order lies in proportion alone. Pointing to a high, straight, naked stairway in Italy, my friend announced himself willing to settle for the unflinching justice of its functional rise. No ornamentation; no curve to no purpose; no dawdling; no piece out of place. That "justice" which gives every element its proper due is, in this view, the key to our deep intellectual satisfaction. In one of his plays Graham Greene has suggested that God is "just" in the way that a straight line is said to be just and that we are at fault when we imagine Him as given over to emotion or susceptible to special pleading. For my friend the beautiful, the profoundly pleasing, began and ended in the assertion of an incorruptible rectitude.

Another man will urge, with as much intensity, the doctrine that the order we seek and find in art is due to its superb management of a great variety of things within a single design. "Variety within unity" here becomes the credo, and we are commanded to give special attention to the one underlying beat that keeps the blood flowing through so many diverse and contending parts. Our lives do seem to be a clutter; to have the clutter reproduced, and to feel an organizing throb coursing through the clutter, delights us beyond belief.

If there is an explanation that contents me more than most as I pick my way through such debates, it is the slightly more complex suggestion that the depth and density of the order that confronts us comes not from a single stroke of the managerial hand—the stroke that stakes everything on simple proportion, the stroke that uncovers a startling oneness in a vast diversity—but from a trio, nothing less than a trinity, of interrelated orders. Here we are forced to talk about three different proportionings that may be discerned in the work: an external order at the surface, an internal order moving "deep down things," and the order that exists between these two orders so that they may properly belong to each other.

The external order is the easiest to see. It is obvious enough that the surface of nature is subjected to an arranging and a rearranging, at the election of the artist, that are almost brutally willful. Though the artist may proclaim that he is "imitating" a certain landscape, it is plain that he has been capricious about the placing of a barn, half a dozen trees, and a hill that one would have thought immovable. He has shifted things about quite as freely as Moss Hart did when he manufactured his own landscape and so moved George Kaufman to remark that "it just goes to show what God could do, if He had the money." Shapes and shades are redistributed without the least qualm of conscience; the object is to make them better suited to their role in a master plan. So far, child's play. And so far, supposing that we are indebted to no further ordering than the tidying up of the external world, we have brought into being little more than mere prettiness.

Suppose, though, that while this sort of gardening is going on, another kind of subtle control is being exercised over the nearly invisible and only dimly perceived interior behavior of tangible things—as much in the secret energies that give birth to the seen landscape as in the secret impulses that make a Rouault clown face so unexpectedly shy. Something stirs at nine fathoms; something *must* stir there or we shall realize quickly that we are simply staring at good housekeeping. It is boring, after all, to listen to an art teacher or a Venetian guide going on and on about the triangular composition, and the mathematical repetition of color, in Titian's *Assumption*. What is specifically triangular could be grasped by any fifth-grader, and the recurring colors have the subtlety of corner stop lights. Surely there is something more interesting to be said, we fume to ourselves, than that geometry has been put to work in the formal scaffolding of this altarpiece. Either it has acquired a buoyancy from some inward source or it is a protractored exercise in the obvious.

Though it is no longer fashionable to speak as though the "content" of a poem or a painting had anything to do with its quality—or even as though a poem or a painting could respectably acknowledge to having any such "content"—it still is easier to conceive an interior order of things as though it were, in fact, an order of subject matter. That is to say, in a novel it is never enough for the syntax to be shapely or the sequence of paragraphs to be just; it continues to be important that, at some level, we recognize and believe in the behavior of the characters. Similarly, there is a substructure in painting, in music, in any experience of the beautiful which whispers to us that it *is* beautiful and not merely handsomely assembled. However this intimated substructure may be defined—whether one wishes to say that it has been truly overheard from nature or that it is a lucky accident come to spontaneous combustion in an artist's brain, brawn, and bowels—it is the penetrating whisper upon which our truly hearing the artist depends, the "inscape" that makes the landscape luminous. Indeed, it is not only a conviction that this interior coherence exists that keeps the artist thrashing at his materials long after he has mastered the trick of duplicating resemblances, it is the command of this hidden coherence that initially sets him to work. The restlessness of the artist comes from his impatience with mere appearances.

But the most difficult order of all, perhaps, remains to be discovered: the order that will flow back and forth, in an effortless embrace, between the supple, secret order of the interior and the ingenious, geometrically defensible order of the surface. Each must be introduced to the other, made into the other. The creation of a perfect intimacy between them, so that every shift of external shape will be the result not of arbitrary management but of a tremor detected beneath the crust of the earth, is the last, most limpid, ordering of all. Because it must flow two ways at once, inward and outward, a facing of mirrors that reflect one another, a loving exchange of identities that dare not be intercepted, this ultimate proportioning is maddeningly elusive. The two prior orders, exterior and interior, are in a kind of constant terror of seeing the light that lives between them go out.

The job is always in danger of being botched, and to botch it is the equivalent of murder. A wrong stroke at the surface can scratch the inner order forever. No doubt that is why Michelangelo turned on one of his *Pietàs* in a fury with a sledge hammer and why Gogol threw the monumental sequel to *Dead Souls* into the fire. What had lured these men on had remained bafflingly buried beneath all their craft, perhaps compromised by that craft.

Conversely, a lapse of vision at the interior level can leave an immaculately-proportioned surface utterly empty. The best draftsmanship, illuminating nothing other than itself, can become a permanent, hollow ache: Robert Browning has made us feel that this was so for Andrea del Sarto, and we know that Wordsworth could occasionally write poetry that merely kept time.

The three orders, if three there are, must touch hands at every dangerous intersection, must know one another in a perfect constancy or in as nearly perfect a constancy as the poor fallible artist—who, it has been said, never finishes his work but abandons it—can manage. Michelangelo's *Pietà* was put together again, by friendly hands; we feel kindlier toward it than he did.

However, all of this is only one more way of trying to account for the proud presence of order in Kant's "agreeable" arts—and "agreeable" is not such a bad word, after all, suggesting as it does that when all things agree with one another they are instantly agreeable to man. It does not much matter, for the purposes of our present inquiry, whether one prefers to locate the origin of his delight in proportion or variety or a round dozen of terms we have blithely neglected. What matters is the clue we have been given to our own natures, to the irresistible impulses and the insatiable needs of the instruments we call our minds.

Man's mind has a bias, a leaning, a predilection: it thirsts, without thinking twice about it, for order. A baby puts up building blocks seventeen times a day; a child cannot keep his hands from thumbtacks and paste or from his parents' staplers; adults progress to doing their engineering with people. The human creature cannot help itself: it has a compulsion to arrange. When arrangements go wrong—when blocks tumble and thumbtacks bend—a spirit dominated by so powerful a compulsion cannot help but kick and scream and swear and despair in just as powerful a sense of frustration.

But—and this is the hint we'd better hang on to—if man has always known he was seeking order, he has also always known where to find it. In his most primitive state, with the fire going out and the flints going blunt and the imposing beast mocking his right to survival, he crawled into a cave and did an inexplicable and apparently unnecessary thing: he drew pictures on the walls. Authorities are not yet agreed as to just what conscious or unconscious motives may have impelled Upper Paleolithic man to so decorate his dark, rough meeting houses. Perhaps he drew a beast with some thought of putting a mark on the beast, so that it should be easier to kill. Perhaps he drew it in triumph because he had killed it. Perhaps he had eaten the beast and was now offering its memory—the memory of its living beauty?—to God as a form of atonement. We'll be a long time being sure.

The one thing that is clear is that he was not careless. The bison is painstakingly, often exquisitely, shaped. At a time when tools were crude and social structures clumsy and refinements of any kind very hard to come by, this activity was astonishingly refined. Lines move in an exhilarating economy, without coarse excess; forms are respected with something like awe; if this was the enemy, the enemy was in some way loved. The bull, the horse, or the headlong deer soars on the wall in its articulated elements, in the admired propriety of its parts, in the plunging, rippling, suspended sweep of its own harmony. It is as much like music, though far more austere in its sound, as Mary McCarthy tells us the fifteenth-century Pazzi Chapel is:

"The continual play of . . . basic forms and their variations —of square against round, deep against flat—is like the greatest music: the music of the universe heard in a small space . . .

"No more exquisite microcosm . . . could be imagined, for everything is here, in just proportion and in order, as on the Seventh Day of Creation, when God rested from His labors, having found them good."

Upper Paleolithic painting and Pazzi Chapel share certain things. The play of basic forms, in just proportion and in order. The sense of rest, of being in the presence of completeness. The conviction, when all is done, that what has been done is good.

It has been man's nature, however thoughtlessly he may first have pared a stick or drawn a picture in the sand, to discover order in the very things he was failing to order. The mind that was trying to arrange things looked back, for a moment, to notice that all things boasted their own inherent arrangement. The vision pleased him, for many reasons, some of them still unfathomable. But at the very least it confirmed his most compulsive suspicion: that order *was* and could be. By renewing his belief in the bias of his mind, it renewed him altogether.

What then? If these observations are acceptable, have we

nothing to do in the process of lightening our hearts and re-freshing our minds but dart off to the nearest gallery and, for a small admission fee and the price of a pamphlet, recover our souls' composure? It isn't as simple as that. We have learned to think too much, and the simplest things are the hardest for us to do now.

5

✬
✬
✬

The Act of Being Pleased

> Poet, never chase the dream.
>   Laugh yourself, and turn away.
> Mask your hunger; let it seem
>   Small matter if he come or stay.

> —ROBERT GRAVES

IT SHOULD be so easy, as easy as falling off a log. Here are two propositions which, so far as they go, are reasonably unassailable. Twentieth-century man is increasingly baffled by the number of things he must work into patterns; his anguish stems from the fact that the erection of stable patterns has come to seem impossible. But close at hand lie a number of curious objects which in themselves constitute evidence of successful patterning and which, by implication, suggest that pattern is a natural property of every movement, or every stillness, of life. (Discouraged man, meet encouraging object. Go home happy. The beliefs that have driven you this far are sound, your instincts are accurate, you can be of good heart.)

It won't wash. We know it won't wash. Each of us has quite deliberately set aside an evening for the specific purpose of sinking ourselves into, and draining something out of, the kind of ordered, harmonious experience we have heard about. We've nodded assent to the proposition. Yes, yes, of course, it's true. We have brooded for some weeks over the fact that we haven't yet found time to sit down and regale ourselves with the rejuvenating patterns we are willing enough to believe in. We have now cleared the decks, already rather angrily disposed of the children, lost the first twenty minutes because someone about us *had* to have the answer to a question before they'd "leave us alone," and we have made sure that the cigarettes and the ash tray and the footstool are in place. We have adjusted the light over our shoulders and picked up *War and Peace.* Here goes.

Sometimes we are feverish within twenty minutes (am I renewed yet?). Sometimes we aren't aware of what a ratchety evening it's been until the evening is nearly over (oh, Lord, do I feel enough better to have lost all this time?). There is a theatrical expression, "flop sweat," which is used to describe the clammy perspiration an actor notices on hands, neck, and brows as a first-night performance begins to go wrong. "Flop sweat" is upon us now. A deliberate evening of relaxation can be as psychologically unnerving, as emotionally disastrous, as any experience we know. And not because we have been reluctant about it; if anything, we have been too much in earnest.

We know—because we have been told so—that there are massive contrapuntal harmonies in *War and Peace.* We are intelligent enough to be able to notice them—once we have got the characters' names straight, which takes a while. Yes, this is interesting, that is well done. The scale! And what time is it?

Interrupted, we leap up, close to delirium in our gratitude. During the weeks that follow, the memory of the evening crosses swords with a certitude. The evening didn't work. No, it didn't, let's be honest. But it *should* have worked. Let's be clear about that. Nettled, we wonder how soon we dare attempt it again or how long we dare go without attempting it.

We continue to give assent to a theorem, without in the least having been fired by the trial run to plunge at once into Cézanne or Stendhal or Bach—certainly not Bach. We accept the premises that have been so patiently laid out for us without having the least knack for applying them personally, much as, shifting our attention from the architectural triumphs of the fine arts to the architectural triumphs of nature, we nod rather worriedly over everything Thoreau is quoted as having said without disturbing, in our souls, a secret conviction that death would be preferable to a week in the woods.

In nervously approving a theorem, we give it a limited, cerebral, ultimately impotent response precisely because it is only a theorem, a mathematical demonstration of what might be good for us. So far from stumbling onto a passion for which we'd fling a number of things to the winds, a fondness we'd indulge whether it were good for us or not, we have drawn the lid from a candy box only to find the chocolates ash-white. We are tackling our pleasure according to the intelligent laws of our work, flirting disastrously with what might be called the IOU theory of the fine arts or the IOU theory of fun.

Consider. Aware that we are in need of an experience of order, and aware that the fine arts offer an experience of order, we march to the fine arts demanding a profit: order on the barrelhead. In this state of mind, we are converting a pleasure into good, solid cash, finding a "use" for it. And the order we speak of has, unsurprisingly, a decidedly abstract ring to it: it is not so much the unnamed and intangible order that makes the roundness of an apple pleasing to the eye as the named order that can define an apple in terms of its line and its mass. We have brought our slide rules and balance sheets with us and applied them to the problem of delight. Though we are dealing with propositions that are perfectly true, we are dealing with them as though they were negotiable; we have not begun to surrender any of the habits of mind that may, in this country, be bad habits.

That there is something wrong here is made plain by the fact that, even when we have discovered our need and discovered where to satisfy it and then done our duty like solid little soldiers, we tend to come away uninvolved, unenraptured.

Henry James warned us that we should. In a letter to Bernard Shaw he insisted that the artist who meant to provide the spectator with "*direct* encouragement" and the spectator who trooped off to art with profit aforethought—looking for just such "encouragement"—would never really become friends. The artist who held his helpful patterning in the forefront of his mind would probably wind up producing something "shallow and misleading," and the spectator would most likely turn on him "with a vengeance for offering him some scheme" that was only an hypothesis and not quite what he was looking for. James did not wish to deny that, brushing shoulders with art, "we can on the whole feel encouraged." But any such benefit would have to be a posteriori, after the fact, almost an accident, a dividend that should not have been anticipated. To demand an accounting a priori, to insist that art should fulfill an obligation before it has had time to kick its heels, is to take a short cut that will keep the spectator forever outside the country of pure contentment.

It would seem that there are certain experiences in this perverse life of ours that will not yield to command; they will yield only to surrender—like Maurice Chevalier's squirrels. M. Chevalier once explained to an interviewer that pleasing an audience in the theater was like feeding hungry squirrels. No matter how hungry they might be, you couldn't foist your treats upon them. You couldn't call to them, urge them, make an obvious offer. You had to pretend to an absolute indifference, perhaps even come to feel something like indifference, before you could reach *rapprochement*. Once you'd settled down quietly and seemed to promise nothing, they would come comfortably to you.

Each of us, whether he is sitting composedly on the park bench or circling warily with the squirrels, is aware that there are desires which can be satisfied only after being suppressed. The one sure way not to have a good time at a party, for instance, is to go to the party determined to have a good time. Fun is a sneak and likes to catch people unawares; it simply will not tolerate wrenching. The one sure way not to enjoy a meal is to attack it headlong. The palate is most responsive when it is pretending to reserve. The worst hour you will ever spend with your children is, inevitably, the children's hour, the hour that has been purposefully scheduled. An adult can unsettle a child utterly by giving him his fully focused attention. Sex? I sometimes wonder if the twentieth century hasn't devised a foolproof method of insuring frustration. Having learned what a good time D. H. Lawrence had, or said he had, and being regularly instructed in the demands we may make of the connubial act both for ourselves and for our partners, we go to "the glory of it"—I have stolen the phrase from Tennessee Williams—better informed than our fathers did; our fathers, however, seem not to have been so disappointed as our novels and plays and columns of counsel suggest we are. We seem to have worked out a technique for approaching one kind of couch that sends us frequently to another.

Still, we know that what Robert Speaight has called "the relaxed grip"—the grip is upon ourselves, holding our powers in abeyance so that, paradoxically, we shall enjoy them more— is a prerequisite to some of our most prized satisfactions. What can this mean intellectually, in the thread of our running argument? It could mean that our minds will meet with no profound pleasure until they have ceased being acquisitive, that they will never be able to fasten firmly upon the very joys they most desire unless they first show signs of a willingness to let go.

We have added up a strange list of demands by this time. We have been searching for an intellectual act that, so far from being dispiriting, might prove restorative. It would have to be a genuine *act*, not a euphoric state: the mind would have to be attending to something, not drugged. The act would also have to be truly *intellectual:* that is to say, it would have to allow the mind to follow its own bias, which is toward knowledge and toward order, in fact toward the knowledge of order. At the same time this act would have to be free of the necessity of creating its own order: the mind's bias would have to be satisfied without exhausting effort, the threat of failure, the penalties of "work." And we now seem to be suggesting that the act should properly belong to that group of human experiences which attain their so eagerly sought objectives by approaching those objectives without evident eagerness, almost in a spirit of reserved, gentle, and generous disinterest.

In sum, we are looking for an act that is thoroughly playful while being thoroughly intellectual. Is there such an act? Of course; there always has been. The men who made the first great philosophical assault upon the mystery of the human condition came upon it quickly and prized it so highly that we now think them out of their minds. "Contemplation" was the name assigned to the act, and for someone like Aristotle it was the clue—the exclusive clue—to "perfect happiness." For us it is either an empty term or, if we can find any specific content for it, one that is meant to describe a near-lunatic passivity.

Norman O. Brown, in his *Life Against Death*, accepts the work of Schopenhauer, done in the first half of the nineteenth century, as "a landmark, seceding from the great, and really rather insane, Western tradition that the goal of mankind is to become as contemplative as possible." Reading the remark, we do not instinctively question Mr. Brown's adjective "insane." What we question, in real bewilderment, is the statement that at some time or other there was a Western contemplative tradition; when was that?

The term has not, of course, fallen from our vocabularies, though its connotations seem less Western than vaguely Oriental; and if we were put to the task of completing a free-association test in which "contemplate" needed to be coupled with something else, we should, beyond doubt, couple it most quickly with "navel." While we have probably not used the word in conversation in twenty years, we remain able to endure its presence on the printed page. We do not necessarily boggle when we read in T. S. Eliot: "It was the Greeks who taught us the dignity of leisure; it is from them that we inherit the perception that the highest life is the life of contemplation." We are nodding by the fire with a poet now; we understand that. Poets tend to go on in this way, especially if they are Anglican and rather elderly, and what harm can there be in one more gesture of obeisance to those remarkable Greeks (isn't Edith Hamilton wonderful?). "Contemplation" is now a word with butter on it; it slides down easily—so easily that, not having to be chewed, it leaves no taste.

If we were to take Mr. Eliot the least bit seriously and begin to investigate for ourselves what the Greeks may have imagined they were talking about, we should be put off at once by the schoolboy preposterousness of it all. Do you know what "logical" structures Aristotle was able to erect in support of his proposition that "perfect happiness is a contemplative activity"? Here is one of them:

"We assume the gods to be above all other beings blessed and happy; but what sort of actions must we assign to them? Acts of justice? Will not the gods seem absurd if they make contracts and return deposits, and so on? Acts of a brave man, then, confronting dangers and running risks because it is noble to do so? Or liberal acts? To whom will they give? It will be strange if they are really to have money or anything of the kind. And what would their temperate acts be?"

Aristotle goes on to suggest that it would be quite tasteless of us to suppose that the happiness of the gods depended in any way upon their ability to control themselves since, after all, "they have no bad appetites." One by one the virtues that we most admire in men must be discarded as possible sources of happiness among supernatural creatures; these virtues seem merely "trivial and unworthy" in gods.

"Still," the argument concludes, "everyone supposes that [the gods] *live* and therefore that they are active; we cannot suppose them to sleep like Endymion. Now if you take away from a living being action, and still more production, what is left but contemplation? Therefore the activity of God, which surpasses all others in blessedness, must be contemplative; and of human activities, therefore, that which is most akin to this must be most of the nature of happiness."

God makes no bank deposits, runs no risks for His friends, establishes no philanthropical foundations, feels no need to join Alcoholics Anonymous. Neither toiling nor spinning, nor yet dozing off altogether, He is confined—by the dignity of His office and a kind of forced unemployment—to a single unproductive activity. This must make Him happy, because happy He is.

The argument has charm, which is not what one looks for in Aristotle (though I must say that few sentences make me happier than the philosopher's observation that "in the theater the people who eat sweets do so most when the actors are poor"). It is not, however, an argument one would wish to develop extensively in a contemporary courtroom or at a cocktail party.

The dictionaries we have at hand do not help very much, should we wish to pursue—in stubborn bafflement—the suspiciously mystical concept that seems once to have been a Western goal. The trouble with dictionaries is that they helpfully reflect a changing language and so can only give us back our own usages; admittedly, the "traditional" understanding of the term we are tracking down passed from our casual comprehension about one hundred and fifty years ago.

Nevertheless, and for what it is worth, Webster: contemplation is "*1*. Meditation on spiritual things" (which is what we were afraid of). It is, secondarily, "musing" or "study." Turning to its verb form, we come upon a few variations: to contemplate is "*1*. To view or consider with continued attention; to meditate on" and also "to purpose or intend."

I have been rash in hinting that few of us have used any form of the term conversationally in recent years. Chances are that we have chanced it, occasionally, in the sense of expressing a purpose or intention, as in "I contemplate going, if the weather is right." The usage, however, falls on the ear with a faintly false overtone; it is a shade pretentious, perhaps even ugly, with its air of borrowed dignity blanketing direct, useful prose. Something is slightly off.

It is also clear that no lexicographer can attempt to explain the term today without rather hastily equating "musing" and "study." These two activities are not, as we commonly understand them, quite the same thing, unless we mean to say that a man who is "musing" is in a "brown study." Certainly we distinguish between the two practices as we send a child upstairs to do his homework: in this case "study" becomes imperative and "musing" expressly forbidden. But the lexicographer is under pressure, in our no-nonsense time, to make his definitions clear and practical; he is expected to find a better equivalent for "musing" than dawdling around.

The pressure, and the direction in which it urges him, is made perfectly plain in a Webster issued twenty years later than the one I have been using (1936 for the quotations above, 1956 for those to come). "Musing" has dropped out of second place now; contemplation is "the act of thinking about something intently; study; consideration."

Need I put the new *thinking* in italics? Is it necessary to call attention to that "intently," the same "intently" that transforms the older "to view or consider with continued attention" into "to look at intently"? A feverish note has begun to assert itself here. Surely those eyes that are fixed so "intently" are doing something more than, and something different from, what was done by the eyes that were simply looking "with continued attention." The drone would seem to have become a surprisingly busy bee.

The opportunities for finding a link here between the word as Webster tells us we use it and the word as it might ever have been used to define a state of relaxed, unproductive, and intoxicating happiness are decidedly slim. "Meditation on spiritual things," missing altogether by 1956, is in any case no part of our quest; that is not what we are looking for, though we behave oddly when a book by a Trappist monk recording the stages by which he abandoned a practical life for a contemplative one attracts us so perversely that we boost it swiftly onto the best-seller lists. The success of Thomas Merton's *The Seven Storey Mountain* may very well be taken as a hint that a considerable number of our contemporaries sense that something is missing in their lives that Father Merton may have found in his. Still, if the book is read with a touch of envy, it is also read at arm's length: we are curious, but not really eager to be convinced. Even a good many members of Father Merton's own Roman Catholic faith, being moderns, remain unclear about the purpose of meditation in a cloister. Explain to one of them that it is not the function of a contemplative religious order to run parishes, give sermons, teach school, or minister to the sick and you will most likely be met with an earnest frown. There is an attempt to understand, an attempt that generally ends in an honestly anguished question: "But, then, what do they *do?*"

The laughter that could be heard a few years ago during a film in which an elderly priest stared at one of his athletic young assistants and mockingly inquired, "You *do* meditate, Father?" was an intelligent, if instinctive, response. The thought that meditation might go hand in hand with the socially useful activities in which the younger priest was so blithely engaged was patently absurd. We sense a similar absurdity, viewed from another angle of the auditorium, in Paddy Chayefsky's play *The Tenth Man* when a young rabbi explains to a colleague that the first step to be taken in developing the spiritual life of a community is to organize a basketball team. We get the joke, in each case; something ludicrous beats its wings in the air just above us. Pressed to analyze the joke, or to explain what is ludicrous, we should, however, be quickly in difficulties; when the singing group is trained and the basketball team organized and every member of the congregation appropriately cared for, what *does* a priest or a rabbi do?

If the contemplative aspects of the religious life elude us even while we are humorously aware that *something* is eluding us, the contemplative possibilities of secular life are equally puzzling. Once again an awareness that one kind of experience is singularly absent from our lives reveals itself in an odd way: a book in which Anne Morrow Lindbergh records her reflections during a few days at the beach, cut off from the occupations of a markedly successful and productive life and with little more than a sea shell to tease her ear, makes its way onto the best-seller lists as Father Merton's book has done. *A Gift from the Sea* is widely read and in many quarters professedly admired. Briefly, a dissatisfaction is brought to light, an appetite stirred. But what, after all, is Mrs. Lindbergh talking about? We'd all like to get away for a few days, wouldn't we? (We'd be terrified to do so; Mrs. Lindbergh can fill the vacant hours by thinking out a book, but what if we were caught without a single thing to put our hands to and with no voices to fill the void?).

Neither the contemplative religious search of Father Merton nor the contemplative natural search of Mrs. Lindbergh is more than a fugitive grace note, heard on the run and forgotten by another sunrise. The most recent abridged dictionary does not take either into account. If we are also to rule out of our accounting those somewhat fretful and familiarly profitable

terms—study, thought, consideration—which remind us so much
of our workaday habits that they seem not at all suggestive of
an older and contrary tradition, what clue is left us? Any?

There is a very spare phrase we haven't taken the trouble to
dismiss: "to view . . . with continued attention." Is it possible
that in these bare bones there is a memory of practices past?
What would it be like simply to look at something, without
fierce concentration, without the effort of thought, without the
urgent need to wrest clear gain from the object or the hour—
only with continued attention? Attention itself requires nothing
more than staying within certain boundaries, such as looking
out of a window without letting oneself be diverted to the
interior of the room; it may be held as lightly as the thread of
a kite. Suppose we were to let ourselves, submissively, be drawn
to a view, and then, with only just so much alertness as is
needed to hear a baby cry in the night, not let ourselves be
drawn away from it. Suppose, in a kind of contented abstinence,
we were to refrain from trying to understand more of the
landscape before us than the landscape cared to display for us,
that we were willing to follow the bend of bough and straggle
of gravel and tilt of pole wherever the bend and the straggle
and the tilt chanced to take us, that we concerned ourselves not
with pattern or profit or even pleasure but merely with watching like a token sentinel in safe country, that we gave our eyes
a quiet carte blanche and permitted our minds to play at liberty
over the face of an untouched terrain? Could that, then, be
called the play of the mind?

Here is a columnist on a small-town newspaper making a
random note:

"Saw three birds abreast, wheeling leisurely in great circles,
the movements of six wings synchronized and perfect . . . as
they momentarily held the morning sun and then winged away
into the distance. . . . Had I been an ornithologist, I would
have identified these creatures on the wing by name, delved into

their family tree, and explained something of their habits. Seeing them in the eyes of a weather prophet, I might have announced them as omens of fair weather or of rain and related stories of the past that would prove my predictions. As a philosopher perhaps I would see them as symbols of peace and harmony and would expound at length the examples that nature has set for mankind. Being none of these, I saw them only as three white birds in a morning sun and thought them beautiful."

Slightly fine writing in a conventional vein? No doubt. But it isn't only small-town diarists who have written in this way or remarked on these things. Joseph Conrad, in his much-admired preface to *The Nigger of the Narcissus*, suggested that the conscious artist was most hopeful of producing in his readers a very similar state of mind:

"To arrest, for the space of a breath, the hands busy about the work of the earth, and compel men entranced by the sight of distant goals to glance for a moment at the surrounding vision of form and colour, of sunshine and shadows; to make them pause for a look, for a sigh, for a smile—such is the aim, difficult and evanescent" of the artist.

But if it is possible, as everyone has always known, to take a certain idle pleasure in glancing at a fragment of the natural world, and if it is clear that this kind of woolgathering bears some relation to the deeper pleasure given us by an artist's headier distillation of the same fragment, are we yet in the presence of anything important enough to be called intellectual and free enough to be called play?

It is obvious, in a most superficial sense, that the mind is playing as it daydreams, jaywalks, and gawks; it is simply skittering about without any particular focus, and that is a kind —a low kind—of playing. How is it still playing as it burrows its way through the composed intricacies of an art form? It would take some daring to pretend, for instance, that the mind of the artist had anything sportive in it as it struggled to conceive the complex, subtle, stable architecture of *The Age of Anxiety, The Hound of Heaven,* or *The Princess Casamassima.*

Yet W. H. Auden speaks of poetry as a "game of knowledge," and a game is a thing to be played. Francis Thompson, in his essay on Shelley, likened the poet's gifts to "the child's faculty of make-believe raised to the *n*th power."

"He is still at play," Thompson said, "save only that his play is such as manhood stops to watch, and his playthings are those which the gods give their children. The universe is his box of toys. He dabbles his fingers in the day-fall. He is gold-dusty with tumbling amidst the stars. He makes bright mischief with the moon. The meteors nuzzle their noses in his hand. He teases into growling the kennelled thunder, and laughs at the shaking of its fiery chain. He dances in and out of the gates of heaven: its floor is littered with his broken fancies. He runs wild over the fields of ether. He chases the rolling world. He gets between the feet of the horses of the sun. He stands in the lap of patient Nature, and twines her loosened tresses after a hundred wilful fashions, to see how she will look nicest in his song."

And it was in the letter to Shaw that we quoted earlier that Henry James raised his plaintive voice to say: "You surely haven't done all your own so interesting work without learning what it is for the imagination to *play* with an idea—an idea about life—under a happy obsession, for all it is worth. Half the beautiful things that the benefactors of the human species have produced would surely be wiped out if you don't allow this adventurous and speculative imagination its rights."

Certain writers have insisted with some exuberance—perhaps in terms too glowing for contemporary taste—that not only the stars in the heavens but the ideas in his head are an artist's playthings, that poetry is the product of a toyshop. We are, by the way, confronted with a small conundrum right off. Haven't we also been told, *ad nauseam,* how difficult an artist's "work" is? The agonies of creation have been endlessly described, and while we detect a trace of self-pity in these men who make moan we are convinced—if only by our own aborted efforts to compose a sonnet or paint a Sunday picture—that the task is not altogether simple. After all, what the artist produces is called a "work" of art, isn't it? Aren't we dealing with something wrought, something made, no doubt with desperate difficulty?

We are, indeed. But what the poets seem to be telling us is that "play" is the first term of a poem and the last. The poet's excursion does not begin in a fierce act of the will, a determination to make a poem. Much as he might like to make a poem, he cannot, until he has idled. In the act of idling, he overhears something. Enchanted, he follows it, more or less without asking questions. Following it, he finds himself wheeling and dipping—but through perfectly real life—in as dizzying and foolish a way as an amusement-park ride does. On one breath-taking descent, though, he discovers something: the apparently aimless plunging hither and yon has followed a pattern that was at first invisible but that was there all the time. It exists now only as a memory—the kind of patterned afterglow that survives the twirling of a Fourth of July sparkler—because he has come so many dips away from the blind spot at which he started. He is at the end of the fun, but he is exhilarated, and just as we feel that we *must* collar a friend after any exhilarating experience and shower him with our enthusiasm if we are not simply to burst with it, the poet must rid himself of his excitement. As he attempts to do this, he stumbles into work—work that he very often wishes he had never stumbled into, it is so impossible. He is faced with the necessity of translating an erratic and unanalyzed flight that is over into a set of obstinate and earthbound building blocks—clumsy words and regulated line lengths—in such a way that the flight will begin again and prove just as unreasonably delightful for someone else as it has for him. His work is the result of his play; and if it is done right, it will turn into play again. We who were denied the first experience, or were not sufficiently idle to have it, are offered the pleasure of playing over his work until we find, unexpectedly, what he has found for us.

If what he has found for us is an intimate, experienced, un-earned knowledge of some sort of pattern *in* things, he will have met the second of our requirements: he will not only have pro-vided a playful outing but will also have provided it at an intellectual level.

We do have some difficulty, as we have seen, in conceiving of the contemplative act—whether it is a matter of looking out of a window or wandering through a poem—as essentially play-ful; it takes a good bit of extravagant shouting on the part of creative people to tell us that this is so. But we have even more difficulty in conceiving of the same act as essentially an act of the mind. If we are lolling on the grass without thinking, doesn't the absence of thinking make us, automatically and for the moment at least, mindless? And in the case of a poem or a painting or an onrush of music, isn't it our senses and our emotions that are most being played upon?

We like to think so, in this age that prefers to think of all pleasure as mindless and, in the sensual sense, self-indulgent. Color is something that simply bombards our senses, perhaps leaving them drugged; melody tickles our emotions until we shudder a bit, and to respond too readily to anything so like an orgasm really ought to leave us ashamed. These are atavistic survivals, relics of war paint and tom-tom throbbings which have become sufficiently sophisticated to enter polite society and are no doubt good for us as means of discharging old urges; but to suppose that they direct themselves primarily to the mind —and to the mind at its most perceptive—seems a sorry rationali-zation.

It is fascinating, nonetheless, to watch our own often violent displeasure when a presumed work of art does succeed in stirring our senses, and does succeed in rousing our emotions, and then does not succeed in meeting the needs of our minds. We do not always recognize our intellectual frustration, in such cases, as intellectual; but we recognize it as frustration and are quick to say so. Not long ago I spoke to an articulate woman who is a fervent theatergoer and who disliked, intensely, the position in which a certain play had put her: she felt obliged to dismiss it in spite of its obvious merits and her obvious emotional involvement with it. Yes, she agreed, it had caught her interest. Yes, it had created a lump in her throat. "But when I came out of the theater, the lump was still there!" she expostulated, angry and dissatisfied. She had been moved; but she remained moved, in a way she did not like; some further agent ought to have intervened to dissolve that lump, to distribute that emotion in some meaningful way.

The play, good as it was in achieving its initial effects, had not gone on to the end that is promised by every play, every poem, every contemplative act: that condition of "serenity, stillness, and reconciliation" of which T. S. Eliot has spoken. That the senses and the emotions play vital roles in every aesthetic experience—whether the experience takes place on a sand dune, on the New Haven railway passing Harlem, or in a gallery set apart for the purpose—is plain enough. That the roles are supporting roles is less clearly, less frequently, realized.

An act that bestows its benefits only upon the condition of "continued attention" quickly cries out for two props. Attention must first be caught, if the act is to begin at all. And it must then be held, protected against distraction, for a certain span of time—a span long enough for any given object to yield its particular satisfactions. The senses do the first job, the emotions the second.

It is easiest to follow this Tinkers-to-Evers-to-Chance sleight of hand in the so-called "time" arts, where things happen in succession. Because plays and novels and extended pieces of music gradually unfold themselves as the clock ticks on, we are reasonably able to chart the growth of our responses. The "space" arts behave a little differently: in a painting or a frieze everything is set upon the counter at once. Here every delight would seem to be simultaneously available, and available as a completed unit: no third acts are hidden from us, no allegros deferred, while intermediate pages are turned. But from the spectator's point of view any very firm distinction between the "time" and the "space" arts is apt to be misleading; both are obliged to tease the spectator, detain the spectator, carry the spectator through time in much the same way.

We readily understand that once we have seated ourselves in the theater there is a pressing need for our eyes and ears to be turned from our fellows—who are still bustling and buzzing about us—and to be fixed on the stage. We just as readily understand how the trick is managed. The designer throws a wash of light over the most arresting shapes he can devise, given the circumstances of the play. The principal actress enters as fetchingly as she dares, dressed all the way up to—and sometimes well beyond—the means of the character she will eventually create. The first line spoken raises a question or makes a tantalizing reference or strives at least to fall pleasantly upon the seducible ear: it had better do one, or all, of these things, because it cannot yet make sense as part of a plot. Few playwrights are willing to settle for lines; it has long been customary to open with street brawls, witches at their brewing, sight gags, agitated figures pacing, or the arrival of obviously ravaged and out-of-breath messengers.

A calculated assault is being made upon our nerve ends, the most commanding assault all of these lures can manage, so that we shall be coaxed into attending to what is at the moment inexplicable. We are being led into the labyrinth by the most provocative of verbal threads, teased into the bull ring by the visual dazzle of a cloak of near-scarlet. Novelists and musicians have their own ways of swiftly touching our no-more-than-skin-deep susceptibilities, and poets become skilled at halting us in our hurry with a salvo or caress, with openings that say "The splendour falls on castle walls" or that mention "When lilacs last in the dooryard bloomed." The artist's invitation is so worded as to make our mouths water: I do not go on with the Whitman poem, after all, because I know or care what the poem is about; I drift to the second line because I have liked, in my primitive way, the soft fall of those *l*'s in "lilacs last."

Again, seated in the theater or holding a heavy novel, it is clear enough to all of us that sensation alone will not occupy us long; we shall soon feel cramped, or weighted down, if those first skin-deep sensations are not succeeded by a power with a more muscular grip. Having been drawn to the party, I must also become a part of it if the occasion is not to pall. I have approved of the eyes of the actress, the stagecoach tumble that sets the novel in motion, the scurry of the orchestration as it makes its opening declaration in a tandem race of chords; now what? With the street fight over, I must become interested in a girl named Juliet or I shall leave the playhouse; six more street fights will not keep me there. With the first thrust of sound past me—the thrust may be dominating or insinuating, it does not matter—I must become sufficiently enamored of the four or five notes the composer has named as his theme to want to know them more intimately under a variety of disguises. With alliteration acknowledged, or with a jack-in-the-box rhythm already sprung in my face, I must wish—I must be *made* to wish—to move with the poet as he quarries, beneath assonances, a lode three layers deeper and closer to my heart. I must become emotionally embroiled if I am to stay the course, and my affective link to the developing scheme of things must become stronger and more tenacious as the scheme, multiplying its parts until it seems they must clash, reaches for its climax, its destiny. In certain of the "time" arts the progression from simple sensory stimulation to deep emotional commitment is transparent enough to make discussion of it superfluous.

But we think less often about the binding process that must similarly take place in the "space" arts. If a piece of sculpture is there all at once, it is nevertheless impossible for us to see it all at once—for quite a long while, anyway. Painters are forced to catch us, too; and they may catch each of us with different fishhooks. It is interesting to watch a group waddle into a gallery, cohesive as ducks, and then disintegrate as though they'd been atomized: one man's eye is drawn irresistibly to a curve in a far corner, another's is transfixed by a bolt of red from the blue. The tug of the senses distributes, divides, isolates, then acts as a private adhesive. A single line may make this gesture of summons, a titillating contrast may do it; even a fragment of content—though content is frowned upon in these years of our sorrow—may pull one of us where he hadn't honestly meant to go. Once this bid to the feast has been responded to, and once the eye has devoured the spill of violet or the strain to the vertical that said "Come here," has the painting been "seen"? No, of course not. It has merely been noted, in part and in passing. Even if three inviting stop signals blink at us from three different spots on a canvas and we leap from one to the other as they contend for our interest, we have still not succeeded in seeing anything steadily or anything whole. Not until a gesture of grace, a guiding strand of filament nearly as invisible as Ariadne's, begins to beckon us from the things that have arrested us to the things that are less immediately arresting do we begin to move with the work into its own recesses. What is guiding us now may be properly called, I think, an emotional line, a kind of quiet companionship that marks the first stirrings of love after an obviously pretty face has been properly appreciated. The painting began by taking our eye; while our eye was upon it—we hadn't meant to stay long—it also took our hand. From the shout that drew us to it we are being carefully, patiently drawn by a whisper that was there to begin with but couldn't be heard for the shouting. We follow, with docility but increasing excitement: one of the shapes to which we so swiftly responded elides, without warning and without resistance, into another, makes way for it. Each gives in turn, seeming to say that they all belong to one another and that there is no need to fear for their privacy. In time, every inhabited spot on the canvas is visited, because the thread we are walking beside has gone everywhere; it is a line with no end to it, like those picture-puzzle lines we used to follow as children, and no matter where we have started from we are given a complete tour of the grounds. All the while, from the moment we began to care and were rewarded by an offer of company, our affection has been growing in accelerated pulse beats—an affection the canvas seems almost to return—and our sense of well-being is expanding so rapidly that we are soon in danger, if we are not careful, of breaking our "continued attention" in order to look quickly for one of our wandering fellows, collar him, and hurry him over to share our near-bursting ardor. But we are careful: the stirred feelings that have so subtly, casually, but bindingly followed our first sharp sensations are still on the rise. So long as they are on the rise, we are waiting for something.

In so much that is compulsively sensual and then much more deeply and more indissolubly emotional, where is there room for intellect to assert itself? Actually, it has been speaking its piece and issuing constant small reminders of its prior claims the whole time. No matter how abruptly a comet's tail of color has coursed into view, no matter what loving and lingering commitment we have made to what seems an unfolding Eden, we have not for a moment lost consciousness of the act we were performing or of the nature of the materials upon which it was being performed. We have surrendered our wills, to be sure—in the sense that we have given in to the impulse to stay, to do nothing, to let happiness happen if such be our good fortune. But we have not silenced our minds, our powers of knowing. At our most enthralled we continue to know red for red, paint for paint, Juliet for an actress, and our animated response for our own so animated response. "To know a story when we see one," Lionel Trilling has said, "to know it *for* a story, to know that it is not reality itself but that it has clear and effective relations with reality—this is one of the great disciplines of the mind." We have not taken to marijuana, and would not if we could: the experience is so delightful that we want to double it by knowing our own delight—now, while it is going on, and later, when it can be remembered. We have submitted our senses and our emotions to an experience; and we have enriched the experience immeasurably by continuing to know it, every inch of the way, as an experience.

But if the mind is in perfect possession of its powers all the time that the flesh is tingling and the blood running faster, it is waiting for something, as we are. It is waiting, precisely, for the moment when the whole painting, or the whole play, or the whole concerto, has come to the precipice of its completion; when each of its not really separate parts shall have been somewhat separately investigated; when the convoluted line that leads us eternally inward shall somehow arrive again at the point of its own departure; when all of the sensual stirrings and emotional attachments that have flared like lucifers and then smoldered like long-lived, ever-growing fires shall have come, with the line, to a point of meeting and a threat of total combustion; when everything that is in the work presses so closely upon everything else that it must, under such pressure, either be satisfied or destroyed; when, finally, all the felt things and all the known things are ready to become known *as one thing.* Then, as aching rhythms and contending colors and factions as opposed as the Capulets and Montagues cry out for a universal satisfaction that can only be achieved by bringing them all into ultimate, exquisite balance, the mind blinks once, stands back, and sees the balance. In this decisive act of perceiving an order among parts, a harmony in differences, beginnings in ends and ends in beginnings, urgency is resolved and passion spent.

Without this *coup de grâce* executed by an intellect that is both benevolent and stern, we should be quite unable to fulfill, or even terminate, the longings aroused during the turbulent journey. It is not in our power to put an arm around Othello and console him for what he has done; he is an actor, or a name on a piece of paper, and we cannot reach him. Nor can anyone offer to console us, to absolve us of what we feel, after we have watched Desdemona die; after all, we did not kill Desdemona. If we are free to go home with the lump in our throat dissolved —as my furious friend was not free to do—it is for two reasons: because we have all along felt something quite different from Othello's love of Desdemona or any love of our own for Desdemona, we have had an emotion *about* Othello's love (we have known a story for a "story") and so played with a "known" object rather than a "loved" one; and because known emotions, coming to birth in the intellect rather than in the bowels, can be resolved by our knowing more, as the cankers beneath our skins cannot. In a piercing vision, and with a gesture of just disposal, the mind—at the crossroads, at the crisis, at the last coming-together of ignorant armies and unlucky lovers—discovers that it knows all.

Without exerting itself, the mind has arrived at a judgment; it has *seen* justice, rather than forged it. In this comprehensive knowledge it finds content, and the content quiets everything that has earlier been stirred.

It has for a long time seemed to me that this is what the earlier analysts of the arts meant by "catharsis." We have trouble with the term today, as we do with so many terms. Contemporary psychology, and contemporary forgetfulness of the nature of the contemplative act, have made us assume that the emotions expelled at the crisis of a play or a great coming-together in any of the arts are the emotions we have brought with us from home, from our pasts and our presents and our pent-up "real-life" yearnings. Viewed as a universal emetic, "catharsis" has been questioned and, quite properly, dismissed. W. H. Auden has dismissed it this way: "If I understand what Aristotle means when he speaks of catharsis, I can only say he is wrong. It is an effect produced, not by works of art, but by bull-fights, professional football matches, bad movies and, in those who can stand that sort of thing, monster rallies at which ten thousand girl guides form themselves into the national flag."

Still, if art does not purge us of our private churnings in the manner of an exhibitionistic revival meeting, it does—as we know from our own best experiences—possess some power to quiet us. Suppose "catharsis" has little or nothing to do, except by way of an occasional accident of time, place, or personal identification, with the unrealized impulses that dog our own hours of sleeping and waking? What if the forces that are "purged" are the forces specifically generated by the symphony or the seascape and generated for the very special purpose of making us listen to the symphony or look at the seascape long enough to arrive at a peace that does not resolve the tensions of our private lives (these must still be resolved in our private lives) but resolves only the tensions stimulated by and contained within the work of art? What if this sensual and emotional exercise does not in the least seek its "cathartic" satisfaction in any sort of direct sensual or emotional release (we cannot kiss the pretty girl upon the stage, we cannot warn Hamlet that the blade is poisoned—or, rather, we can, and intelligently refrain from doing so) but looks for "cathartic" satisfaction in the reconciling powers of the mind? Dare we say, then, that whatever purgation takes place takes place at one remove from the flesh, that it is essentially an intellectual, rather than an intestinal, cleansing—and that whatever soothing unguents at last reach the intestines are the by-products, the after-effects, of a harmony perceived by the mind?

If a kind of "catharsis" does really take place, but is a shaking-up and a settling-down brought about not by the gratification of feeling but by the gratification of knowing, then the mind has indeed discovered for itself a sport not unlike the exhilarated athlete's. The athlete accepts, for the purposes of his play, a set of fanciful and arbitrary rules: he makes obstacles for himself, hurdles to be got over, so that in spanning them— so freely and so gratuitously—he will engage his body as fully as possible, purifying it by actively honoring the miraculous articulation of its parts. He will, at the end, be in harmony with himself because he has reasserted, had fresh experience of, the natural harmony that was given him. The contemplative, similarly, exposes himself to arbitrary challenges—to sensations that lure without promising immediate relief, to emotional disturbances that may even be painful—so that the ripple of his nerve ends and the ground swell of his emotions may be brought to the poised perfection of a majestic whitecap, known in its mass and its balance and its shivering harmony during the long moment of its climactic suspension, exercised and then exorcised by a perceiving intelligence. Parting company with the athlete, the contemplative does not bestir himself physically. But he has submitted more of the whole man to the joyous whipcracking of the intellect: he has brought the senses and the emotions dancing into the ring, for the specific purpose of letting his mind draw a ring around them.

His mood is playful, though the things to be played over include the whole of the world in which he normally works. His activity is ultimately and essentially intellectual, though all sorts of passions are made to dance to the mind's tune. How can he be sure that by letting his mind go a-roving, forbidding it the while to do any of its own housework, he will have the experience of watching it come home to him, healthy and refreshed and sounder than a dollar? What guarantee has he that order will be the reward of an uninhibited romp?

He will have to go on faith, for a bit. "The delight we find in art," says Rebecca West, "amounts to recognition of a saving grace, to an acknowledgment that the problem of life has a solution implicit in its own nature."

☀ *Good Lord! The thing was*
a mystery and we measured it.

—Eric Gill

I have been watching a baby lately, and I find his behavior instructive. It is the practice of the household at the moment to give an eighteen-month-old infant the freedom of the living room for twenty minutes or so each evening as temporary release from the safe prison of his playpen. Since I take the precaution of removing everything that is easily breakable, he is permitted to touch what he likes. I notice that his noisy happiness increases in direct proportion to the number of textures he can sample in quick and varying succession. He slaps his palm down on a mahogany coffee table, draws it along the surface with that moist sucking sound that is slightly unnerving to everyone but himself, then bunches his knuckles to give it another trial run with his fingernails. Immediately he lurches three feet away to a travertine coffee table and repeats the entire process, obviously delighted by the fact that one of these objects yields entirely different sensations from the other. Having established his tactic for testing the surprising solidity— and the surprising dissimilarity—of things that go to make up the world within reach, he applies it everywhere: he scrapes palm and then claw against pillows, chairs, books, lamp bases and the piano bench. Sometimes he enriches his experience by opening his mouth wide and laving the object with his tongue.

He has virtually no words as yet, and I am making the mistake of encouraging him to acquire a few. Last evening, somewhat thoughtlessly, I began to overarticulate the syllables of "ta-*bul*" for him while he was paying his respects to the glories of mahogany. He looked up and smiled, possibly because my helpful tone seemed to approve of his pleasure, but he didn't say anything. As he bounded, ritualistically, across to the curve of travertine and began to give it the same admiring if reckless caress, I once more pronounced "ta-*bul*" with all the clarity at my command.

But I had made a mistake. He looked up at me again, though not with a smile. He didn't exactly frown, either: he gave me that straightforward, rather piercing look that babies make such shattering use of and that does not so much suggest a failure to grasp on his part as a deliberate incoherence on yours. He understood that something had been said, and that what was said was meaningless, perhaps baitingly so.

I had offered him an absurd equation. I had said that the name for an object that was brown, rectangular, grainy, and held up by eight legs was "table." And I had said, almost in the same breath, that the name for an object that was white, circular, slippery and held up by five legs was "table." I was being ridiculous, and he knew it. Any fool could see—with his eyes and his fingers and his tongue—that the two objects had nothing in common.

And the truth of the matter is that, taken as single concrete objects, they have very, very little in common. They are not made of the same materials, they have neither the same color nor shape, they are not even of the same height, and it just so happens that they have utterly different decorative objects on top of them: one displays a few odd pieces of silver plate, the other a plant. Furthermore, the infant who is now enjoying them so much never will come to see what they do have in common until he has learned to drain them of all he now enjoys and to treat them as featureless multiples.

He is not yet ready for intellectual work and cannot even imagine how it might be done. We are so used to it that we forget how it *is* done. It is done, as the philosophers say, by abstraction from multiples. I cannot arrive at an intellectual concept that will be of valid use to me so long as I confine my observation to a single sample of anything. This holds true not only for laboratory scientists making thousands of repeated tests before they dare announce that they know something to be a "fact" or for public-opinion samplers going to great lengths to be certain that their pollings are extensive enough and representative enough to constitute a "finding." It holds true for the simplest, most casual, most primitive judgment I make as I wake up, wondering, to the world about me.

If I confine myself, with the baby, to a single table as the source for my idea of a "table," I shall quite naturally conclude that a table is a round, white, slippery substance with flowers growing out of it. Or, contrarily, I shall decide that it is brown, rectangular, and rough. And if I happen to run into a friend who has defined his "table" on the basis of a single table that is different from mine, we shall find ourselves in instant and hopeless argument worthy of *Waiting for Godot*. I may do worse. If the only table I ever happen to see happens to have nothing at all on it, I shall have been led to a most interesting proposition: that a table is an object on which nothing is ever placed. There is a door in my house that does not lead any-where; it does not even open, though it was certainly first built as a door. I should be ill-advised to draw any conclusions from it.

Plain enough. Until we have learned to deal with multiples, and with multiples that vary so wildly from one another that their differences outnumber their similarities ten to one, we are prohibited from calling our knowledge "useful," perhaps even from calling it "knowledge." We are not only obliged to investigate a vast range of samplings but are also required to dismiss from consideration anything that is singular about any of them—any particularity of shape, color, height, material, texture. We are forced to break down and to banish all that is concrete about all actual tables, robbing them of the fascinating solidity by which we have first come to "know" them, until we are at last left with a handful of disembodied—and hence trustworthy—principles they hold in common. *Principle:* a table is meant to support other objects. *Principle:* to make it easy to reach or see the objects, a table had best be elevated. *Principle:* to support the objects safely, a table had best have a flat surface.

With these principles, we now possess a knowledge of the nature of tables that enables us to make tables and to use tables. We also possess three strangely faceless, colorless, tasteless terms: *support, elevated, flat.* It may be noticed that while these terms define all tables, they describe none. They embrace everything and alight nowhere.

Because they are, in effect, in constant motion—testing tables everywhere but refusing to rest in any one of them—they belong to what philosophers call the discursive reason. At first sight it must seem strange that the word "discursive" should be applied, philosophically, to so strict a process as "going from premises to conclusions in a series of logical steps" (as the dictionary has it). For "discursive" means wandering, and we do not think of thought as being so foot-loose.

But foot-loose is what thought—reason, logic—is. Thought wanders from table to table, as from house to house, in order to eliminate what is misleading about every actual table or every actual house and to arrive, if possible, at a clear statement *about* tables, *about* houses. The movement is around. The statement is about. The method is roundabout.

All of our thinking is done in this roundabout way. Instead of leaping to conclusions in the presence of single objects, we circle all such objects warily, keeping a discreet distance from them, squinting our eyes so that we shall blur what is "real" about them and see only what is general or "universal" about them—until their repeated essentials can be added up in the countinghouse of the abstract.

The method is rather like that of a man-made satellite, eternally revolving about the earth in the stratosphere. It is capable of sending back valid and valuable information. But it can get the information only by keeping its distance. It is odd, and it is suggestive, that all of man's intellectual work should have to be done under the command that exhausted Peer Gynt: "Roundabout, Peer, go roundabout."

To play, like the baby, is to come home again. But how shall an adult, after his long years of residence in the logical stratosphere, come home?

He must, it would seem, stop thinking. It was Aristotle who noticed that the contemplative power, the power that produces pleasure, "seems to become stronger when the reasoning power is relaxed."

The notion horrifies us, even as it beckons us. Relax our reasoning powers? It would be nice if we could: we are so tired of having to take thought. What, relax our reasoning powers? Unthinkable: it is all we can do to hang on to them. Between a yearning and a shudder, we draw a blank.

We understand the conundrum that is posed for us. If the contemplative act we need so desperately to perform is truly a kind of intellectual play, it is obliged to offer us knowledge. Otherwise it could not be called intellectual. At the same time it must not embroil us in what has been described as "the laborious procedure of discursive knowledge." If it did, it would not be play.

For the contemplative act to hold up its head as a happy deed in this insufficiently naughty world, it would have to promise us apparently impossible things. It would have to give us knowledge without making us slave for it, it would have to do it on contact without making us wait for it, and it would have to bring off the whole improbable benefaction without sending us on that lonely journey into the discursive never-never land. It would have to permit us to resume our childhood love affair with single, concrete objects: with one coffee table, with one back yard, with one human face.

Our bafflement is not at once relieved by hearing the name a growing number of contemporary philosophers are willing to give to the easy and presumably thoughtless knowledge we are seeking. It is becoming a philosophical commonplace, in the quiet of the academies, to speak of "discursive" knowledge on the one hand and "intuitive" knowledge on the other, quite as though the thinkers in their towers hadn't heard what the rest of us think of "intuition." The rest of us know perfectly well what we think of "intuition": it is the idiot claim a woman makes to conceal her intellectual incompetence—either that or a damned lucky guess. Even the Encyclopaedia Britannica continues to devote the largest part of its article on the subject to people who have hunches on horse races.

The term has had a troubled, groping history, and the groping is not yet done with. Many earlier philosophers who were admittedly in search of an intellectual experience "superior to reasoning" did not use the term. Many of those who did use it understood it to mean a bewildering variety of things. Francis Bacon thought that we knew only one thing intuitively: our own existence. Spinoza, abandoning Aristotle's search for something "greater than reason," thought that intuition itself must be conceived as an extension of reason, a final leap into the air from a discursively-built springboard. Kant, not wishing to make room for it at all, wondered at last if he might have to. Schopenhauer, making plenty of room for it, supposed that it was not intellectual; quite a few men have held it to describe something sensed in the bowels rather than truly known by the mind.

The pressure these days, though, is to move for its admission into polite society. "Intuition" is in the wind, fore and aft— among those looking forward to the twenty-first century and among those looking backward to see what our spiritual fathers may have meant. Emmanuel Chapman does not hesitate to paraphrase St. Augustine to the effect that "intuitive knowledge" is an experience in which "the mind, without any effort of abstraction, is irradiated by an intelligible light which is delightfully apprehended." Leonard Callahan, in summarizing Aquinas' understanding of "aesthetic" knowledge, uses the words "spontaneous, intuitive, in a manner perfect" and reminds us that the Doctor preferred to speak of such knowledge as *"vision . . .* to convey the idea that there is no need for effort at abstraction, no labor, no discursus of reasoning."

F. S. C. Northrup, looking to that hopeful time when the Orient, with its emphasis upon the concrete and the visual, and the Occident, with its emphasis upon the abstract and theoretical, will at last bring their respective insights together and so make the world a true sphere, proposes that knowledge reaches us in two different ways, through two distinct—though simultaneous—"continuums."

There is a "theoretical continuum," a face of the world that is revealed to us by discursive thought. And there is an "aesthetic continuum," a face of the world that "must be immediately experienced to be known." These are not interchangeable; neither one tells the whole story or the same story; neither can be substituted for the other.

That is why, Northrup reminds us, "no amount of verbal description will enable one to convey the sensed color blue to a person born blind." For some things we must have eyes to see. Nor do we truly "know" everything when we have broken blue down into its disembodied ratios. The valuable figures on our scratch-pads do not add up to blueness: "neither mathematical calculation nor logical deduction can ever take one from the theoretically known number of the wave length for blue . . . to . . . sensed blue." The wave length is something borrowed; but the blue is something blue.

The very advances of science have helped us to see what science misses. "In science we try to trace phenomena back to their first causes, and to general laws and principles," Ernst Cassirer explains. "In art we are absorbed in their immediate appearance, and we enjoy this appearance to the fullest extent in all its richness and variety. . . . Even art may be described as knowledge, but art is knowledge of a peculiar and specific kind."

It is time for us to ask what kind. Obviously, if what we have been saying is in any way defensible, the intuitive knowledge promised by the contemplative act must come about through a return to concrete singulars. "Surely a poet *has* to treat the concrete as primary," Randall Jarrell has exclaimed.

But what sort of reversion to the womb, or at most to the status of happy but uncomprehending toddlers, is this?

Are we obliged to abandon the gains we have made with such agony, to rid ourselves entirely of the abstractions we have acquired, to reduce ourselves—forcibly, and as best we can—to the mindlessness of children chewing cheerfully on furniture? In order to rid ourselves of our misery, must we pretend to deny our maturity?

Surely not. While it is true that unless we become as little children we shall not enter the kingdom of heaven—or even, for that matter, the kingdom of earth—there is a difference in merit between returning to the openheartedness of children and returning to the empty-headedness of children. It is patently virtuous of us to strive to reacquire innocence—by cleansing our minds and hearts and wills of what is not innocent but conniving. There can be no virtue at all in willfully wiping from the slate whatever we have truly come to know, however we have come to know it. No abstraction need be ground to a fine dust and swept under the rug.

Though there is no simple way of describing what does happen, the simplest I can think of at the moment is to suggest that, as we return to the concrete singular from which our abstraction was in part derived, the abstraction comes to rest in its source and so do we.

It is as though all we had learned about the essence of coffee tables had slipped silently and snugly beneath the skin of one coffee table, where it could no longer quite be identified but where its vibrating presence seemed to radiate outward through its fresh-found and comfortably warm clothing of thick brown wood. In effect, the universal has nestled down *inside* the singular.

But this is, of course, much too simple a way of speaking of what has been called "the most humanly complete object we can attain," even though it does inch us toward Goethe's assertion that the genuine poet is one "who contemplates the universal in the particular." My example fails to describe exactly how this very strange meeting of matter and form comes about, since it assumes that we bring to all of our concrete experiences as adults the ready-made abstractions that fit so neatly, so invisibly, inside them. In point of fact, I do not have to come to my pleasure so handsomely equipped: the universal may be lying in wait for me where I have not encountered it before. I do not have to know what the Parthenon was used for in order to admire the Parthenon; in some way the Parthenon supplies its own guiding principle and, rising, fulfills it.

We are forced into analogy. Intuitive knowledge is, in a surprisingly strict sense, "almost like falling in love." The comparison is not so sentimental as it sounds. To fall in love with someone is, in a real but maddeningly inarticulate way, to know someone. There is, to begin with, a personality to be known, provided that we are in some way tempted to undertake the project. The personality, however, is not to be known in terms of its height, weight, coloring, ancestry, intellectual quotient, or acquired habits. These things are easily known, early in the game, but they never do constitute a satisfactory summary of the identity that is beginning to enchant us. They are not dismissed or forgotten either; because our increasing affection urges us toward ever more intimate contact, they remain eternally present—either as aids to our affection or as obstacles to be overcome. A person who is "known" is known *through* these qualities but never simply by them. There is flesh to be dealt with (it may be exceedingly tempting or slightly scrofulous), there is speech to be deciphered and returned in code (it may be delightfully revealing or disturbingly opaque), there are eccentricities of behavior to be countered, as in a dance (mostly fun, but how often we stumble). Still, no one of these things—nor all of them together—precisely identifies the single, simple vibration that gives us such joy in the meeting of eyes or the lucky conjunction of interchanged words. Something private and singular and uniquely itself is touched—and known in the touching.

There is no explaining it to others, because this is not the kind of knowledge that can be formulated discursively: we can know "girl" discursively but not Jenny; we can know "friend" discursively but not Leo. In our exuberance, of course, and made foolishly confident by our utter certainty, we try to explain it to others, whereupon we find ourselves falling back on "such a sense of humor" and "I can *talk* to her." After we have given up babbling, and gone away with all the best things left unsaid, our patient acquaintances will confide in one another, "I still don't see what he sees in her."

"Sees" is quite the right word, because the lover's knowledge is a seen knowledge, never an abstracted one, and it is not shared by those who are still looking on with a judiciously discursive detachment. For all that, it is knowledge—more knowledge, more intimate knowledge, more complete knowledge than the ringside people possess. It may be called, to be sure, a knowledge of the heart: "the heart knows reasons reason doesn't know." But it is also a certainty fiercely held by the mind, albeit by the unreasoning mind. Indeed, until the mind can be made up —until the mind can be *sure*, however mysteriously and unscientifically the sureness is brought into being—the heart will not be given away. It is knowing that opens the floodgates.

We are speaking of a unique, hence unmeasurable, personality living within and giving external animation to a body of physical and psychological properties that can readily be measured. It is the *élan vital* that enchants us, and we go about our lives in the unshakable conviction that the private absolute can be discovered through the fleshly particulars. We hold our flesh in common and our identities individually; we are confident, in spite of all of our personal failures, that identity may be known without divorcing it from the flesh, that the whole man may be grasped—intuitively—in his wholeness. Our greatest happiness has come from just such moments of conscious possession; we know that we know, and our very being expands.

Let's veer a little and try to look at this notion of a complete object completely known—with its vital principle radiating splendidly through all that is matter-bound about it—in yet another part of the forest. Let's also look at it backward, as though it weren't a matter of burrowing through possibly misleading flesh to a shining essence within but as though the whole object could be built up progressively from its internal principle to its external wardrobe. We have quoted a description of a work of fine art as "the most humanly complete object we can attain," and we might well ask just how such a thing is attained by a man who is forced to construct it.

In *The Voices of Silence* André Malraux speaks of an extraordinary discovery made by Gothic art. "Hitherto a painted or carved personage had always conveyed his feelings . . . by *symbolical* gestures. In Egypt, Greece, Assyria, China, India and Mexico art had known two forms of expression: abstraction and symbolism." The face of reality was rendered not in its fleshly fullness but by "a system of signs," and such signs "always had a logical basis." That is to say, the discursive reason had taken many samplings, isolated what was common about them, and expressed the commonness by lines and gestures from which most concrete trappings had been stripped. Never so naked as a dollar sign or an ampersand, these paintings and carvings nevertheless signified an object in something of the same disembodied way.

However, "Christianity's supreme discovery in the field of art was that the portrayal of *any woman whatsoever* as the Madonna had a stronger emotive value than a would-be exaltation of the role to superhuman heights by means of idealization or symbolism."

Malraux is tracing, historically, a process by which the natural object was indicated by a sign and then, *without loss of the sign*, was restored to nature again. First the outline of a head. Then, within the outline, a mask. Then, over the mask, a face—but with the mask and the outline still glowing, like a buried phosphorescence, deep inside. "The scene was rendered abstractly at first, then gradually 'came alive.' "

If the struggle to achieve the greatest possible degree of completeness in a man-made object can be seen as part of one historical movement, it can also be seen in a single painter's movement as he labors to produce a single work of art. In the volume devoted to Thomas Eakins, for instance, in the Great American Artists Series, two facing pages offer us *The Gross Clinic* in two different stages of composition. On the left we are permitted to see a preparatory "sketch" for the painting: one head and one hand are already visible, though only as structural elements in a nearly abstract pattern of lights and darks which we should be unable to recognize as anything humanly meaningful if we did not have the completed work, on the right, to guide us. The completed work, on the right, is so thoroughly realistic as to seem photographic—even offensively so to contemporary taste. It is also realistic enough to seem almost devoid of "abstract content." Yet it was abstract before it was concrete, and it is now a fusion—whether in good proportion or bad—of both. The most casual glance through any painter's preparatory sketches will, of course, stir echo upon echo of this architectural sequence: first shapes that are not much more than signs, then glowing and most earthy substances in which the signs are simultaneously hidden and not hidden. Abstract and concrete interact, play upon one another.

"Art," Malraux continues, "sometimes has recourse to a symbolical rendering of emotions that we know (a method involving logic); but sometimes to an irrational, vividly compulsive expression of feelings that we all can recognize (as when Giotto shows Mary watching the Ascension with an expression not of ecstasy but of sorrow)." We accept a halo in a painting because we are agreed, abstractly, on what it stands for. That is one kind of knowing; we bring it with us from the agreements of our work. But to recognize something—without having agreed upon it, without even having discussed it—is knowing, too. The mind is stabbed on a spot it did not know was vulnerable. This is knowing by contact, on contact.

We have neglected knowledge by contact in our abstraction-centered lives, have in fact almost persuaded ourselves that it does not exist. We watch the baby and do not even envy him his happiness: he is not yet intelligent, we say; his joy in the real is an ignorant joy that cannot be recaptured by thinking men. When we say "intelligent" or "intellectual," we simply mean "rational," and nothing other than "rational." The mind seems to us to function—validly—by discursive thought alone, as though it possessed but a single power, a single tentacle for searching out truth. Our conviction finally reduces the world about us to the flat lines and empty spaces of the one method we acknowledge.

I should like to record here the first faint flush of hope I've had about one of my own more "knowing" children in some time. A ten-year-old has just brought me a "story" he's been writing. It isn't, of course, a story at all. The boy is one of the new breed I've been talking about, and his eighteen-page manuscript is actually a speculative essay with a couple of conventional thrills thrown in as sops. His mind, at the moment, is a fascinating clutter of Genesis and contemporary paleontology, and he seems to have wanted to weave a few of his beloved dinosaurs into the post-Eden adventures of Adam. He writes, and the spelling is his:

"Our story begins with creation. The Bible tells us that Adam and Eve lost for themselves and all who preceeded them the great gifts which God had blessed them with. One of these was the throne over the animals. How can we judge their sense of communication with other animals. Most certainly they were able to converse with these lower creatures. Then we must be aware of a degree of inttelligens to which these animals were capable of inhabiting. This is necessary before we can continue in this saga. Refering again to the Bible we aknolege that God banished Adam from the Garden of paradise. Now here we admit the only flaw in our tale. I am unable to explain the manner in which Adam managed to secure such itteligent but monstorus creatures. There were five of them and their names were such: Zeta, Balt, Nappricondos who was the strongest, Lestar who was the craftiest and Bareen, leader and oldest. Some prefer to associate them by initials though I will continue to use there full names. To retern to Adam we find he has lost his great knowleg and also his great memory. . . ."

The author has, you see, an appalling problem on his hands. He wants those dinosaurs to be able to communicate with Adam and Adam to be able to communicate with the dinosaurs.

He is much too honest a craftsman to gloss over the difficulty. Instead, he repeatedly calls our attention to it, as in this excerpt from page five:

"Now and always we must keep in mind the superior intellect of these creatures and also their ability to talk a half and half language similar to that of their time. . . ."

Perhaps you see what has cheered me. A child I know is, in his candid yet confident way, groping for a "half and half" language, looking for a break-through that can be accomplished without words. He is determined to get through to his dinosaurs or to have them get through to us; he is perfectly aware that he is never going to make it by means of the verbal abstractions we now use; so he simply and honorably posits another possibility and goes on writing. That boy is on the trail of intuition, and I must say I'm proud of him.

I'm supplying him with my prejudices, of course. But there is something decently heartening in his improbable try. He is unwilling to equate "inttelligens" with the capacity for handling abstract counters, even though he'd better improve his own capacity for handling abstract counters or he'll never get published. He is contending, wildly, with an ultimate truth: that the intellect is not simply what thinks. It is something more than that. The intellect is what knows—whether by thought or by some less circuitous process.

To be perfectly plain about the matter, we are here positing that the intellect is capable of grasping the knowledge it seeks in at least two different, mutually exclusive but happily complementary, ways. It can come to possess knowledge by a discursive method, by thought, by logical deduction from defined abstract principles. This method is laborious and constitutes "work," the exhausting work of "proving things out." When things *are* so proved out, they are ready to be used; because the knowledge can be demonstrated, on paper or in the laboratory, it can be profitably employed in the strict disciplines of all our further work. The method is itself work, and it is the cornerstone of whatever other work we do.

The intellect can also come to possess knowledge by a simple, submissive, eye-to-eye contemplation of the object to be known. It possesses the knowledge by gently and quietly possessing the object—not in the fragmented state in which the object's concrete clothing is forcibly divorced from its informing principle, but in its whole or "natural" state, with its informing principle resting comfortably, invisibly, and quite unmolested deep within the nest of the tangible. Because this knowledge is singular and must be eternally private, it cannot be proved out. Because it cannot be proved out, it cannot be used in our work. Intuitive knowledge is knowledge without a future; it has only a present. The object known is not known for the sake of some other gain; it is known in itself, as itself, for itself alone. The act of knowing is not in this case grasping; it is gratuitous. Its end is not profit; it is love.

We do not have to go all the way with Aristotle and say that man's happiness consists *entirely* in this second kind of knowing. We need only realize that unless a man is able to satisfy the dual powers of his mind, unless he is able to move freely and frequently between knowing by roundabout and knowing by head-on, he is probably not going to be happy because he is not going to love very much. This is, of course, the source of the aridity we have come to feel in our time. From Bentham onward we were warned against any participation in acts which "rest in the understanding merely." Such acts, we were told, were without value. Being unable to "prove out" a value for acts which, by definition, refused to enter the proving ground of the discursive reason, we permitted our intuitive powers, and any contemplative habits we may have had, to atrophy. Now, later in the day and startled to discover ourselves loathing the values we thought were secure, we begin vaguely to realize that it is in acts which "rest in the understanding merely" that our repose, our content, our very delight in being alive, reside.

Do we have the right to reverse Bentham, are we any farther along than John Stuart Mill was when he made his unacceptable defense of such acts on the grounds that the best men had always approved them? Will we ever be able to assert with complete confidence the "value" of something that cannot be placed on a scale?

How are we to go beyond Francis Bacon and say, firmly, that it is possible to have intuitive knowledge of something other than ourselves? That we know ourselves, and our own existence, poses no problem for us. No one has to prove to a baby that he has fingers and toes: he has known those fingers and toes from the moment he was able to see them even if he didn't know, or care, what other people chose to call them; when, eventually, he is encouraged to identify them by words, it is obvious that he regards this new process as strange and unnecessary. A baby isn't even bothered by his own image in a mirror, a fact which has never ceased to perplex me; I should think he would be terrified of such duplication if he couldn't be given a reasonable explanation of it, which, at his age, he cannot be. But he is quite unfussed. There he is. Of course. What else? The certainty that one is, and feels, and knows, is a private certainty that permits of no contradiction. One's being proclaims itself; the proclamation is, without further discussion, certain knowledge.

But how can we know, in this same unproved yet self-confident way, the pieces of the world that don't belong to us, the separated substances that are not part of our own animation? These things are outside us, as we are outside them. Aren't we condemned, intellectually, to remain outside them and to get to know them only by going "roundabout" them?

Perhaps not. Communion may be possible even with coffee tables. St. Francis, after all, did not have as much trouble with birds as my ten-year-old son is having with dinosaurs. The speculative possibility that philosophers have been exploring for a while now is, in a much oversimplified way of putting it, just this: in addition to knowing our own being intuitively, we may also have valid intuitive knowledge of everything that holds being in common with us.

It may, offhand, seem most unlikely that I hold enough in common with a lump, any lump, of inanimate matter to be able to know it by partially identifying myself with it. But why shouldn't I feel some closeness to, and affection for, the hot or cold stone I rub my palms against as I brace myself against a boulder to look out over Long Island Sound or along the Isthmus of Corinth? (The charm is not entirely in the view; it is also in the substance that surrounds and supports me, and I like the feel of it.) After all, we share the same responsiveness to heat or cold; we are both permeable. We both possess weight. We both occupy space. We both rest on the same resistant mass. We both owe a debt to gravity. Chemically, we are at least distant cousins. My animation does distinguish me from the boulder, but not to the point where I can claim to be disembodied. And whatever is bodied about me stems from the same first impulse that produced all solid bodies, whether they be foreign bodies or no. In fact, I am not really at liberty to describe anything in the universe as a foreign body absolutely; and to the degree that it is not foreign I am able to know it by affinity.

As all the things about me advance in the scale of matter, they really advance toward me: they edge closer and speak more familiarly because we have so many more mutual interests to gossip about. A beech tree and I not only possess weight and usurp space in much the same way but also grow up and grow old most similarly: I am not being entirely sentimental in mourning the red maple that has just died in the yard. Too, I am at least as productive as the Seckel-pear tree that feeds the local squirrels. And by the time I have got round to looking at the squirrels, or the cat that pretends to chase them, I have increased the resemblances that enable me to recognize them without effort and with an affection born of consanguinity once again.

I probably did come the same way, up the long lane of evolution, as the cat. If I have landed, through no fault of my own, at a luckier vantage point that seems nearer the goal, I may still do well to remember that the cat got halfway home before I did. It was the dog, the cat, and the dolphin, working out their own destinies, that taught me how to play. "In the behaviour of a cat, a dog, a dolphin," writes Teilhard, "there is such suppleness, such unexpectedness, such exuberance of life and curiosity! . . . It takes interest, it flutters, it plays. . . . Around it an 'aura' of freedom begins to float, a glimmer of personality . . ." If I sometimes find it easier to "play" when there is a dog or a cat around, it is no doubt because I am entertaining, and being entertained by, the companion who discovered playfulness and left it to me as a legacy—a legacy I have neglected and of which I need to be reminded. Though my son will never be able to play with dinosaurs, much as he rashly thinks he might like to, I have met a man who enjoys the off-and-on company of a group of five-foot iguanas.

The submerged oneness that enables me to know another form of being nearly as intuitively as I know my own being—because certain aspects of being are common to both of us—becomes increasingly intense as we ascend the scale from "inert" matter to living tissue and at last to human personalities. Meeting Jenny or Leo, I meet more of myself and am freer than ever to know by identification rather than by analysis. No longer confined to a limited sharing of chemical properties and mechanical stresses, or to a structural homogeneity that sends sap through a tree as it sends blood through me, or even to that greater kinship I have with a dog because it is blood that is coursing through both of us, I arrive now at the nearly un-limited commonness that embraces all of these things and then adds the common property of intelligence, the joint capacity to know things in the same way. Our minds cannot help reaching out to one another any more than compatriots can help hailing one another when they are abroad, whether in Harry's Bar or on the Via Veneto or in the lobby of the Grande Bretagne (this is thought to be vulgar, on the sound theory that what one ought to be doing abroad is speaking to strangers in the language of the country; but the pleasures of recognition are an unalterable fact, a swelling of the heart due to affinities between minds, and might just as well be enjoyed between the vocabulary lessons). It is easy for knowing eyes to look into one another when the habits of knowing, and the yearnings of the intellect, are identical—provided that communion has not been blocked by the abstractions we erect as barricades to protect our privacy and our purposes.

Paradoxically, even our capacity for abstraction may link us, since it is one more polarizing principle: knowing how to play the same tricks with the same tokens, we are able to see through one another, or perhaps through *to* one another, be-cause we recognize the trickery and can so take delight in it. All good conversation, really, depends upon our joy in being able to *match* wits, to make our own manner of juggling ab-stract counters conform as closely as possible to someone else's so that the two manners will mate, for a time. Indeed, it is to describe just such playfulness, and just such adroit players, that the epithet "intellectual" is most often used nowadays. I have employed the term initially to describe anyone who works with abstractions, in an effort to make plain the degree to which all of us are engaged in activities far removed from the physical. But in *The House of Intellect* Jacques Barzun draws an apparently odd distinction between intelligence and intellect, going on to say that while politics has obvious need of intelligent men it has no need at all of "intellectuals." What can this possibly mean but that an intellectual proper is someone who loves the play of the mind for its own sake—and who would not be likely to "get on with things" because he takes such delight in exploring further, and possibly endless, permutations of principle and combinations of corollaries? Our recent much-advertised suspicion that an intellectual, above all an intellectual who makes jokes, would prove a dilatory and much too light-minded President reinforces the view that an intellectual is, per se, something of a cerebral playboy. Well, we shall have to skip over that—at least until we have learned to respect the dignity of play as much as we urge the dignity of work. The meeting of minds, when it is only a meeting and not a matter of mutual rape, constitutes an obvious pleasure. On this we may agree.

We are, to be sure, divorced at the last by our separated identities, by the fact that each of us—no matter how many times related—is unique. But, to admit to the argument one last paradox, the fact that each of us is unique is also a fact that makes us similar. And if it is similarity that enables us to know things intuitively, then this ultimate obstruction becomes an ultimate invitation to lean on the back fence and chat with our like, until unique and like become almost interchangeable. At the very least, our separateness can comfort by its commonness; it is another way of knowing not by circuitous detachment but by kind facing kind and confessing that two secrets are the same secret.

Abstract knowledge is arrived at by making things as unlike themselves, and as unlike ourselves, as possible: by isolating them from all concreteness and all flesh, by reducing them to disembodied principles—which the things of this world are not and which we are not.

Intuitive knowledge prefers not to make this forced march. It adheres, instinctively and with great warmth, to whatever most immediately resembles its own manner of being. In Bergson's words, "We have here the indivisible and therefore substantial continuity of the flow of the inner life. Intuition . . . signifies first of all consciousness, but immediate consciousness, a vision which is scarcely distinguishable from the object seen, a knowledge which is contact and even coincidence."

Blood brothers meet and merge—because they are blood brothers and because the mind cannot resist reaching out to whatever is perfectly adapted to it, perfectly consonant with it. "Perfectly" is no doubt too strong a word: things can, and do, stand in the way of swift marriage. Still, we are poised on the shore of a knowledge that is as embracing and as exhilarating as the sea: the knowledge of immersion, of recognition that may be instantaneous because it is based on family resemblances.

It is a knowledge that breeds affection, what Conrad called "the latent feeling of fellowship with all creation." It renews our pleasure in the universe. More than that. As our being touches other being, and lets it flow into us, we are mysteriously aware that our own being has been increased. From having discovered ourselves in a multitude of things we have made ourselves more, or at least have become more amply ourselves. Something like re-creation runs in us like a tide.

6

✦
✦✦
✦

The Prohibitions That Become Freedoms

Edgar Degas purchased once
A fine El Greco, which he kept
Against the wall beside his bed
To hang his pants on while he slept.

—RICHARD WILBUR

THE HABITS that keep us alive are the habits that keep us unhappy.

The one thing, really, that stands between the mind and its pleasure is its powerful drive, developed over the long struggle for survival, toward possessing and devouring whatever promises it pleasure. The mind grabs out at goodness to be able to feel its presence in the fist, after which the treasure is hoarded in the attic; it is in the fist and in the attic that it loses its charm.

This may seem perversely put. But have you ever noticed that, of six or seven books lying about on the living-room table, the one you own is the one you will defer reading? You may offer several most plausible reasons for this state of affairs. The fact that it is owned means that it needn't be read just now, it can be read at any time (which very often means that it will never be read at any time, and the longer it is owned the slimmer are its chances). The books that are not owned—that are borrowed or rented—ought logically to come first on any virtuous man's list. I should give my earliest attention to a book that has been borrowed in order to return it at the earliest possible moment, shouldn't I? But do I really read it now out of consideration for the friend who has loaned it, racing to get it back to him? Or do I read it now and forget to get it back to him for months and months? Similarly, I am simply behaving sensibly if I first pick up the lending-library book that is costing me five or fifteen cents a day. But just what was it, earlier this afternoon, that made me pluck that volume from the lending-library shelf when I knew perfectly well that I had a new and unread book of my own at home? I behave perversely.

The painting I own is the painting I should need to be born again, with new eyes, to see. I loved it once, of course, or I should never have made such a sacrifice to seize it and carry it home. For a day or two my delight in it seemed almost to be increased by the exhilaration of my owning it. Lately, though, it is only a visitor who has never visited me before, or who has not visited me very often, who sees it. I do indeed continue to point it out, to answer questions about it, to show it off—and in doing these things I glance at it. But no glance could be more glancing. My eyes flicker, familiarly, across its surface with some pride, some animation, some bonhomie, but not with love. The painting does not still me. On the contrary, I am to be heard babbling away for as long as seems socially suitable, after which I go mix the drinks. And when no visitor is there, the painting is not there, either. I pass it a dozen times a day as though it were a nondescript stranger. I own it. It is mine.

Sometimes a domestic cliché is revealing: the one I am thinking of is that breakfast-table triangle that appears so often in syndicated cartoon strips. Blondie and Dagwood, or whatever their names are in all those inferior imitations of Blondie and Dagwood, are having coffee. That is to say, Dagwood is having coffee: the cup is at his lips. Blondie, across the table, is staring straight ahead, trying to burn a hole—with the intensity of her glare—into the newspaper that has risen between them. They are married. They belong to one another. That is why they no longer look at one another mornings.

There is something about possession that diminishes, when it does not intercept, pleasure. The possession of a woman's loyalty diminishes the pleasure of her company. We know this, just as we know that "seats now available" in a theatrical advertisement means that here is one show we no longer have to see. We are quick with conventional excuses: familiarity dulls, an appetite satisfied is an appetite gone limp, whatever is readily available is only moderately desirable. But, apart from the woman possessed and the painting bought, what about that owned book that has never been read at all? Here is an appetite that has not been satisfied; it has been short-circuited.

Is there something about permanence, or the promise of permanence, that is opposed—in essence—to the experience of pleasure?

This may, in a strange way, be so. The contemplative act, the sustained and loving surrender of attention to something no more than intuitively known, yields its profound gratifications only at the price of certain peculiar sacrifices. I suppose "sacrifices" is itself a peculiar word to be applying to the beginnings of pleasure; surely the search for delight should be the one search of our lives that ought to be conducted with abandon, without thought of restraint, without giving up anything.

To put a finger on the "thou shalt nots" that circumscribe, and thereby protect, the possibilities of pleasure, we are forced to turn to the contemplatives who have most assiduously analyzed the nature of the act they are performing. These are, of course, the religious contemplatives, those who have spent their lives rather than their Sunday afternoons attempting to perfect a kind of knowing. The object of their knowledge is, to be sure, quite different from the object the rest of us are normally after: they are preparing themselves for an intimate, immediate experience of God, whereas most of us will be content with an intimate and immediate experience of creatures like ourselves and the common earth we walk. But the intellectual acts are themselves deeply alike; and the greater passion has produced a readier vocabulary.

What have these professed contemplatives to tell us about the possible guarantees of a possible happiness, apart from the fact that all infusions of joy are bound to be separated by long dark nights? The first thing they have to tell us is that there are no guarantees. The happiness of union with something other than oneself is indeed possible. We carry within us the capacity for receiving an impress of delight. But we are unable to force the experience. Unlike the force we apply to the universe when we are intent upon wresting from it its working secrets, the power we exercise now is a simple power of sensitivity—of being able to respond rather than ravage. We are engaged in an act of submission, of invitation, of biding our time until the forsythia blooms. Armed attack will get us nowhere, which is why the party that everyone tries to make "go" is the party that will leave everyone's nerves shattered and why the determined evening of quiet with a rewarding book will so often undermine its rewards and make the quiet intolerable in direct proportion to the vigor of its determination. We cannot ourselves create what recreates us. We can only lay ourselves open to friendly invasion, aware that we are subject to the most extraordinary impressions of pleasure and equally aware that the visitation comes from without, touching the within of its own volition.

This sounds rather as though we were talking about an Oriental quietism, a passive drowsing in which both intelligence and feeling abdicate their seats in the human parliament—and as though we were utterly helpless in our pursuit of pleasure because pleasure must come as an accident. In point of fact, we have all had experiences of unbidden pleasure, surges of something close to ecstasy that came with as little warning as a car hurtling out of a driveway. What one Ionesco hero remembers is probably remembered by all of us:

"It's such an old story, I've almost forgotten, it might have been an illusion; and yet it can't be an illusion when I still feel the loss of it so badly . . . It happened as spring was ending, or perhaps in the very first days of summer, just before midday; it all came about in a way that was perfectly simple and perfectly unexpected as well . . . I was in a little country town . . . Somewhere in the South, I think . . . It's of no importance anyway, the place hardly counts. I was walking along a narrow street, which was both old and new, with low houses on either side, all white and tucked away in courtyards or little gardens, with wooden fences, painted . . . pale yellow, was it pale yellow? I was all alone in the street. I was walking along by the fences and the houses, and it was fine, not too hot, with the sun above, high above my head in the blue of the sky. I was walking fast, but where was I going? I don't remember. I was deeply aware of the unique joy of being alive. I'd forgotten everything, all I could think of was those houses, that deep sky and that sun, which seemed to be coming nearer, within my grasp, in a world that was made for me. . . ."

It is also clear to us that such experiences are so rare as to offer us no real hope in the dilemma of our dailiness. Renewal must either come oftener or be dismissed as having no sustained role to play in the rhythm of our lives. If, as the religious contemplative is entirely dependent upon a stirring of God, I am entirely dependent upon the stirring of a Monet—I can do nothing to improve the painting; no honing of mine will make its shaft pierce me deeper—am I altogether impotent? Can't I *help?*

I can help by learning how to keep my helpful hands out of things. This is a more active procedure than it sounds. Out of the goodness of our hearts, or of gratitude for favors not yet bestowed, or perhaps in the hope of being invited again, we feel a powerful urge to bring to the feast an imposing bottle of wine or a carefully selected ornament to be hung on the wall. This creates complications. The host has a wine of his own; dare he serve it now (it is the only suitable wine) or must he honor the donor by breaking out his, thereby destroying the scheme for the dinner? When an ornament is obviously expensive, or even obviously good, must it be hung on the walls that one means to live with and that one had so wistfully wished to display as personal? Some guests are nuisances because it is impossible for them to be guests. They are hosts and hostesses eternal, and in many mansions.

The contemplative act rigorously requires that all who seek its benefits come empty-handed. It is very hard for God or for Daumier to put anything into a closed fist. I am not thinking only of those men who march to an experience in stern self-interest, ready to add up the specific moments during which they enjoyed themselves and then to subtract from this total the number of moments when they did not enjoy themselves and finally to regard the net as a fair estimate of the kind of time they had. Self-interest asks: Am I happy, when am I going to start being happy, what is it that will make me happy?

I am thinking of something less obvious: a perfectly generous interest in other persons and things that may just as effectively erase the experience as such. If I go to a play written by a playwright I know and am concerned about, or a play performed by an actress of whom I am personally fond, my chances of seeing the play are slender. I may come away relieved or depressed, exhilarated or unnerved, but the state I am now in is the result of a dozen things, not one of which is an unobstructed vision of the work performed. Caring— whether ingrown or outgoing—is a menace to the strange kind of meeting we are trying to define: that of an unconcerned heart laid bare to the uncompromised fullness of an object wholly known and disinterestedly loved. Sheer delight must always begin in sheer disinterest, so that there shall be room for all of it to enter. No corners dare be marked "reserved."

Specifically recreative pleasures are dependent, paradoxically, upon a kind of death. Perhaps there is no real paradox here. How should one be reborn without first dying? If the death is figurative, it is nonetheless firmly insisted upon by those who, with Thomas Merton, see clear parallels between religious and natural contemplation. Contemplatives have forever spoken of the initial necessity of "losing the world." Merton makes explicit some of the things we must lose if we are to open our faculties to an experience of disinterested love:

"The one big obstacle to 'unitive' or 'connatural' or 'affective' knowledge . . . is attachment to human reasoning and analysis and discourse that proceeds by abstraction . . . and by syllogizing, to conclusions." A man may do one or the other, but if he chooses always to reason things out, " all right, it is no sin. But it will take him much longer and cost him much more effort to get to his destination, and he will have a much more limited view of things along his way."

The writer is here speaking of intuitive, or mystical, knowledge of God. But the resemblance between the processes involved in such knowledge and the processes involved in an intuitive knowledge of nature, or the intuitive knowledge communicated by a work of art, is strong:

". . . a genuine esthetic experience is something which transcends not only the sensible order . . . but also that of reason itself. It is a supra-rational intuition of the latent perfection of things. Its immediacy outruns the speed of reasoning and leaves all analysis far behind. In the natural order, as Jacques Maritain has often insisted, it is an analogue of the mystical experience which it resembles and imitates from afar. Its mode of apprehension is that of 'connaturality'—it reaches out to grasp the inner reality, the vital substance of its object, by a kind of affective identification of itself with it. It rests in the perfection of things by a kind of union which somewhat resembles the rest of the soul in its immediate, affective contact with God in the obscurity of mystical prayer. A true artist can contemplate a picture for hours, and it is a real contemplation, too. So close is the resemblance between these two experiences that a poet like Blake could almost confuse the two and make them merge into one another as if they belonged to the same order of things. . . ."

What we are trying to deduce from the comparison is the set of conditions under which we may help the sources of our delight to move toward us. If the first of these is a readiness to acknowledge that the delight is in the source and not in ourselves, that we are the sensitive agents rather than the dynamic masters of the experience, the second is a willingness to put down our workaday tools. We are accustomed to understanding things by reasoning about them, by analyzing them; but if we bring reason and analysis to the duration of our delight, we shall have become critics of our pleasure rather than participants in it.

Criticism is a legitimate and valuable activity, but it is labor toward a future purpose rather than playful give-and-take between the responses of our own being and the realities of all the being around us. What we want to do is lock arms with the world, not keep it at its distance so that we shall make no mistake in measuring it. Christopher Fry, in *An Experience of Critics*, speaks of a time when he went to a play not as a member of the audience but as a pressed-into-service reviewer. "I could scarcely hear a word of the play for the noise of my own mind wondering how I should write about it," he says.

This can be translated to fit any pleasurable experience one cares to name: "I could scarcely hear, or see, or feel the world about me for the noise of my mind wondering what I should think of it." When thought takes precedence over every other possible response, as it must during the hours when we are trying to think out our practical destinies, it does more than dominate the intelligence. It occupies it wholly, shutting off alternate supply lines in much the same way that a dishwasher in the kitchen, when it is going full blast, eliminates the possibility of anyone's taking a shower on the third floor.

It does not make a great deal of difference what kind of thought preoccupies a man; any preoccupation, even with the object at hand, places cataracts over his eyes. If the preoccupation is external, busy with matters unrelated to the experience, the defeat of the experience is automatic. If the preoccupation is directly concerned with the matter of one's pleasure—if one's thoughtful mind is centered on the party or the painting—virtually as much static is threatened.

Perhaps in order to get the most out of an experience, I take great pains to "bone up" on the experience. I read the play carefully before I go to see it. I read the long introductory critique to a classic before exposing myself to what the author has written. I read program notes at a concert. I learn all I can about the background of someone I am going to meet, in order to be able to draw him out about his "major interests." The result is that I never do see or hear what is happening; I see or hear, or perhaps am dismayed not to see or hear, what I have read. I go looking for landmarks; if the landmarks appear, they balloon out at me in such vast disproportion that I might as well be peering into an amusement-park mirror; if they do not turn up more or less as I have imagined them in the possible error of my preparation, I feel either that I have been incompetent and missed them or that someone else has been incompetent and failed to supply them (though they may have been supplied in a manner for which my homework has not prepared me). It is not really possible to hear "To be or not to be" any longer; we know too much about it. To hear it, to attend to its meanings as they are and not as we have endlessly analyzed them, we should have to listen to the speech in French or in German, or, perhaps, in that strangely alien arrangement of words and implications which constituted its first printed appearance in English:

> *To be, or not to be, aye, here's the point,*
> *To die, to sleep, is that all? Aye all:*
> *No, to sleep, to dream, aye marry there it goes,*
> *For in that dream of death, when we awake . . . [etc.]*

Now, having shocked our heads clear, we may return to the familiar text with some hope of noticing what it is saying.

And we might pause, at this point, to offer sympathy to the newly-met stranger who is asked all the "right questions" in order to put him at his ease. He is being asked to deliver his standard lecture about himself (and his work) and his weariness is immediately transparent. What he really wanted to meet was you. What he really wanted to talk about was anything at all—even the weather—but not the so intelligent subjects that have been introduced.

Some knowledge of the people one is going to meet and the places one is going to visit and the books one is going to read is unavoidable. Furthermore, whenever a man falls in love with any of these things, his knowledge of them is going to increase: he is going to think about his passion, read about his passion, take his passion apart and put it back together as every child does his most beloved toy. But passion depends upon an inflexible rule: Let there be a first time.

It should be stressed, too, that the more a toy is played with, the closer it comes to breaking. I have a toy. I am especially fond of certain comedians of the silent films; whether this is because I grew up feasting upon them, or because they were truly as good as I think they were, is beside the point. I collect prints of their films when I can, the acquisitive impulse in this case being too strong for me. The first time I thread a print into my projector, and sit back to enjoy myself, I am honestly entertained. The second time I notice a great many more details and begin to think about them. The third time I find that I have begun to be restive: I know not only what is coming but what I think about what is coming. The temptation to run the film a fourth time makes me feel slightly ill; I know now that I shall have to put it away for a year, after which, with luck, my mind will be quiet enough to let my eyes open once more. There is one interim possibility. If I can persuade a friend to drop in and join me for a showing, life instantly returns to the screen. I am creating, by proxy, another first time. I know perfectly well that I should be far better off if I collected no prints at all but contented myself with rare and inconvenient museum showings or occasional visits to the homes of a few friends with the same acquisitive habits. In someone else's house I can enjoy what he cannot, thereby benefiting us both.

The fact that possession deadens even more than familiarity does is a surface manifestation of something that goes clean to the bone of the contemplative problem. At the vital center of the experience stands a sign reading "Hands Off." This is not simply a warning against acquiring what one wishes to continue to love. It is a warning against *wanting* to acquire it, even in the privacy of the mind. The will to possess must be quieted at the core or regenerative pleasure will be denied us.

To put a philosophical platitude as simply as possible, and to explain why the discursive and the intuitive faculties cannot be engaged at the same time, a rudimentary distinction must be made between the "good" and the "beautiful" aspects of any one object. It is easy to say that all things are both good and beautiful at once and that these qualities exist in nature simultaneously. It is not possible, however, to enjoy what is "good" about a thing and what is "beautiful" about it at the same moment. A pear is good: to know its goodness I must eat it. A pear may be beautiful: to know its beauty I must not eat it, I must resolutely refuse its goodness, I must let it alone.

Goodness yields itself to use; the reason I am justified in calling a pear "good" is that when I do use it, when I eat it, it proves to be good for me. But in the process of eating it, of using it up, I am of course destroying all of the properties that enabled me to call it "beautiful." It is the nature of use to benefit by destroying, transforming. In order to build a house or a fire, I must destroy what is pleasing about the trees with which I build.

Now it is true that eating a pear or having a roof to shelter me gives me a certain kind of pleasure: my will to be fed, my will to be warm and dry, the insistent demand of my practical appetite, is satisfied. This is, quite clearly, the kind of "pleasure" on which Bentham erected his—and our—system. But if we have never tired of repeating, even in the hour of our accumulation of crusts, that man does not live by bread alone, it is because he does, in fact, possess yet another appetite: an appetite for the untouched, for the virginal if you will, for that primary, natural, unmolested radiance in the presence of which his aggressive will is quieted and only his mind is pleased.

This is an appetite satisfied by admiration alone. The goodness of the object is held in abeyance while the glory of the object is feasted upon. But one feast precludes the other, for the time being. Indeed I must erase from my mind, as best I can, the very possibility of possession, must teach my will to say "no, absolutely no," if I am to enjoy the simple, happy act of breathing in and out with things. Even the faintest yearning, the least trace of desire for Bentham's kind of "pleasure," will so scratch the glass of my vision and set up such contending emotions within me that the damage will be all but irrevocable. How much chance has a starving man of admiring the contours of a peach?

In a once much-quoted passage, Ruskin explained that "any natural object which can give us pleasure in the simple contemplation of its outward qualities, without any direct or definite exertion of the intellect, I call in some way and in some degree, beautiful." Our starving man apart, how much "simple contemplation of its outward qualities" is likely to be given to a landscape or perhaps to the face of a pretty girl by a man who, though far from starving, has admitted into his mind the merest possibility of subdividing the landscape or seducing the girl? Even a very mild toying with the prospects of goodness— both the subdivision and the seduction have an obvious goodness about them—compromises the moment, rules out the pleasure that had nothing to do with profit. The man who permits himself to speculate on the availability of the girl is no longer in a mood to look at the girl; he wants to get her into a dark corner where he will see very little of her. We are unluckily equipped to operate only on regulated frequencies.

The impulse to seize and to deal with the world in its wholeness, to return its potentialities for usefulness and for delight to their original fusion and to manage them "in the round" as it were, is an old one. It gives rise to a kind of iconography which employs, but in the end tramples underfoot, the "beautiful." There is, for instance, the iconography of the liturgical symbol in which the wings of a dove reach out to form the curves of an intertwined and dominant alpha and omega. Or there is the road sign in which what begins as a little picture of a picket fence bleeds swiftly into a triangular warning that a train crossing is near. In each of these there is a partially-completed concrete image, a trace of the "beautiful," and a partially-completed useful message, an indication of the "good."

There can never be a question of the winner between these two. The dove and the fence are semipresent, but they serve only to catch our eyes. They dare not be finished as images if room is to be left for a good and useful purpose: if they were finished as images, our eyes might rest on them and we should be neither exhorted to pray nor warned to slow down. The exhortation and the warning—the messengers of the "good"—

are only semipresent too, not spelled out. But they are triumphantly semipresent, the crown to which the curious work aspires, the purpose to which the less "useful" half of the object is subordinated.

Deliberate combinations of the beautiful and the good invariably become sacrifices to the good. The contemplative image refuses to perfect itself in order to be able to yield to the urgency of the more profitable symbol. Such a sequence is wholly proper to that somewhat ambiguous but essentially useful device known as the icon: the dove, having caught our attention, generously loses itself in a thoughtful, abstract reminder of first and last things so that we shall be drawn away from earthly concerns and urged to pray; the picket fence is quickly atomized into a meaningful formula so that we shall not be caught napping if the railroad gate is down. But there is no combination of these two properties that does not, in the end, behave as the intentionally-designed icon behaves. Man's habits of usefulness cannot be teased, or even half wakened, without insisting upon priority. The recurring urge to wrap all things together into a single cohesive package—to draw the concrete and the conceptual into the same frame, to pay homage and to draw pay in the same gesture—cannot help but arrive at payday. Man's mind has been returned to its tread.

The contemplative act, then, requires not only that we come to the party with empty hands but that we allow them to rest quietly in our laps for the whole of its duration. That this posture is not entirely passive should be plain enough. It takes some effort to drop the tools of our work. It takes some courage to quiet the energy of our wills. A third condition which is imposed upon us is that we be willing to sustain this posture of alert restraint for as long as the occasion requires to fulfill itself, that we do no more than "view with continued attention" until the informing experience can make its own inroads upon us; but we have spoken of this necessity. There is a fourth. We must be prepared, after all our preliminary sacrifices, to come *away* empty-handed, with nothing left to us but a memory of delight, an increase of well-being so deep and so central and so invisibly distributed throughout the psyche that it cannot even be located, let alone measured and codified for future use.

An experience of profound pleasure has the revivifying effect of an electrical charge. Like a current leaping to life between a positive and a negative, it brings into the here and now a powerful racing from pole to pole that is truth personified, truth knowing itself by becoming identical with itself in an uninterrupted exchange of familiarities. But on the instant that the positive is withdrawn, the power proper ceases to be. An after-effect lingers, an echo of fusion, an aura of wholeness. Reassurance is born of it. But what was actual in the flaming arc is no longer possessed in any practical way. Intuitive certainty ends with the breaking off of contact; when the contemplative act is over, the special knowledge that has been inhaled is breathed out again, never to be recovered in that form.

Let us try to be literal about this. Throughout history men have spoken of the "pleasure and profit" to be taken from the arts, which is to say from intuitive experiences. To suppose that they were using "profit" in the sense in which we understand the term—as an advantage or gain in the abstract processes of our work—would be to land us at once in all sorts of difficulties. At the most obvious level, it is clear that the man who "profits" from Shakespeare by learning that Bohemia has a seacoast is a wayfarer who is going to lose his way, just as the man who learns from Botticelli that the Annunciation took place in a Florentine villa is going to be a misleading teacher at Sunday school. It should be remembered, in passing, that neither the inadvertent error of Shakespeare nor the deliberate anachronism of Botticelli does any damage whatever to the "truth" of the work in question; what is true in a play or painting is simply not viable as geography or history.

Well, we know that. But if we sometimes behave as though we did not know it—if psychiatrists can still complain of arts that "teach" crime and if sociologists can still urge dramatists to "teach" social responsibility—it is because we are nowhere near strict enough about what constitutes profitable, or working, knowledge. We are not privileged to say that we know something, or have learned something, in the scientific sense until we have derived an abstract universal from its thousands of misleading particulars. But a play or a painting is not only composed of particulars; it is composed of one single set of particulars, inside which an as yet unabstracted and hence rationally undefined universal is somehow intimated. To attempt to seize and to use this scientifically untested universal as though it were a factory-inspected tool is close to a form of madness; it is only madmen, or the spectacularly ignorant, who have been so convinced that the villain is actually injuring the heroine that they have leaped to the stage to intervene. The novelist or dramatist who offers us sociological or political "instruction" in the set of singulars he has devised is behaving very badly indeed: he is urging us to believe that we have acquired a principle which may be practically applied from a unique experience whose circumstances he has wholly faked. The man who flies to action from an experience of fiction has been encouraged to take "responsible" action. But any action he takes on the basis of the evidence offered him is in fact irresponsible. He has not subjected the principle to proof.

There are qualifications that might be entered here. An intuition of nature may leave a tantalizing memory, the memory may itch in an analytical brain, the brain may force the memory in time to the series of laboratory tests that will prove it useful or no; a good many, perhaps all, scientific discoveries have begun in this way. But the useful knowledge was not useful knowledge so long as it remained an intuition. The intuition produced nothing but pleasure, and the pleasure was ended before analysis began. Again, a man who has exposed himself repeatedly to intuitive pleasures, without ever wishing to translate any such experience into laboratory gain, may in time acquire a reputation for a kind of wisdom, may in fact possess a real wisdom. But wisdom, properly speaking, is not the same thing as the possession of a vast accumulation of scientifically-known premises. It is the ability to respond, as a whole man and with some serenity, to the fresh challenge of the previously unknown. That a contemplative habit should help produce such a quality in a roundly-experienced man need not be denied; nor should it be regarded as in the least surprising. But the "profit" is no more tangible than the quality of wisdom is free to be precisely measured: it is a readiness, a suppleness, that comes of exercising all functions freely rather than fastening inflexibly upon the demonstrable advantages of one; the profit, if profit there be, goes to the faculty and not to any particular act. To live in part contemplatively is indeed humanizing, in that it brings into play an aptitude men actually possess; but it gives them nothing practical to hoard.

It is advisable, even when some interaction has been allowed for between active and contemplative practices in so complex a creature as man, to insist upon the distinction between the two kinds of knowledge involved. One is meant to be available, all of its information intact, for future use: that is why its findings must be checked out and reduced to intelligible formulas. The other exists entirely in the present tense: a knowing now, while the light is upon us, filling us with warmth against the return to the dark and the wrestle with cold counters tomorrow.

Our own problem, of course, is not that we overvalue the yield of the intuitively known, in spite of some of the claims occasional didactic novelists and Marxist theorists continue to make for it. Our problem is that we overvalue the productivity of the theoretically known, the merit of the useful equation. By making usefulness in the future our single talisman, we find ourselves without a present or imprisoned in a present in which nothing real can be known—a present that is empty of everything but our despair. We go to our pleasures, when we dare go to them at all, demanding that they surrender to us a kind of knowledge that is not in them. And so we kill them.

We also kill in our pleasures the effect we expect of them: tranquillity, composure, that unruffled expansion of being we are inclined to call happiness. Serenity is what is asked for, whether after a walk around Walden or an afternoon at the National Gallery. As Mortimer Adler has remarked in his *Art and Prudence*, a work of fine art has been traditionally prized because it "is not only good in itself as a source of contemplative joy, but through its purgative efficacy, is itself a means . . . to assure both interior tranquility and exterior peace." We have come face to face with a knowledge that has not resisted us, has not had to be wrestled with; it has blessed us with its easy amplitude and not even asked to be remembered on its next birthday; having neither to contend with it nor to take care to memorize its formula for future reference, we can do little more than rest content in it—enjoying its self-satisfying splendor for so long as the splendor lasts. Such emotions as it has aroused in us it has also dispelled: for each impulse in the pattern there has been an answer in the pattern. Such intellectual ferment as it has stirred in us it has also fulfilled: being whole, with all of its parts perfect, it could leave no agitating parts dangling.

But it is not possible to come away tranquil from a work that has had as its object the stirring of our wills to action. When a poet or a painter tells you that his purpose is to "agitate"— toward whatever political or religious or social end—you had best believe him; you had also best know, believing him, that whatever else you get from the experience he offers you, you are not going to get what you mean by "pleasure." It is not possible to come away tranquil from a work that promises you "education" or "enlightenment" in any specific sense; it will be better if you do not believe the novelist or dramatist who promises you this, for he is offering you the profits of hard labor under the conditions of pleasure and he is, in the process, corrupting both. By engaging your greed, he is roiling your mind against the contemplative possibility; and by sending you away convinced that you have "learned" something useful, he is degrading the intellectual disciplines of actual learning.

Neither is it possible to derive an exhilaration that is also serenity from a work of genuine regenerative power, a work that is not at all compromised by the promise of dubious fringe benefits, if we bring to it our own restless grappling hooks and spades. Each party to the experience must be content, for the moment, simply to be; renewal rises from the gratuitous flow, back and forth, of this shared being.

To regain some delight in ourselves and in our world, we are forced to abandon, or rather to reverse, an adage. A bird in the hand is *not* worth two in the bush—unless one is an ornithologist, the curator of the Museum of Natural History, or one of those Italian vendors who supply restaurants with larks. A bird in the hand is no longer a bird at all: it is a specimen; it may be dinner. Birds are birds only when they are in the bush or on the wing; their worth as birds can be known only at a discreet and generous distance.

To make a kind of pun, we must learn to live with the fact that nothing "good" is going to come of pleasure. Delight is probably the one thing in the world that may honestly be said to be its own reward; we must not ask that it do the washing, too. When an impressionable child named Jane Reis was six years old, she wrote the following poem:

I had a dream
Not mean things this time.
There was music crying last night
I held a lot of things belonging to spring
But when I woke up
They would not come with me.

It is enough to remember that the dream wasn't mean and that the things belonging to spring did, for a while in the springtime or a while in the night, exist; it is no cause for regret that what has pleased us cannot be carried in our pockets to spend. If the music is crying somewhere, we will be wisest to approach it making very little noise of our own, to attend to it in the stillness that does not disturb, and to retreat from it, in the end and with some awe, without having made our presence known. "I wonder if the gratuitousness of a work is not often the measure both of its potency in depth for human beings as well as its ability to endure in time?" François Mauriac has asked in his *Second Thoughts.*

☼   *I'm somebody else now.*
       Don't tell my hands.
            —THEODORE ROETHKE

Most of us have known adolescents who were compulsive eaters. The compulsive eater, stuffing himself so urgently and inattentively that he scarcely notices what he devours, imposes upon himself two quite serious penalties. Though vast quantities of the truly "good" are being crammed into his body, he is all the while becoming less and less fit. And he is, alas, not enjoying what he eats; he scarcely remembers to taste it.

As twentieth-century adults, we have become compulsive users, with approximately the same results.

The fault is not in our craft, not in our increasing capacity for extracting the maximum use from a useful world, but precisely in the compulsiveness—in the fact that we have permitted ourselves no freedom of choice between using and not using. Our inability to respond selectively to our experiences and to our opportunities for experience is, in a real sense, neurotic, as should be clear to us from our feelings of guilt in the presence of possible pleasure and our feeling of being justified only when we are engaged in despoiling ourselves. Disinterestedness is now beyond us; we do not know how to perform gratuitous acts or to deal with gratuitous acts performed by someone else; the contemplative experience frightens us more than more work does. Falling off a log is not, after all, always so easy. A man who has held himself in a single position for a very long time may become so rigid that he dare not let go without risking injury. He may learn, from others who seem somehow to have been luckier, the conditions under which a safe tumble may be taken; but he does not himself feel flexible enough to attempt the feat.

Strictly speaking, the feat has never been so matter-of-fact as all that, not even for those societies that prized the contemplative act highly or pretended to. From the very beginning the problems of survival have tended to fix men's minds toward the entirely necessary profit to be taken from things. It is not really possible to imagine an Eden, since Eden, when a woman —in a man's eyes—was not almost instantly a potential cook, a potential mother, at the very least a potential conquest. Need brings its objects into quick, sharp focus.

We should be sentimental in supposing that a shepherd in the earliest unnamed Biblical hills did not know what a sheep was for, or that Cain was not behaving with some degree of naturalness when he saw in Abel's offering of prime meats a practical waste. The Greeks were not generally so Platonic as Plato. It has forever been hard for a man to see the beauty of a fire when it was his forest that was burning, to see the beauty of a field when it was time to cut the wheat, to see the vaunted loveliness of trees when the weather was getting colder and a supply of kindling was needed.

It may have been a little easier to drink in both aspects of the world, in some sort of regular alternation, during some earlier ages for the simple reason that a degree of contemplation, or at least a degree of watchful waiting, was enforced. When men lived close to the earth, and earned their sustenance by tending it personally, they could not help but be more conscious than we are of the nearness and the thickness of things. More than that. They could not spend all their time taking dividends. They had to spend some of it being patient. A farmer could not reap the day after he had planted (though we can do just this in the stock market, provided we know how). Once the sowing had been done, a period of mild supervision and much quiet observation ensued. The farmer was apt to look at his field, just look at it, because for such a long time there was nothing else he could possibly do with it. He had other chores to perform, to be sure. But even as he turned to these he was subjected to restraints that allowed time for looking. He could not kill the calf until the calf had been fatted, he could not milk the cow until the cow was ready to be milked, he could not gather eggs until chickens with habits of their own had laid them. Nature stood between him and his profit with a solidity he was forced to respect and could not help noticing. Unlike those of us who are now free to exploit the physical world without actually being exposed to the physical world, he was trapped in the tangible present and thereby tempted to sigh and see it.

This difference between us was nicely illustrated by a brochure that came in the mail not long ago. An acquaintance who works in an investment house, and who keeps thinking that investment would be good for me, has formally invited me to become a farmer. He foresees no difficulties in the fact that I have never been introduced to a cow or mired in topsoil. I can become a farmer very simply. I send him some money— no, I do not even have to do that; I can acquire my homestead for "*no money down*" by taking out "a 20-year mortgage @ 6%"—and he does all the rest. I do not mean that he goes out to the farm and digs around in the loam. He writes a number of letters to other people in which the abstraction @ figures prominently, and somehow or other the farm loses money for three years (no panic need be felt; the investor's "*farm losses are fully deductible from his salary income*"), after which it begins to show a profit and can be sold immediately at a capital gain.

I am especially interested to read that the government will permit me to engage in this absentee husbandry only provided that I can show clearly that I am "*operating the farm for profit*" alone and that I am not incidentally enjoying it. I must be careful to have "no extensive social or recreational facilities" on the property or my loss deductions may be disallowed; it sounds as though if I dared set foot on the farmland I would quickly be in trouble. The invitation ends with a warning: "*Remember*, this is not a do-it-yourself area. You must get expert legal and investment advice. Your lawyer and investment counselor will be able to set you on the track toward being a successful executive-farmer." I am glad I did not order overalls.

The likelihood that one of my forebears had more opportunity than I to stare at the "timber, buildings, livestock and unharvested crops" is apparent. Even so, he was no mystic. If he was often mean and grubby and grasping as peasants are rumored to be and to have been, if he looked no richer in spirit or happier of mien than Grant Wood's gaunt ghost with a pitchfork, it was because he was compelled—as all men have always been compelled—to root even among droppings to see what use might be made of them. There has never been a moment, surely, in the catalogue of men's days when the urgency of use did not tend to usurp the varied powers of the mind.

What may more truly distinguish the mood of most ages past from our own—and help account for a neurotic compulsion in us that did not always exist in them—is a difference in our respective determinations to discover the precise room at the inn in which pleasure is lodged and in our respective determinations to enter that room boldly, slamming the door behind us.

I shall have to dwell upon this notion of slamming the door. The door that must be closed behind us, of course, is the door that reopens onto the possibility of use, of work, of profitable labor. So long as it stands ajar, we will be sucked back through it by the winds of our need and the reality of our worries; we are built that way. The problem, then, has forever been simply this: since all things are in some way useful, how does one go about reducing useful things to a condition of utter and exhilarating uselessness? How *does* one shut the door tight for a time?

The problem can be solved only by the erection of vise-tight patterns which become absolute barriers, barriers against profit-taking. These barriers need to be so formidable, so beyond the possibility of our scaling them or dissolving them, that even if we wished to snatch a profit we should find ourselves restrained from doing so. I suppose the whole process might be compared, halfway anyway, to that familiar and friendly Colonial device known as "bundling," the business of popping a boy and a girl into bed of an evening where the quilts will keep them warm and the proximity will keep them happy and the slat of hard wood between them will presumably keep them from being of ultimate use to one another. In the last analysis, no doubt, the comparison is as inadequate as the slat:

profit-taking is made difficult, but it is by no means put out of mind.

From the beginning, however, mankind in general has been extraordinarily ingenious at inventing much more reliable patterns of resistance to use. Many things have been found to help.

Preposterousness helps. If the village can be persuaded to grease a pole and the village men can be persuaded to try to climb it, one chance at delight has been born. The pole is only a pole, without a purpose. It supports nothing. It leads nowhere. If a man does succeed in climbing it, he has accomplished a glorious nought. He has also been made to behave absurdly on the way to achieving the absurd. The ordinarily climbable pole has been made as unclimbable as possible; its function has in every way been denied. The man's ordinarily strong and serviceable hands have been violently robbed of their talents, made wonderfully and ludicrously impotent. The man can take nothing but delight from this wrestling match with the worthless. The women watching him can take nothing but delight in the fool he is making of himself. A Maypole, supporting nothing but streamers which are nothing but pretty, is equally preposterous; there isn't a thing to be done with it, once the irresponsible dance is over, except to put it away until next year, when it can be made happily useless once more.

Arbitrariness helps. Any degree of patterning which has no purpose but to *be* a pattern makes a swift contribution to the gaiety of nations. A game is invariably hedged in by rules: the rules are carefully arranged to signify nothing other than themselves. There is no *reason* why a baseball game should go for nine innings, a football game for four quarters, a game of table tennis for twenty-one points. The nine and the four and the twenty-one do not correspond to or reinforce any of the practical habits or profitable virtues of tomorrow's labor, do not suggest how a day or a business deal might best be conducted, do not inculcate principles of thrift or teach mathematics in the manner of those insufferable children's games our educators have now devised. (Children are encouraged to encourage their parents to sit with them in the evening shuffling out cards in a contest that is partly Old Maid and partly third-grade arithmetic. The "game" is irritating and depleting precisely because a source of pleasure has been robbed of its very pointlessness. It is not possible to *play subtraction*.) The purpose of game rules is to circumscribe the play as arbitrarily as possible, to make it as much unlike the productive conduct of our labor as the overhead flight of a chess knight is unlike the conduct of a horse (and since when have bishops always gone straight to the point or kings been the least mobile figures in the land?). Hoyle is a wonderland of rigid irrelevance, a sober treasure house of logic founded upon premises that vanish as the dice are pocketed and the board folded away.

Nor is there anything more relevant in the fact that a two-step is a two-step, a schottische a schottische, a conga a conga and not a cancan. These things are counted differently and with such precision that they are often difficult to master; but when the precision is attained, it is also seen to be purposeless— except for the pleasure our bodies may take in altering the rhythms of their unproductive passage through space.

How entirely arbitrary the strict patternings of dance are may be seen in the fantasies of limitation invented by isolated ethnic groups. There are nations in which it is an honor to make no movements with one's hands: an Irishman's jig is performed with his arms utterly limp. There are nations in which the head must never be moved, except perhaps slightly sideways. There are nations that insist no noise should be made with the feet. Something, everywhere, is always saying "no," as a hint of the "no-ness" that lies at the heart of delight. "No trespassing" on the part of those workaday boots and cunning heads that have "seared with trade; bleared, smeared with toil" is what these otherwise quite meaningless restraints are so politely whispering. A gesture, a power, a greed is held back in order to help avoid that coming, awful moment Gerard Manley Hopkins foresees, that moment when

> . . . *the soil*
> *Is bare now, nor can foot feel, being shod.*

A token prize that cannot be translated into real reward helps. The laurel wreath thus comes to be esteemed much more highly than a bag of coins or a goose that can be taken home and cooked. When the coin is spent, so is the pleasure. The victor has been able to use his reward and now has nothing left of his victory. The laurel wreath, untouched on the wall by virtue of its valuelessness, remains as a memory of the splendidly useless thing that was done. It was appropriate to the occasion and appropriately loses nothing it never had. It is a common joke among motion-picture actors that they use their Oscars as doorstops. But this is a sly, shy means of denigrating them, of deliberately reducing their value by putting them to inappropriate and indeed degrading use; perhaps motion-picture actors have no other way of calming their consciences. But where the trophy is genuinely valued, it is elevated to a position of aspiring uselessness at the highest visible point in the house.

Closing real doors helps. When a holiday is declared, it becomes impossible or at least flagrantly self-seeking and antisocial for a banker to go to his bank, a shoemaker to his hole in the wall, a teacher to his classroom. (There is always something vaguely indecent, something that violates good taste, about a teacher who summons his students to meetings during the Christmas or Easter holidays, even when the students deserve punishment; he is trespassing upon ground that one feels to be sacred, not because of the religious associations of these odd weeks of freedom, but because of the spirit of release that has been promised each student's heart. The teacher may be doing the right thing, but a sinking in our souls tells us that he is doing it at the wrong time.) Earlier societies did tend to declare more frequent festivals, whether they were declared as holy days or holidays, and to respect them more firmly, than we do. The proliferation of public occasions during the Middle Ages became so marked that a special calendar was needed to make note of them all; today a Corpus Christi is a mere date on that calendar and a Feast of Fools no more than a footnote in a history book. Lost altogether, too, is a medieval suggestion—most likely never put to widespread practice—that the day be divided into "three eights": eight hours work, eight hours play, eight hours sleep. "All work and no play . . ." is advice still on our lips but lost to our lives; we have spoken of the crushing burden that Christmas has become, and we are not altogether certain that we will not seem pompous and old-fashioned should we decide to run up a flag on the front lawn for July Fourth. Being nervous of seeming fools, we do very little feasting.

The connection, by the way, between holy days and holidays is obvious, and we should be less puzzled than we are that so many sports and even fine arts seem to be entangled, at the roots, with religious ceremonies. We draw odd conclusions from the circumstance, at times, assuming that art itself is in some way a religious observance or that religious experience is essentially aesthetic experience. What happened, of course, is that religion, having closed the door to work for a day in order to protect an activity of the spirit, completed its own activity without having occupied the whole day. The worshipers were now turned loose, with their banks and their workbenches still sealed safely away, to engage in another—and in most ways quite different—exercise of the spirit, the spirit being free. They played games, and invented drama, and got drunk. How far the two gratuitous, nonprofit activities grew from one another, while still belonging to the same day in time and the same arbitrary divorce from labor, is easily observed. The Greek dithyramb was a religious chant and also the seedbed of drama; but it became drama only as one of its transitional practitioners, Archilochus, was reported to do his best and most inventive work "while drunk." The medieval trope was once more a part of the liturgy of the church and also the forge from which the spark of drama flew off; but as soon as the spark had succeeded in setting a flame, the bonfire had perforce to be hustled out of the interior of the cathedral because it was patently leading "to boisterousness and laxity in church." As Newman has pointed out in *The Idea of a University*, painting and sculpture and music may all serve, for a time, as handmaids of religion—so long as they are content, in an unfinished state, to remain servants and not become principals:

"But the case is very different when genius has breathed upon their natural elements, and has developed them into what I may call intellectual powers. When Painting, for example, grows into the fulness of its function as a simply imitative art, it at once ceases to be a dependant on the Church. It has an end of its own, and that of earth: Nature is its pattern, and the object it pursues is the beauty of Nature, even till it becomes an ideal beauty, but a natural beauty still."

To put the point in another way, it should never surprise us that one contemplative act, no matter what object it may be dwelling upon, should help bring into being yet another contemplative act, albeit one with a quite different object. The mind has been set, as a camera is, for a certain admission of light. Without altering the aperture, we shift the view. The light itself has come from a uniformly cloudless sky, the overcast of our labor having been banished by fiat in the formal declaration of a "day off."

I have often found myself wondering, as I glance at a newspaper, whether much of the irrational violence that marks our time—the unpredictable and random bursts of fury that find both adolescents and adults striking out at what has not injured them—may not be due to the loss of all other opportunities for exercising unreason. The irrational is not in itself despicable; it is an assertion of that aspect of personality which the limited tool of reason is incapable of grasping or satisfying. Nor is it in its essential nature vicious. It is playful and may become vicious only when it is denied its proper playground, its happy exercise.

Even with all of the formalizations thus far suggested—the occasion on which work is prohibited, the pursuit of a prize which has no resale value, the erection of patterns as arbitrary as the one-foot side steps to nowhere called hopscotch, the reduction of familiar objects and familiar powers to impotence through the greasing of poles or the divorce of the horseshoe from the horse to which it belongs—the itch to turn things to advantage does continue. When the itch appears during a game, it corrupts the game, as college basketball has so often been corrupted or as a "poor loser" spoils our pleasure because he has had his mind set on gain. It is a natural characteristic of sport that it should breed in us a resistance to the man who abandons his amateur standing in order to turn "pro"; we sense a fall from grace, perhaps in both senses of the word. The term "amateur" has continued to mean "lover" to us, even if we should be embarrassed to admit it, and we cannot altogether destroy a fundamental conviction that sport is something invented by and for love, no matter what livelihood may sometimes be drawn from it. Still, the temptation to make a good thing of holidays or a side bet on the turn of another man's card persists like a canker sore; the festivities remain vulnerable, in some degree, to those unquiet virtues that have elsewhere made us good providers.

It is perfectly possible for us to derive contemplative pleasure from a walk in the woods or even a walk on asphalt, from a day at the shore or even a day spent dawdling down the main street of a city, from the act of simply sitting in a chair doing nothing at all until something is done to us by the possibilities outside ourselves or from the more active act of doing nothing vigorously by engaging in an irrelevant game. We neglect each of these opportunities at our peril. But if we do find ourselves neglecting them, or if we experience considerable difficulty in taming our present tensions to the demand for sustained patience these forms of idleness make, it is because there is still a certain looseness about them: their boundaries are not yet defined absolutely enough to close us tightly, and safely, in. We tend to find such experiences both interruptible and corruptible. An advertising man going for a drive in the country can always appease what nags at him by counting billboards along the way. We have still not come upon a landscape sufficiently protected against us to resist our habits and to enforce its own laws.

Mankind's search for a condition of uselessness that could not be reconditioned to use by a clever secondhand dealer led it ultimately—whether by an accident of instinct or by conscious design—to the most nearly useless of all human activities: the making of imitations. We have always understood, from Aristotle onward, that "it is natural for all to delight in works of imitation," that "imitation is natural to man from childhood," that man "is the most imitative creature in the world." The delight we take in watching a mimic, any mimic, need not be brought into question here: until we stop laughing at men who try on women's hats at parties or at dialect comedians or at friends who are able to reproduce the speech patterns of other, momentarily absent, friends, we shall be in no position to challenge the proposition. What needs emphatic restatement just now is the further proposition that our predilection for imitation is a predilection that produces delight *and nothing else*.

This isn't immediately obvious. One first has to forget the various contrary claims that have been made for the most fully developed of imitations, the major forms of art, and think rather plainly about the commonest substitutes for the real thing that we come across. When one reaches for a bottle of lime soda he is reaching for something with "artificial coloring" and "imitation flavoring," as the label will tell him. He does not suppose that the imitative factors—that bright green hue, that exceeding sweetness—have any useful, nutritive value about them. Nor have they anything "natural" in them: a lime is not so sweet; the only thing that is truly green about it is the one thing he would never eat, the rind. If he reaches for the soda anyway, it is not with the hope of profiting by what is imitative in it but simply because the bright green color, which is altogether absurd, is pleasing to him.

Any household is stocked with useful things which imitate, superficially, other things they are not: ash trays in the shape of copper frying pans, catsup holders in the shape of tomatoes, saltcellars that look like kittens and that may even squeak as the children overdo the salt. But the irrelevant image is every-where an excrescence, yielding nothing in the way of im-proved service. It is merely mildly pleasant to the insatiable eye. Indeed, a purist would insist that whenever a mimetic factor is added to a useful object there is great danger of vul-garity, of denial of function and hence form, of embroiling oneself in the ersatz—as in the cases of imitation marble and imitation leather. No profit has been added—only a playfulness that may in the circumstances be inappropriate.

It has often been suggested that the imitative antics of chil-dren are not only fun for them but a part of the learning process they must undergo. The notion needs serious re-ex-amination. Children do make mud pies, and eventually they become intelligent enough not to eat them. But nowhere along the line, imitate though they may, do they actually learn any-thing about making actual pies. When the day comes for a daughter to be instructed in pie making, she will have to begin over again; she will now have to be taught, carefully and laboriously, how to perform the chore, and she will bring to her present industry not the least bit of profit from her earlier activities in a wet back yard. Children play "house," but according to their own rules, which are the splendidly useless rules of play; when they are finished playing "house," they will have to be taught table manners.

Nor does learning take place even where it seems most obviously to take place: in the acquisition of words. An infant does indeed begin to pronounce syllables by repeating what he has overheard or what has been strenuously drilled into him—in much the same way that a parrot acquires a mock vocabulary. But repeating "Mommy" or "Daddy" or "snow" does not in any sense constitute understanding. The process of associating a familiar sound with the object it is meant to signify must still take place—secretly, and with a surprising expenditure of effort—in the labyrinth of a developing brain. The infant I spoke of a chapter ago has been able to pronounce "Daddy" and "snow" quite clearly for five or six months past; but "Daddy" remains variable enough to include visiting strangers of both sexes, and I have only now, in the spring, discovered that if "snow" signifies anything, it quite mistakenly signifies "outdoors." The child has been a good mimic for half a year; soon he must get down to work.

In equating mimesis with learning, we are not only superimposing an alien task upon an instrument of play but are also once again being dangerously careless about the quality of our work. Genuine learning is not even a lucky by-product of mimesis. Some thinkers seem to have hoped that it might be, no doubt as a justification for so much time wasted. Other thinkers, politicians in particular, have snatched at the imitative processes as the shortest cut to a desirable conformity and hence a desirable efficiency. But Toynbee has called attention on several occasions to the "perilousness of mimesis" as a teaching method:

"The Achilles' heel in the social anatomy of a civilization is . . . its dependence on mimesis (imitation) as a 'social drill' for ensuring that the rank and file of Mankind shall follow their leaders . . . but the avenue thereby opened for a social advance may end in the gates of death . . ."

The historian is not here suggesting simply that the kind of leader who would organize his society by arranging that it Heil when he Heils, that it hate what he hates, that it believe what he believes, is a leader likely to plunge it into mindless excesses. We may assume, for our purposes, that the leader is intelligent and well-intentioned, that his ideals are worthy ideals. To the degree that he relies upon mimesis in order to consolidate his following, he is bound to fail.

A society is not truly alive as a human society so long as it is functioning as an echo. Until each of its members has himself grasped, analyzed, and criticized the propositions put before him, until he has given assent that is born of logical conviction, until he has assimilated unto himself not only the gestures of meaning but the vital musculature that gives the gestures interior support, the society will be hollow at heart no matter how loudly it roars. Collapse must come, sooner or only slightly later, because the successive steps by means of which all solid structures are built have been bypassed. Indeed, it is only "when an inevitable failure has bred an equally inevitable disillusionment" that "the discredited leaders are apt to resort to force in order to retain an authority that is morally forfeit."

The authority is forfeit because the proposed ideals, good or bad, have never been subjected to that slow, tested growth of understanding, that organic development, by which stable "learning" comes to birth. Nothing useful or productive has been acquired—only empty patterns of borrowed behavior. At the core of such a society, as in the heart and mind of each unit in that society, there is a creative vacuum, an absence of real energy which may be briefly concealed by an animated shell. Any time that mimesis is accepted in lieu of learning, or as learning itself, we are dealing once more with that shell, and we will do well to listen for the first sound of its cracking. For it is the distinction, and even the glory, of mimesis that it has succeeded in freeing itself from the possibilities of profit.

With the discovery of imitation, man had found for himself that experience which, by most firmly separating itself from the temptations to use, was readiest to yield him his purest delight. What intuition led him to it we do not know; it is not to be supposed that he reasoned the matter out, certainly not in the terms we are using. But the man who scratched a bison on the wall of a cave had done an astonishing thing. He had summoned before him a bison that could not be eaten, that could not be skinned, and that need not be feared. He had isolated the beauty of the beast from all the good or all the damage the beast could ever do him, and, in the act, he had plucked the cataracts imposed by a lifetime of forced labor from his eyes. He had won the battle of the world by making the world his without the sickening fears that compromised his vision of it as he most often encountered it: the fear that it would turn on him when he wished most to admire it or the fear that it would elude him when his spear was desperately hungry. Nor was he engaged in an anatomy lesson, learning tonight what would help him tomorrow. As Malraux has remarked, "The surgeon who removes a cataract does not interpret the world to his patient but gives it, or restores it, to him." This was the universe restored, unrobbed and un-robbable, suspended where it could be seen and only seen—an object of sheer interest, or, better, of that sheer disinterest that deserves to be called love.

Then and there the man who drew the bison became a con-templative who could not be distracted from his delight by a warning flick of the mane or a teasing envy of the hide. It is, after all, an extraordinarily lucky thing that we cannot kiss the woman in the portrait, that we cannot pluck one of the succulent apples from the order of the still life, that we cannot plant the sun-warmed landscape, that we can hear no law from the Moses of Michelangelo, that we cannot intrude as a marriage counselor upon The Moor's Pavane. All of these have been placed just enough beyond our reach to keep our wills, perhaps the best wills in the world, quiet; they are accessible only to the seeing eye, to the intuitively knowing mind, safe in that snug harbor where, in Aquinas' phrase, "that which, being seen, pleases."

The ingeniousness of the imitative act does not end with the reduction of so many Venuses to the eternally chaste sexuality of marble. It goes well beyond the isolating of bridges from actual traffic, tenements from actual tenants, battles from actual victims whose rhythmic falls we should be unable to enjoy were we given any opportunity to bind up their wounds. It not only seizes upon natural objects originally so sentient as to involve us, recasting them in dimensions which prohibit our touching them either charitably or in the interests of plunder, but also snatches from our hands the very tools with which we normally perform our acts of charity or plunder, those abstract concepts by means of which the world's good work is done.

Words are tools of work, of course. Yet ways have been found of using these abstractions in constructions which quite take their working powers away. Poetry plays with words in a manner that flatly defies their greatest virtue: their individual precision of meaning. We know, for instance, what we mean by the word "convulsed" and are therefore able to use it in our daily battle to communicate accurately. But what has happened to it in E. E. Cummings' irresponsible hands?

> *notice the convulsed orange inch of moon*
> *perching on this silver minute of evening . . .*

Even "inch" has ceased to mean what it does mean, and in some hopelessly impossible way a minute has been silvered over. Our dictionaries will tell us, explicitly, what a broom is for, what the act of sweeping consists in, what an industry is. But in what industry is an emotion swept up? Emily Dickinson:

> *The bustle in a house*
> *The morning after death*
> *Is solemnest of industries*
> *Enacted upon earth,—*
>
> *The sweeping up the heart,*
> *And putting love away*
> *We shall not want to use again*
> *Until eternity.*

The words have not, of course, lost all of the associations we should bring to them in a business letter. They have not been emptied of content. They have been emptied of work content. The power of the term "industry" to signify a specific reality in a legal document is here mocked: surely no legal document has yet been framed in which the aftermath of death was described as an industry, and surely none ever will be. The word has been ripped from its orderly position in the processes of discursive knowledge and hurled at a subject with which it has nothing to do—thereby to create an intuitive explosion. Instead of being soberly aligned with one another in logical sequence, words are now played *against* one another—"convulsed orange inch of moon" is literally a collision of meanings cut loose from their moorings—and what leaps into the air as a result of the crash is a knowledge every bit as real as the old knowledge but a knowledge that is now intuitive, immediate, indescribable, and good for nothing but an intelligible shock of delight. Imitation has used a series of crowbars to create a symphony, just as an actual symphony—elusive to the last—has employed some of the same fractions that Einstein used to keep the universe from eluding him. The profitable has been shorn of its share-taking so that pleasure may come to be.

In the past, at least, man has restlessly put his shears to virtually everything at hand to see whether or not a good clipping mightn't bring him a brief good time. Aristocrats, imprisoned on the estates that set them apart from the earthier laborers they ruled, devised for themselves a number of wonderfully foolish compensations. Hierarchically divorced from the woodland greenery the local poachers enjoyed, they arranged their own greenery. "Arranged" is the right word here, for they so manipulated the growing things about them into wildly useless patterns that we have thought them half insane ever since. About their formal gardens stood curiously shaped mockeries of nature: not only box hedges cut to a neatness that no natural forest ever tolerated, but hedges and trees cut to the shapes of horses and ships and hoop-skirted girls. Impotence was compounded; the trees they saw weren't useful trees, the horses they saw weren't useful horses. Beneath this gallery of grotesques the residents sometimes played at being the milkmaids and milksops they were not. The form of the greenery, as well as the form of the gambol, nowadays strikes us as absurd. But that is what it was meant to be. It is not until the useful has been made in some way absurd that we are able to deny ourselves its practical opportunities and indulge ourselves in its charm.

I have mentioned along the way the embarrassment we feel about committing ourselves too openly to celebrations on shipboard, celebrations on patriotic holidays, celebrations that involve even the elementary patterning of "black tie." "It's all such nonsense" is the phrase that comes to our minds as we try to avoid abiding by one or another rule of stylization—

whether in clothing or guided conduct or any sort of "marking the occasion." And, truth to tell, it *is* nonsense: nonsense deliberately devised to extricate us from the sense we make all day long when we are wearing our working clothes or performing our chores with a slide-rule efficiency rather than with a soul-saving eccentricity. But the psychological resistance which the twentieth century has built up to every form of arbitrary patterning does not end with the nervous abandonment of costumes and traditional capers—those things that help to say "Stop that" and "Start this." It has extended, now, to the denial of that last and most important leap into the useless, imitation itself.

Characteristically, we have come to question whether the concept and the practice of "imitation" can be said to have any value at all. That the term should have got itself into certain literary and pictorial difficulties in our time is in many ways understandable. The arts, suffering during the late nineteenth and early twentieth centuries from the scientific insistence that they reproduce phenomena as literally as possible, had become uncomfortably photographic. As rebellion stirred against the "slice-of-life realism" that obviously could be better managed by the camera, a battle cry began to be heard more and more frequently. We had been "imitating" too much. In order to break with the slavish copying of a factually-measured nature, we concluded that we must break with the notion of "imitation" altogether. To continue defining any one of the fine arts as an imitation of nature was to condemn it to that cheap illusionism of which we had grown so weary and so wary. We needed another concept, we thought, of how a fine art came to being; or perhaps we'd be better off having no concept at all. As Harold Rosenberg has said, "The big moment came when it was decided to paint . . . just TO PAINT. The gesture on the canvas was a gesture of liberation, from Value—political, esthetic, moral." And natural.

Strictly speaking, the conclusion was a *non sequitur*. We had been imitating not too much but—paradoxically—too little. An imitation, if the term is to mean anything, must be conceived as a similarity plus a dissimilarity. It must be in part like some other object and in part transparently unlike it, as the child who is imitating the smoking of a cigar is in part like his cigar-smoking father—insofar as he is making a single reminiscent gesture—and in a thousand ways utterly unlike him, including the fact that he is not smoking the cigar. The charm, the special illumination, even the very existence of the imitative act depends upon our intense awareness of its strong differences from the object imitated. It is because I am so certain a circus clown is not a dog that I am enchanted when he behaves like one. A dog behaving like a dog would not do the trick for me; he would have to get on his hind legs and walk like a man to delight me as much. Contradiction is of the essence here. The quality being mimicked must be mimicked by something that does not normally possess that quality, as paint does not have the dimensions of flesh or catgut access to the emotions of a soul. Imitation implies, to be sure, an echo—but always an echo that has been displaced.

Whenever these strong differences are diminished, whenever our awareness of them is subtly reduced, whenever a work seems to be becoming more and more like its source and less and less distinguishable from it, we are becoming not more "imitative" but less. We are moving toward identity, which is the negation of imitation. And it was toward identity that naturalistic art was moving, just as a popular orchestral composition I used to hear as a child moved from the near identity of horses' hoofs produced on a drum (the horses, if I remember correctly, were chasing a fox) to the absolute identity of an actual gunshot at the climax of the rousing piece. I am sure that none of this can have been music; but certainly the gunshot wasn't. Art had aspired for a while to the authenticity of that gunshot, and we were aware that something was wrong. What was wrong was the absence of imitation; but we got the point backward.

In all probability, however, there were deeper reasons for our rejection of imitation than a simple misreading of the errors of literalism. One of them, I venture to suggest, was a deep and distressing conviction that nature, human nature included, was not worth imitating. Having lost its value for us as we sickened in our hopes, it could no longer be recommended to the poet or painter as a source of *his* value. Hence Mr. Rosenberg's "gesture of liberation" from value of every kind: it would be little more than hypocrisy to go on echoing entities in which we no longer believed. If man seemed a cipher to us, we had best paint the cipher. If nature seemed an accident of atoms, we had best paint the atoms. Better still, paint the accident. Or, to be more consistent about the matter, we had best forget about the imitation of the unworthy altogether and, in a defiant ultimate act, simply thrust our arms toward a surface and strike it.

One last reason for our rejection, the reason we are most concerned with here. The imitative arts had achieved their contemplative power by stripping from the universe, and from the observer, all other powers. Focus was complete, protected, unblurred by concern for our daily bread. And it was this insistence upon a momentary impotence, this uselessness, this banishment of our hands and habits, that baffled us most fiercely in an age convinced that all virtue was in use and all happiness the product of our acquisitive energies. We were in no position to resist the onslaught upon the imitative principle, wherever the pressure might come from. We knew no grounds on which it might be defended. It might still strike us as funny that Jack Benny should pretend to be a miser, or as interesting that Marcel Marceau should pretend to be a mask, but these things were inconsequential; the time we gave them stirred some feelings of guilt, of shiftlessness, in us, but we did not give them all that much time or more than half of our minds while we *were* giving them time. As for the arts that took themselves more seriously, that did strive for consequence, what could we do but shrug and try not to show our ignorance in their presence? Plainly, they resembled less and less what we could, or cared to, recognize. They conformed less and less to a principle we could grasp. Upon what principle of our own could we call them to account? Uneasy and alienated, unable to imagine a value which might be assigned to pure imitations, we simply let them go.

The imitative principle, let it be said, has by no means vanished from the main body of contemporary art. Abstract art continues to imitate a structural element that exists in nature, whether in the mathematical architecture that underlies the universe or in the logical architecture that buzzes in our brains. Most contemporary fine art contents itself with rigidly imitating what we most rigidly prize: abstractions. If it can be accused of anything, it is not of running away from us or turning irrelevant but of serving our predispositions too slavishly and, yes, too literally. Who dares show surprise that, increasingly, painting should display on its surfaces isolated letters and ampersands and fragments of words, when these are the things to which our vision is truly restricted? Why should not Mr. Rosenberg say that "every modern work of art is in essence criticism: the artist paints it as an assertion in paint about painting, and the audience admires it as an assertion in paint about words" when we are determined to live with equations only? Nor is the exclusive imitation of the abstract necessarily invalid; it is probably merely thin. Where, as in the example quoted earlier from Malraux, a Gothic artist overlaid an abstract pattern with a surface of flesh, now sustaining both patterns in a give-and-take unity, we confine ourselves, ascetically, to a single layer. Where an El Greco or a Brueghel found his abstract patterns within the lift or the tumble of dimensional life, we tend to find our patterns only in patterns. "What Piet Mondrian did as framed 'pictures,' Horace's decorators put on his floors," Gilbert Highet has observed. There is clearly nothing wrong with looking at Horace's floors or at Hadrian's. But the view, made universal, is something less than we might demand, something less than most men have demanded, of the attainable world. It is precisely the less of our lives.

It is not until we have gone beyond the more or less intelligible equations of "abstract" art to the uncompromising performance of the "action" painter or the "anti-dramatist" that we come close to completing the intended destruction of the imitative principle. The painter refuses to entertain an image, in his mind, of what he means to do: blindly, he attacks the canvas to see what entirely new thing may come into being as a result of an unpremeditated meeting. The composer is careful to avoid that complex of notes that may, inadvertently, suggest a harmony and so remind one of a balance known to exist: the recognition of anything prior to the experience must be strenuously avoided, for it would bring the hint of imitation into play again and corrupt the purity of the experience as a new, independent, unindebted one. The anti-dramatist does not, as a rule, write more than two lines in succession that may be said to follow one another—or, if they seem to be in sequence, then the second must contradict the first—so that not even the abstract processes by which we engage in thought are imitated. In each case the artifact stands alone, its own creature, without obligation to a nonexistent value beyond itself.

Even here, even in a surface or a sound that prides itself on having no allusive content of any kind, the question of whether or not imitation has been wholly banished remains a matter of conjecture. The artist may cleanse his mind, as best he is able, of the images that tend to lodge there, and strike while the emptiness is hot. Is the unguided, surprising, apparently random movement of freed muscle echoing nothing, not even the pulse throb that animates it, the muscular structure that makes it possible, the very will that has been so determined to act without commitment? No one has ever supposed that imitation was entirely, or even importantly, a matter of surface fidelity: when nature was imitated in the traditional sense, it was thought that she was being imitated not in her strictly measurable effects but, as Aquinas preferred to say, in her *manner of operation.* If no painter has ever counted the leaves of a tree, it is because what truly concerned him was the utterly invisible movement of its sap. "My great desire," Van Gogh said, "is to learn to make such inexactitudes, anomalies, revisions, changes, give birth to lies, yes, call them lies if you will, but lies that are truer than the literal truth." It is not impossible that nature's method of work continues to dominate the motor impulses of the man most determined to give resemblances no quarter and that imitation will survive in the teeth of its last enemy's defiance; it is also not impossible that when we find ourselves taking pleasure in such work, as we sometimes do, it is this last, hidden bond that coils about us.

But let us suppose, for one moment, that the artist does succeed in performing an act that is solely an act and in no degree an echo of some other act. We are, in this case, confronted with a non-imitative experience which is as directly challenging to us in the course and conduct of our lives as any other non-imitative, or actual, experience: a windstorm whipping at us, a street fight we have stumbled into, a face looming into ours, or a stucco wall against which we have braced our hands. The contact we make is not contemplative but, if I may use the word, sensational. The responses we find ourselves giving are real responses, ready, unformed, undistilled by detachment: we feel anger, dismay, irritation, shock, apprehension, excitement, avidity, sensual restlessness—whatever interesting or terrifying or ambiguous emotions we should feel in the presence of an unresolved and continuing *event*.

Most of the men who have struggled to turn the arts into an engaged activity rather than a contemplative one have been frank about this. They have not promised us pleasure. They have promised us agitation. Some have explicitly offered pain. None has been so dishonest as to speak of tranquillity, the traditional residual experience of the fine arts, as a possible or even desirable end to the meeting.

Continuing to suppose that what is actually an artifact can in some way become as much an event as a burning loft or a bull-fight or a forced march in unpredictable weather, the twentieth-century observer is now given a clear choice. He can choose to cease thinking of peace or of pleasure, to cease thinking of himself as an observer at any time, and plunge further into that committed restiveness toward which his conscience is already driving him until he becomes an eternal participant. Or, wondering whether it is truly his nature always to be at the self-consuming center of things, he can raise certain questions. *Is* there, at the very least, an imitative rhythm still coursing through the apparent blind chance of the most independently conceived artifact? Does this rhythm, when and if he finds it, correspond to any inhalation-exhalation he finds in himself, and finds satisfying in himself? Is it related to, and does it seem to become more pronounced in, works that admit to a greater degree of imitativeness? Is he entitled, at any level at all, to demand for himself the benefits that imitation confers and that actual events, as such, do not?

For one thing is agreed upon, by both parties to the present debate: that the purpose of imitation is to give pleasure, that the breaking down of imitation does mean the breaking down of pleasure. Art itself is broken down, banished; for it is only in the term "imitation" that art finds itself defined. It cannot be defined in terms of the "beautiful," even though it be in fact beautiful: many things which are not art are beautiful, too—waterfalls and faces, for instance. It cannot be defined in terms of craftsmanship, of things well made: many things are not art which are wonderfully made—automobiles and typewriters, for instance. To know itself, to proclaim its unique identity, art must look into the arbitrarily-patterned boundaries and the impotently-reflective mirrorings that belong to mimesis alone.

One may elect, under the pressures of the day or in the absence of belief, to do without mimesis, to exchange art for an event, pleasure for agitation, artificial boundaries for no boundaries. The man who does so will not be surprised to see a painting leap its frame and slither to the floor.

One may also cling to mimesis as something both unique and real, as he clings to his copy of *Oedipus Rex* or his memories of Bobby Clark—as something which can easily be rejected but cannot under any circumstances be replaced. He knows that a defined experience, even if that experience should be thought out of date, can be neither equated with nor superseded by its opposite. It remains what it was.

The man who takes this second course will find himself in certain difficulties just now; certainly he will feel old-fashioned. The imitative arts have been explored, catalogued, and exhausted long since, he will be told: what Goya did, or what Spenser did, belonged to a time and an inexperience that cannot be retrieved. (It is always said that art is exhausted, never that the artist is; that is a curious circumstance.) And it will comfort him little to remind himself that the inevitable staling of every cyclical impulse in the life of art does not mean the death of art itself, that the decay of one kind of imitation need not imply a reluctant but total surrender of the imitative principle proper. He can sense that we have not yet the least notion of what new materials the impulse may seize upon to assert itself freshly, as music surprised us all by imagining the symphony such a short time ago. (What a discovery the true novel was in the eighteenth century, and what incompetents we are not to conceive this instant the forms that are going to enchant the twenty-second!) But he is whistling in a dark that may get darker.

Is there nothing in the here and now to give him heart? I know as little about quantum physics as I do about the car out of control, or the friendly stranger, or the next astonishing insight of philosophy or science, that is coming around the corner ahead of me. But I am interested to read, in *The American Scholar*, the following remarks by Douglas Angus:

". . . quantum physics has made possible the view that all phenomena, from star formation through chemical and biological evolution to the forward groping of human intelligence, form a single unitary process from simplicity to complexity and ever increasing consciousness. Since man is, by this view, no longer an insignificant accident in a vast and indifferent cosmos, but the very foreshoot of evolution in a universe no longer entirely purposeless and meaningless, one may expect that the profound pessimism and analytical disintegration that has characterized modern art will presently give way to a more positive evaluation of man and a more harmonious unity of design."

There is a rumor of spring in that.

Even in midwinter, a man can choose. The effort to discover what his preference may be will itself embroil him in almost unbearable hardships; he will be forced to wrest himself free from a single, specialized bent of mind, to submit himself to the possibility of an intuitive knowledge he has never earned, to let himself fall headlong into games that make him ridiculous and imitations that make him impotent.

But he can test for himself the promises that have been made.

7

✵
✵
✵

The World with Both Eyes Open

*When you got to ask what it is, you
never get to know.*

—Louis Armstrong

ERIC GILL once said that it was a sin to eat inferior ice cream, and he was serious when he said it. If the statement shocks us, or strikes us as the remark of a man given to silliness as a form of self-advertisement, it is partly because we have ceased to believe in sin and partly because we have ceased to believe in ice cream. Mr. Gill was being strict about both.

Sin, by definition, is a defect in the quality of an act, a deliberate failure to perform a natural act perfectly. When I am treacherous enough to tell a substantial lie, I am not so much making something up as I am letting something down. In fact, I am letting several things down. I am using my power to communicate in order not to communicate, which means that I am depriving that power of the one thing that is good about it. I perform an act while destroying the purpose of the act, and this is stupid of me because it embroils me in a negation, in a diminution of my abilities which must become a diminution of myself. More fatally still, I am lowering the flag of my intellect: what I say purports to conform with what I know but is actually less than what I know. I have committed myself to a deformity, a lack, a lesion. Sin is always less than the occasion requires.

And there is only one conceivable reason for making or eating ice cream: to give or take pleasure. No one goes to the trouble of churning ice cream for the sake of its nutritive value; all that is nutritious about it can be had with less effort. Nor does one gobble it up as a means of building a sound body; one first takes care to have his carrots and steak, after which he can, if he likes and if he isn't overweight, indulge his childish fondness for the superfluous.

But what happens to this hedonist when, for reasons of economy or perhaps just plain carelessness, he buys and spoons into himself a product short on real cream and shy of real flavor? In point of fact, we know what happens to him— because he is ourselves and we do just this all the time. He comes to hate himself. He sits there eating, unable to resist the next mouthful because he has a memory of ice cream that once satisfied him deeply and because he is entitled to some kind of pleasure, and at the same time seething because it is perfectly clear to him that he isn't enjoying a single spoonful. He feels a fool. He knows he is a fool. If only it tasted like something, he tells himself, the calories might be worth it. But to add the calories and have it taste like paraffin, that, *that* is intolerable. He knows what he should do, of course; he should put the dish aside, leave half of it behind him. When he doesn't, which is most of the time, it is because he will not surrender the right to eat ice cream even when the ice cream isn't worth eating. On he plunges, more irritated by the minute. He is, and he isn't, doing what he wants to do, and the contradiction drives him wild.

Mr. Gill was right, and his rightness has nothing to do with calories or ordinary human perversity. It is a moral matter, a matter of intellectual honesty. The man who rises from his dessert feeling that he has degraded himself has in fact done so. He *is* guilty. At the back of his brain two propositions are clear to him. Under certain circumstances it is entirely proper to eat inferior bread, as Mr. Gill has remarked; bread is a necessity of life, and if one cannot afford or obtain the best bread, one must perforce accept a second-best. But the purpose of ice cream is simply to give pleasure; no circumstance forces a man to submit himself to a second-best, a third-best, an unpleasing pleasure. To eat ice cream that displeases is to engage in an act which denies its own nature, as surely as a lie denies the nature of the truth. Furthermore, the man who does so has been fretfully conscious of what it was he was doing, and he did it anyway; the act has been willful. How should such a man feel himself in a state of grace?

All of this would be little more than idle verbal sparring if it weren't for the fact that we now spend a good part of our lives impotently raging against our complicity in fraud. We buy toys for the children that we know are going to come apart in two minutes of play. We complain that the bonbons we purchase in candy stores seem lately to be covered with plastic and we go right on munching them. We like to talk about these things; but we should be uneasy doing anything about them.

To do anything about them, in a determined way, would be to brand ourselves as eccentrics. The man who does go from store to store insisting upon a particular bitters or any one brand of cocktail cracker swiftly marks himself a faddist. Should he wish to pursue his preference, he must adopt a deliberate posture that will help carry off his quirks. He must become amusingly, defiantly eccentric, make the most of his peculiarities. He must let himself become a "character" and pretend to take pride in what secretly shames him a little.

For he is, after all, behaving irrationally. It is irrational to demand what pleases us and only what pleases us because our tastes in such matters are bound to be subjective; they are not susceptible of proof. The clerk behind the counter can smile in a paternal, forgiving way and explain patiently the superior ingredients of a soft drink or a chocolate sauce his customer doesn't want, ingredients that can be tested "in any laboratory." To maintain a quixotic insistence upon the article one came for is to fly in the face of sanity.

Nor can we believe that taste in general is a quality to be respected; it is the finicky caprice of a crank. Our embarrassment in the face of any pursuit of perfection extends, however, only to the area of our pleasures. The moment we turn toward useful things we are quick to demand quality and unselfconscious about doing so. If we are buying a new stove, a new steam iron, or a new car, we do not feel fools as we examine the product's credentials. We may very well bide our time while we wait for an issue of *Consumer Reports* that will exhaustively analyze the steam iron's performance. We will most likely interrogate a variety of friends who own a variety of makes and weigh each answer carefully. We will drive the car before we buy it, insist upon the longest possible guarantee before we accept the stove, and, should a new typewriter or a new vacuum cleaner prove in any way unsatisfactory, phone the dealer or manufacturer who has "sold us a lemon" almost before he has succeeded in banking his commission. It is not thought quixotic to question the durability of carpeting; it is thought intelligent. It may often be difficult, in these days of calculated obsolescence and a waste economy, to discover the trim, stable, and efficient useful object we are looking for; but we will try, and try persistently. Though the acquaintance who is an authority on wines or illustrated children's books may be something of a pet because his tastes are so charmingly preposterous, the acquaintance who is an authority on power lawn mowers is a man we can talk to seriously—and trust.

Our passion for sound performance begins to weaken as the objects under consideration are related to the good times we hoped to have. We are not so careful about the sturdiness of porch furniture as we are about the sturdiness of kitchen furniture, even though the porch furniture *ought* to be better made because it is going to take a harsher beating from the weather. We buy it more casually, accept an inferior grade more readily, and guard it less faithfully once we own it. It does not matter so much when porch furniture breaks down: we only meant to enjoy ourselves in it.

How much was it we paid for the last pack of playing cards we bought? With money in our pockets, did we buy ivory chessmen in honor of a game we like or did we scrupulously confine ourselves to routine pieces made of plastic? Have we dared to attach to any game *that much importance?* Does it tear at our souls to part with three dollars and ninety-five cents for a work of fiction or are we deeply grateful that all fiction can now be bought—after a little waiting—in paperback form for less than the price of a short taxicab ride, its approximate value in any realistic scale of things?

Few men are thought to be stingy these days. They contribute generously to charity, vote to increase their own local taxes, assume rather more burdens than are easily tolerable. They are only niggardly when it comes to being nice to themselves. Certainly they are not niggardly with their friends, though whether or not they are nice to them may involve us in further shades of meaning. It is customary, when entertaining, to be as lavish as one's budget allows; but how many of us are specifically lavish with what our guests might like? (Not long ago I attended a party at which the host insisted that all of his guests drink champagne throughout the evening, though many of us were yearning for beer or for rye.) We are fond of farewell gestures, sending to our departing friends ready-made vacation baskets in which cellophane-wrapped figs predominate. (I have a nightmare image of all the stewards, porters, and chambermaids in the world living exclusively and forever on the handsomely packaged figs that have been left behind.) Very often our very generosity—a generosity that would not stoop to a bargain—indicates unmistakably the unimportance of being pleased.

The unimportance of being pleased is a conviction so close to us that we wear it as unthinkingly as a saint might a hair shirt. About functional objects we are strict; taste and judgment are here exercised. About less functional objects, in and around which we might laze, we are less strict; the uses to which we put these things are not so legitimate, and it would be self-indulgent of us to take care for their quality.

By the time we have arrived at objects which are not in the least functional, as ice cream and fiction are not functional, we are ready to accept any shabby substitute that will free us of an inconsequential fuss. Confronted with an experience that promises us nothing but delight, we are casually and un-heroically prepared to endure an absence of delight. Consider the docility with which we go to the theater, when we do go to the theater. We do not search out the kinds of plays we like, particularly. If we like mystery melodramas, we do not insist upon mystery melodramas: that would be low-brow of us. If we like tragedies, we do not insist upon tragedies: that would be high-brow of us. In general, we insist upon nothing for ourselves. We wait to hear what the critics like. If they like it enough, it will no doubt *do* for us. We wait to hear what our friends like, or say they like, or seem to take some pride in having seen. If enough of our friends mention a play, so that it seems to be in the conversational air, it is filed in the memory as a possible play to attend. In effect, it is jotted down on a pad more or less neutrally, as one would jot down a routine reminder that, one of these days, the children's teeth should be inspected. In due time we go to the play, making arrangements for tickets as mechanically as we make train arrangements for an unavoidable trip to Boston. On the way into the theater, we glance at the photographs and the newspaper quotes painted above them with the detachment of a child memorizing the multiplication tables: we are storing up information about the responses we are expected to make. In the theater, barring a disaster or an unexpected windfall, we attend intelligently, with some curiosity, watching what we have heard described and noticing that at some points the reports and the actuality coincide. "That's the actor John was talking about," we say to our wives, quietly leaning toward them. At intermission our conversation is ready, if reserved. It is for the most part serious. "Yes, it's good," we say sagely, as though giving assent to a proposition in geometry, with all three words equally unstressed and almost never a shocked "It's *good!*" Later on, we, too, will be able to refer to the play in conversation, easily, judiciously, as though acknowledging that we had noticed an item in the morning newspaper that someone else has mentioned. If our response to the play should vary rather markedly from the response announced by a friend, we shall make whatever counterstatements we care to make in a tentative, already conciliatory, fashion; or we shall suppress our own views altogether. (It's not worth a fuss, is it?) We are generally co-operative; we perform our social obligations, including going to the theater, as a preparation for social conversation; we play along. It does not often occur to us to confess how bored we are or even to notice that we are bored. Should we expect something better?

That we are as gentlemanly, and as effectively anesthetized, in our conduct as we turn to literature (*Doctor Zhivago* is this, *Hawaii* is that) or dance (wasn't the Moiseyev fine on Ed Sullivan?) or music or painting or any of the other experiences offered us as pleasure is clear not only from the uniformity of response that generally greets the more newsworthy events but also from the temperate tenor of the response even when the response means to be adulatory. These are facts that are being taken into account, and weighed, and perhaps recorded in our daybooks, which are no longer quite diaries. (We may very well write: "Saw *Becket*, L. Olivier, dinner Frank & Joan, D. Moore's after, note expenses, call Ken about car insurance," but it is not in us to write "*Twelfth Night* . . . is but a silly play" and "one of the weakest plays that ever I saw on the stage.") We know that we are accountable for a degree of acquaintance with a degree of "culture," and we find it possible to keep an even temperature while we meet these minimum demands; but it is evident from our reasonableness that we do not hold any part of "culture" accountable to us.

In none of our responsible "keeping up" does it seem to occur to us that our tastes may be being violated or even that we are entitled to have independent tastes. How should we begin to assert ourselves in the face of the highest forms of pleasure when we have not the wills to assert ourselves in the lowest? Buying bargain ice cream and asking nothing of it, how shall we rise to the effrontery of asking something of Faulkner, or Inge, or Van Cliburn? If a little taste is unimportant, a lot of taste must be twice as unimportant.

I don't suppose any of us really phrases that last proposition in just those words, though our determination to be pleased— if we have any—certainly decreases in energy and confidence as we advance from the simple matter of orange juice to the more complex matter of Glenn Gould playing Bach. Having quit while the cornerstone was being laid, we are not going to be critical of the vault. And the thought that our own tastes might have anything to do with that misty, alien, and obviously un-reachable abstraction called "taste" rarely enters our heads. If we are timid, or rather tepid, about our personal satisfaction in areas with which we are personally familiar, we are terrified of venturing into that stratospheric band of diffracted light that seems the proper and exclusive territory of astronauts.

As pianist Abram Chasins was saying to columnist John Crosby one mid-March morning, "What is so bad is that the average man, who is more tolerant of art than at any other time in history, finds himself farther away from it rather than closer. He can't respond emotionally. . . . The men who sell music have implanted the theory in the minds of both the critics and the public: 'Be very careful. Just because you don't like it doesn't mean it's not great.' The complexity of modern music frustrates the average music lover who listens, grins and bears it and says, 'I don't know. Maybe it's great.' He's never been more tolerant because he's been intellectually conditioned to be careful." He is, in short, unable to respond emotionally—even when the music *is* great—because he has suppressed all response for fear of betraying his ignorance. Mr. Crosby adds that it is "one of the strangenesses of modern times that incest is perfectly proper dinner table conversation" but that to question "the competence of de Kooning would be a social gaffe of colossal proportions."

There is a triple divorce here. The individual is divorced from his own taste, first from insisting upon it and finally from so much as remembering it. The individual is also divorced from "taste" generally, whatever and wherever that phantom may reside. Further, if the individual did begin to demand that he himself be satisfied, or if he dismissed himself and read long and hard to discover what others called "taste," there would still be an unbridgeable gap between his taste and "theirs."

The origins of this apparently irreconcilable series of breaches may be located easily enough in the sorry progress we charted earlier. Believing, with Bentham, that only the useful could be measured, we abandoned the folly of attempting to evaluate the useless. What difference did it make if one useless thing was better than another? It could not, in fact, be better, because better implies good and all good lies elsewhere. Since the pleasure of tasting one ice cream rather than another is a pleasure that rests in the understanding merely, and since what rests in the understanding merely can be no part of our discussion, we can have no defensible reason for selecting among

ice creams. Or, for that matter, among non-informative works
of fiction.

Accepting this logical sequence and acting upon it, we discovered, with Darwin, that our tastes in such things, and for
such things, had atrophied. What is not exercised becomes
sluggish and then impotent. An unused faculty, dying quietly
on the vine, no longer calls attention to itself; we forget what it
was like ever to have possessed it. Thus what began as a prohi-
bition ends as a paralysis. We are not only forbidden to dis-
criminate among intellectual pleasures but also incapable of
doing so. And should the subject of intellectual pleasures cross
our paths in conversation, we can only be embarrassed by it.
Darwin, his son tells us, considered in later years "that in
matters of literary tastes he was quite outside the pale, and often
spoke of what those within it liked or disliked, as if they formed
a class to which he had no claim to belong."

Noticing that the pleasures are somehow still there, but
knowing ourselves incapable of evaluating them, we have nowhere to turn for an opinion about them—should we nervously
want one—but to the voices of those very few men who were
once outlawed for continuing to cherish their idle preferences.
Shall we ask advice of Bernard Berenson or perhaps Sir Kenneth
Clark? Is it possible to read Bosanquet, do we dare trust Harold
Rosenberg as he leads us across the room toward the sort of
"action painter" who, in the words of one American artist,
"assumes that his own ego and unconscious are more worthy of
contemplation than the objective world"? Unable to choose
among the works for ourselves, how shall we choose among
the men who choose the works? These men are isolated from
us; they have been for a great while. They are aesthetes, and
they frighten us, sometimes for good reasons. They seem to
speak a private language, a language we find it most difficult to
decipher. It is a long time since we cared to listen to them; it is
a long time since they cared to speak to us. When the great

division of spoils was made, when the useful took over and the fine took flight, all of the poems and plays and canvases and scores were placed in their hands. Because these distant authorities have held them ever since, and have alone tasted them regularly, they are now the sole owners of "taste." They are very far away.

The quickest method of re-establishing communication, no doubt, would be quite literally to halloo them, in the most vigorous and challenging tone of voice possible. That is to say, if every "average man" were suddenly to shout, at the top of his neglected lungs, "Whatever you say out there, this is what *I* like!" and be utterly honest in naming the things he likes, the thunder would surely be heard in the rarefied galleries of the custodians. Instantly fearful not so much for their own skins as for the unvalued "values" they have all alone preserved and nourished, the masters of taste might then be expected to make a desperate effort to render themselves intelligible, to forge a workable common tongue in which the delights they actually experience could be conveyed to men not yet on easy terms with them. Since there can be no question whatever but that the insiders *do* possess a taste superior to the outsiders'—simply from having been inside—such a flare-up and its aftermath might possibly do some good.

But there are dangers in such swiftness, and I am not thinking of the obvious ones: the mass vulgarity that might fill the air at least temporarily, the corruption that might come of trying to speak too simply of things that are not that simple, the interim name-calling that might result in an increase of wounded feelings rather than in renewed friendliness. The most serious danger is that the long-isolated specialist, choosing his words more carefully and with some consideration for his listeners' ears, might succeed in reaching the "average man" before the average man was ready to be reached. He might be able to enunciate a set of standards so clear and so imposing

that the inexperienced listener would nod in cerebral comprehension and accept them—without having arrived at any of
them for himself.

That is what is always wrong with the deliberate attempt to
acquire taste by reading books in which men of acknowledged
taste tell us what is good and what is not. It is easily possible to
come to know what is most admired by the well-informed and
even to grasp—in a rational way—why it is so admired. Study of
this sort will keep us from making social *gaffes;* it will also
place at our finger tips a sort of musical scale in which the
higher and the lower will fall intelligibly into place. More than
that. By establishing a hierarchy of values, with Goya a "must"
and Latour an interesting "maybe," it may very well send us
in search of the best—with what is established as the best already
clear in our heads. By going to Michelangelo first, it is hard to
see how we can go far wrong.

But we may very well have gone wrong because we have
elected to act upon someone else's "taste" rather than upon any
joyous choice of our own. It is one thing to admire Michelangelo's Moses, a rectitude that does not look at us but bids us
attend only to the law, because a hundred authorities have
already admired it. It is another to admire it out of a spontaneous uprush of awe and affection, a swelling of heart and
mind that would have come if no authority had ever noticed
the work.

For taste is either personal (yours, mine, Henry's) or it does
not exist. There is no chemical element in the universe that
invariably produces it in a certain solution, no band of diffracted light that always gives the same reading provided that
the meter is set right. Taste is never a law. It is always an
entirely private love. Each of the authorities one may have read
is himself bound by this living limitation: his own taste is either
personal or it is academic, which is to say fraudulent. True,
the authorities have upon occasion banded together in an effort

to abstract from their joint tastes an absolute taste, a taste to be engraved on the books for all time. They did just that in seventeenth-century France when the Academy decided that it would rule not only for the past but also for the future. Almost immediately they were embroiled in a battle with a popular dramatist—Corneille—who was patently violating their absolutes. Corneille, of course, won, not because he was any "righter" than they were, but because he was loved. The actual taste of a vast, unmistakably common audience insisted upon delighting in what he was doing—however tasteless his practices might be, his practices were very much to *its* taste—and the Academy was forced to surrender its grip upon the abstract definite. It is interesting to remember, today, that the real taste of an outspoken, openhearted multitude became part of the continuing and accumulating historical taste that is our heritage; ever thereafter taste itself had to allow for the peculiarities of a man who seemed to be defying it. (The storehouse that is our heritage is not always filled in this way; a single passionate partisan, assuming authority, may badger a society until it is willing to attend to a given body of work; but only when he succeeds in making it attend to the work and not to himself, so that it begins to grow its own affection rather than parrot his, is his mission accomplished and admiration made permanent.)

There are, I think, two conditions upon which taste may be said to rest. One of them is affinity, the other exposure. Of these, affinity need not detain us long. It is plain enough that men's psychic constitutions differ. Each of us is born with a neurological and psychological radar on which some signals are readily received and others remain faint. We are complexes, here and there sensitive, here and there not; and there is little we can do to alter our natural wave lengths. Samuel Johnson, though possessed of a far more than ordinary range of responses, could not hear music. He understood that it was pleasing to others, much as he might joke about the sopranos inflicted upon him, and he would not have denied its exalted role in the production of general human happiness. But *he* could not hear it. For some of us the sound of poetry is effectively cut off by a faulty connection or by a connection that is not so much faulty as effectively overpowered by a closer and more clamoring one. All of us are, in varying degrees, nearsighted or farsighted, and the nature of our equipment will have much to do with whether our eyes fix most readily upon chiseled stone or mixed paint. A mind may be born visual or born aural or born with an intermingling of both in such odd proportions that it can insist upon drama but abhor ballet. No mind can be all minds at once; all-encompassing sensitivity is reserved to divinity.

There is nothing distressing in this. The man who does not hear a telephone ringing when he is deeply engrossed in a book is indeed engrossed; his mind is wholly filled. He could not be made more happy than he is just now, even if the call was from a cherished friend. For every partial deafness or partial blindness there are three or four sights or sounds ready to raid our consciousnesses and claim everything for themselves. Nor do we have any difficulty in recognizing these. At the age of three or four or five we begin to feel the pleasant prickles of the signals that suit us, whether they suit our differently constructed parents or no. A child taken to the theater at the age of seven does not have to decide whether or not he likes the theater: he may find himself enraptured without in the least understanding what has caused his rapture, or he may be as bored—now and forever —as he would be in school. A farm boy of twelve may cadge a ride into town to spend his Saturday afternoon looking at paintings in a gallery. I am acquainted with one who did. He was not instructed to do so, had in fact never known anyone else who wished to; this was simply the invitation he heard. Such an invitation is so entirely interior that a child may reach for paint before he has ever seen a painting or before he has observed much about people or cats or trees; the paint itself seems to stir his excitement. That each of us is invited to a variety of parties —not all, but enough—is obvious before the first of our toys has gone to the attic. It is only by losing the invitations that we miss out on the fun. The very diversity of art forms suggests that favors have been provided for everyone and that no temperament need go away unblessed.

If affinity limits, it also commits—as love always does. But the matter does not end there; it has barely begun. Puppy love is in many respects real love. It is often more generous, more selfless, than adult love. But it is callow; though it is charming and unaffected, it is ignorant. It has not yet fought its way through any degree of knowledge. It is not a love that has survived exposure.

Taste is the love that survives exposure. Affinity is, at first, undiscriminating, because it is as yet unsurfeited. The child who discovers that he loves reading adventure stories will read any and all adventure stories that come to hand. He will coax them from friends, exhaust the shelves that hold them at the public library, badger relatives for more of them as his birthday approaches. In his untamed passion, he will like all of them equally. He may be fond of asking companions who share his enthusiasm "Which do you think is *best?*" as he rattles off the titles in various series, but he isn't truly trying to arrive at a judgment. He is simply smacking his lips over the full list of his enchantments, recapitulating for the pleasure of remembering. He almost never does arrive at anything like a decision, and should he seem to do so the prize will most likely have gone to the last story he has read. He is gloriously at sea in a pea-green boat, riding the waves of an appetite that is uncritical because it is insatiable.

His first step in taste is the result of a sorrow. One day he finds he has read one too many of his very favorite kind of book. Something about this last one seemed a letdown: it didn't catch him unawares or wholly carry him off, it "wasn't up to the others." Shortly no further sample will be "up to the others." Literally, a flavor has palled. Through tasting so much, he has become analytical and detached, has come to recognize as routine a group of effects that once compelled his belief. He has become objective about an experience that must be subjective if it is to succeed with him, and he must now face the fact that he has exhausted a pleasure. He has exhausted it, be it noted, in a rather nice way; by indulging himself wholeheartedly, he has got all the good out of it that ever was in it. If he can never return to it with an unjaundiced eye, it is not because he was born a doubter but because he was born a true believer. There were delights of a certain order to be had for the taking, and in his avidity he has drained every one of them dry. If he now suffers a sense of loss, it is because he once found so much—all the pleasure there was to be found at this level.

What is he to do now; where can he turn? There is only one place for him to go, if he has his wits about him and if he means to continue to please himself. He must go where more, not less, pleasure is: to work that may be of the same general kind but that has been done at a level of greater complexity. Only by immersing himself in an experience that has more *in* it—a new subtlety that may succeed in surprising him, a richness of narrative organization he is not able to anticipate, a compounding of effects as astounding at first sight as a three-decker sandwich is —can he be made happy again. If he has begun by despoiling the Hardy Boys of whatever charm was in them, he may discover that joy is not dead on the day he is handed Sherlock Holmes; if he has read through, and seen through, Edgar Rice Burroughs, he may be ready to be bowled over by Jack London or Rudyard Kipling. Somewhere there is a second stage to his happiness, a stage that does not deny the delights that preceded it but multiplies them as fantastically as squaring a number does. There is now a new amplitude to be greedily appropriated and lovingly devoured. Once it is devoured—and always provided that no unnatural restraint has cut across the process to abort it—the search must begin again, and in the same direction: toward the ever-growing complexity that moves closer and closer to wholeness, toward the added dimensions that end in an increase of depth. The reader does not tell himself he is looking for "wholeness" or "depth." He tells himself that he is looking for more fun, more excitement; he has been gratified before and would like his gratification intensified. But, with his experience, his desire can now be satisfied only where a greater richness actually exists. Without really changing course, or in the least meaning to, the Hardy Boy fan is probably now in the hands of John Buchan and getting ready for Graham Greene. In due time he will be forced to take from the shelves *The Brothers Karamazov*. Nothing short of *The Brothers Karamazov* contains enough that he hasn't tasted and grown accustomed to. Here the universe expands again. So does his pleasure. So does his taste.

Taste is a progressive raiding of the Garden of Eden, beginning where one truly cares to begin, satisfying oneself until satiety leaves only a rind in one's hands, and then moving on to the fruit of another and stranger tree. The discarded rinds mark the trail; the trail itself inevitably leads, at the last, to the bush or branch bowed down by the most delicate and hence most durable of flavors. The raiding cannot be anything other than progressive. No natural man confines himself nightly to a meal that has grown tasteless through repetition, however delightful it may once have seemed. And if he cannot tolerate a present level of wrung-out pleasure, he has even less desire to revert to a pleasure wrung out long ago in a nearly forgotten past: however dull the dinner tonight, he is not going to ask for porridge. The man whose passion for enjoying himself has finally and voluntarily driven him to frequenting the concerts of the New York Philharmonic does not readily submit himself to an experience of Mantovani.

This sounds exceedingly simple. Taste is no more mysterious than leaping to what one likes without thought of apology, liking it to such excess that the daylights are literally hugged out of it, and, when the daylights have indeed gone out of it, leaping to what is liked still more. Since the only thing one can like still more is something that actually possesses more, a man's taste can do nothing but advance in wisdom and grace.

Too easy? In toying with the notion of a purely natural flowering, born of exposure that becomes overexposure and so sends the enthusiast a step higher up the ladder with no guidance at all from "authorities" already at the top, are we sinking sentimentally into a gross idealization that will not bear inspection? Or was Bernard Shaw right when, wishing to urge his passion for painting upon all the rest of us, he abandoned the dictatorial habits he had employed in the theater and said, without qualification and with great kindliness, "You will learn all you need to know by looking at pictures"?

If we cannot bring ourselves to believe in this generous invitation, if our own experience has taught us that learning to love painting or anything else is never so simple as all that, it may be because in some most careful way we steadfastly refuse to let the process be simple. We have become extraordinarily talented at interfering with the movement forward, often under the pretense that we are trying to make it move more rapidly forward; our very earnestness makes us practiced abortionists.

Consider the two beginning conditions mentioned above. If exposure is to do the self-propelling work claimed for it, there must first exist a strong predisposition toward a certain form of pleasure, a running toward it that is gleeful and unaffected, and there must follow an exhilarating period of time in which the uninhibited liking is freely indulged. Without the first, there will be no real love to be remembered; without the second, there will be no satisfaction to the point of satiety and therefore no need for a further search.

In practice, and at every level nowadays, we do our virtuous best to see that neither condition will ever be met. Let us glower for a moment at the lowest conceivable level: that of the terrifyingly available comic book. Our instinct, on seeing a child curled up with a comic book, is to rip what is obviously crude and vulgar from his hands. We are distressed that anyone for whose future we are responsible should waste his time and degrade his mind in this fashion. It does not occur to us to ask whether or not the child likes what he is reading, at this moment in time. We know that he does and that he shouldn't. It is our firm opinion, swiftly acted upon, that there is *no* time in a child's development when he should be free to like comic books.

Further, we have an alternative ready. Confiscating the badly drawn and garishly colored pages of pulp, we tell the child what he can do: he can go upstairs and read a "good" book. It is plain enough to us from the face he is making and from the weary way he is getting out of his chair that although he may indeed be going upstairs obediently, he isn't going to attend very willingly to any "good" book he picks up. Nor are we stupid enough to conceive that he imagines himself on his way to a pleasure. It may even cross our minds, as we envision the fretted and resentful half-reading that is going to take place during the next fifteen minutes, that the child is learning to define a "good" book as something he doesn't like and that it may take some powerful persuasion a good many years later to break down his conviction—provided that it ever can be broken down. But no matter. One must be principled.

Occasionally we are a shade softer-hearted or a shade softer-headed and we grudgingly permit him "to finish just this one." Or perhaps one a week, or one a month, with an extra thrown in on train trips. But our very permissiveness, however great or little, carries with it an implied—or, more probably, firmly stated—warning to the child. What he likes is bad. Bad in itself, bad for him. It is a sign of weakness that he should be indulging himself just now: a weakness in him and a weakness in us. He is never behaving well when he is actually enjoying himself.

The results? I don't think we need worry too much about the traditional aftermath of such strictures, the strong likelihood that the child will become a secret reader, drunk on the sly; generations have bragged of reading Nick Carter in their attics without apparent moral deterioration, perhaps because they read enough Nick Carter to get him out of their systems. I am disturbed by a recent memory of a figure who seemed strangely contemporary. He was a well-groomed, well-dressed young man, between twenty-five and thirty years of age. There seemed nothing in any way underprivileged or retarded about him. He looked as though he had come from a reasonably responsible junior-clerk job in a central Manhattan bank, or law office, or large stationery-supply store. He did not look married or fatherly; he looked placid and composed and unhurried. He was standing at a Grand Central magazine rack quietly leafing a comic book.

I would like to have asked him why, but of course I didn't, and so still don't know the answer. What dim memory of something that had once interested him, truncated almost at its inception and never openly responded to since, could have lured him now, so soberly, to attend to the immature with such calm absorption? Had he never had his fill? Had he never found anything more interesting? If he had ever been handed a "good" book, it clearly hadn't taken or he would scarcely have been confessing his tastes in so public a place. But there was no air of embarrassment, or even of self-consciousness, about him. There was only a clear brow that might have meant innocence and might have meant intellectual checkmate.

The great danger of attempting to impose a higher taste upon a lower one at any time is the possibility of paralyzing both the higher and the lower responses. A child may be suspended—possibly suspended forever—in a never-never land in which he is immobilized between a lower pleasure he has been taught to suppress and a higher pleasure he does not yet need. He will survive the loss of the lower; children grow up and get jobs anyway. But it is most unlikely that he will ever feel the need for the higher. Why should he, when he has never finished the one pleasure he began and has now lost all sense of his right to pleasure, of his possible taste for it? What has vanished in the process is the direct, continued experience of pleasure, and that is vital.

I wonder if anyone has had the courage to take the obvious course in this matter. The obvious thing to do, coming upon a child with a comic book, is to smile at him and hand him twelve more. Give him another twelve on the following Saturday, twenty or thirty on his birthday, and all he can carry at Christmas—until he is inundated, waterlogged, up to his ears and ready to drown in the experience. Liberality should accomplish the true end in view more efficiently than any other conceivable tactic. It is bound to achieve at least one thing: it will make the child weary of comic books. And if the child has shown any sign of enjoying the deluge at any point along the way, and if some sign has been given him that it is perfectly all right to enjoy what one really enjoys, he may have an itch left over.

We do not do this because we do not believe that pleasure is proper and because we cannot imagine that pleasure might—left to itself—bring about any sort of progress. Pleasure retards, leads to slackness. Even in its own domain, it tends to corrupt: "taste" is acquired not by being pleased but by steadfastly refusing ever to be pleased. The thought of handing a contented child so much as a second comic book makes us shudder. There might be more logic in the gesture than there is in our present patently damaging procedures, but we are stubborn. We insist upon a cleavage between what is enjoyed and what is possibly praiseworthy.

Our sense of a sharp break between the delightful and the

respectable does not end with our behavior in the matter of
children's reading habits. We keep it sternly alive in relation
to our own. Let us say that we have got at least as far as Graham
Greene now. If we find ourselves reading Greene with something of the delectable suspense that once kept us tingling
through yarns loved in boyhood, and if we realize vaguely that
Greene is considered to have literary merit by a body of rep-
utable literary critics, are we at last content with ourselves and
our activity? Have we finally arrived at a fusion of fun and
acceptable taste, so that we can indulge our yearning for excitement and still hold our heads high? Are we now both happy
and virtuous?

Not at all. Our consciences at once cut through the experience to tell us that insofar as we are enjoying the experience we
are enjoying an inferior aspect of it and that ideally we should
prefer to have the thrills suppressed and the novel written at a
level that did not pretend to entertain us. Nor is this a mere
private puritanism, a sobriety of our own imposed upon the
author. Mr. Greene is himself ready to underline the distinction
for us.

In recent years he has adopted the practice of dividing his
output—past and present—into two categories. On the flyleaf
of each new work appears the customary list of "other books
by the author." Half of these books are now listed as "entertainments." The other half are listed as "novels." A difference between the two groups is discernible. The "novels" are richer in
psychological complexity, dwell longer on specifically moral
crises.

But a persistent reader of Greene may notice that the divorce
between the two sets of books is not so final as it seems in the
cataloguing. Shuttling back and forth between them, one has no
sense of entering separate worlds: the same chases (there is as
much of a chase in *The Power and the Glory* as there is in
This Gun for Hire), the same betrayals, the same chilling iro-

nies serve as structural architecture for both. Nor are the moral dilemmas confined to the "novels." They invariably appear, in a less developed state, in the "entertainments." Environments, events, and even characters change little; they are simply, in the "novels," more deeply pierced.

This is a difference of degree, not of kind. The "novels" are the "entertainments" more patiently listened to. But Mr. Greene would have it otherwise. Nor does his insistence upon the distinction seem to me merely personal and idiosyncratic, the device of an author for telling us which books he likes best. So far from being idiosyncratic, it is symptomatic—an echo and a reinforcement of the premises we have taught our children and the convictions we cling to ourselves. For one of the things the distinction says to us is this: no book good enough to be called a novel should be thought of as entertaining.

Once again, it is implied that fun is for the feeble-minded; fineness washes its hands of it. One must approach what is worth-while in a spirit of resignation. The invitation reads: give over the promise of joy, give over the memory of pleasure, and come with me to the stake; there you will be rewarded, though not in a way that you will likely find rewarding. The promise is Spartan, a promise of purity unstained by delectation. If one does not feel up to it, he can go back to his adored second-rate.

Embarrassed now to discover that something he has liked is second-rate, twentieth-century man feels obliged to surrender it or at least to indulge it sparingly. At the same time he is apprehensive about what is described to him as first-rate, for it is described to him as something he will probably not enjoy. Having given up the one, he feels not up to the other. Between two negatives, he hesitates, bites his nails, does nothing.

If he has been promised novels that will not be entertaining at a level he thought he could manage, the invitation to still higher reaches is still more forbidding. So far as he is aware that higher reaches do exist, he is also disturbingly conscious of what the map to that country looks like: it is a map that shows danger on the left hand and danger on the right and, straight ahead, a stretch marked "terra incognita."

Although only a specialized audience may have read "Mass-cult and Midcult," Dwight Macdonald's two-part article for *The Partisan Review*, the twin terms of its title have reached everyman's ears. These have got into the air around him, and he is well aware that there is a vast area of popular manufacture in the field of the entertainment arts too close to sea level to be worth his exploration. "Masscult," or whatever other phrase he knows it by, includes servant-girl romances, Erle Stanley Gardner, *Life* magazine, most Hollywood movies, and *I Love You Truly*. He understands that, and if he still does leaf *Life* or go to spectacles starring Kirk Douglas, he realizes that he is killing time and possibly, as Thoreau warned, injuring eternity.

However, he is not yet hopelessly oppressed by the slogans that confront him, though he is probably being kept from a thorough testing of what he thinks he likes at this level. What begins to dismay him is the discovery that "Midcult" is no better. It may be worse. Midcult, or middlebrow aspiration to rise above Masscult, includes John Steinbeck, John Hersey, *John Brown's Body*, *Harper's*, *Horizon*, "Omnibus," H. G. Wells, and Max Lerner. A flutter of fear runs through him. Had he better get that handsomely illustrated—and very expensive—art book off his living-room table? And not renew *Atlantic?*

These are not only the things he has spent most of his time with; they very much constitute his *effort*. It wasn't easy, after all, to remember to tune in "Omnibus" or to finish an article on architecture in *Horizon;* but he had rather prided himself on giving up something he wanted to do more in the interests of his soul, or his intelligence, or his public duty, or his taste. What has he been fighting for?

On reflection, however, he understands. He is able to see what is meant by pretentiousness, by a partly jolly and partly academic compromise between the truly good and the halfway palatable (though he is uneasily forced to conclude, again, that what was wrong with all of these things was that they *were* partly palatable). He does not want to be a hypocrite, making a pretense of possessing what he does not genuinely possess, and he is able to give worried assent to Mr. Macdonald's proposition that Midcult merely repeats the come-ons of Masscult while decently covering them "with a cultural fig-leaf." Very well. Away with Midcult.

But he is now without a compass, for there is no third catch phrase he can hear. Typically, there is no third part to Mr. Macdonald's survey. The air about our "average man" has been noisy with two prohibitions but silent on the subject of what may be permitted. Working with the terms he has been given, our man broods and, brooding, struggles to a conclusion. Masscult is out. Midcult is out. What is left? Cult?

He wants no part of that, sensibly enough. (He realizes that valuable contributions have come from one or another cult in the past, but he also realizes that they have been contributions *to* some less insular and more centrally located body of work, and it is this central location he is looking for.)

He is now at a standstill, fearful of moving in any direction. If he should pursue his inquiry beyond the stage of grasping negative slogans—in most cases he does not, being a busy man and already sufficiently badgered about the matter of his questionable tastes—he might in time come upon a phrase or two suggesting an acceptable terrain. Mr. Macdonald, for instance, does not move on to Cult but posits the existence, though in passing, of an admirable High Culture. Here is a lead. But High Culture has an unpromising sound to it, bringing to mind as it does high church and high tea and that one sorry try at Trollope. Is there nothing that reeks less of incense?

There may be. Even at the highest reaches, one or another critic seems to be making room for Krazy Kat and Charlie Chaplin, as Mr. Macdonald is swift to justify Edgar Allan Poe.

With these barriers down, what can High Culture mean? For Mr. Macdonald it comes into being whenever we are made to feel that a *person* is vigorously present. The Masscult writer is all impersonality, grinding out a standard product "like Kleenex," whereas Poe, even when he is writing for money and working as a hack, retains "an extraordinary ability . . . to express his own peculiar personality. . . ." The contrast is capped by a quotation from Wordsworth: "What is a poet? . . . He is a man speaking to men . . . a man pleased with his own passions and volitions, and one who rejoices more than other men in the spirit of life that is in him."

That is not so formidable. Taste is highest when the sense of being talked to is strongest. It is even rather appealing. I may be free to judge the quality of what I think I like by the intensity of the dialogue that goes on between us.

But how am I to recognize a personal tone of voice? An answer suggests itself. How do I ever recognize a personal tone of voice? Am I not able, day after day, to detect without difficulty a true or false inflection on the other end of a telephone?

"What didn't he tell me?" is often the thought left hanging after a prolonged conversation with a friend. The conversation went swimmingly—too swimmingly. There was an extra measure of affability there, a quickness at picking up threads that suggested that an unlucky pause might let the enemy in, a faint but unmistakable falsification of personality. At one time or another the ruse has been transparent to me: a lame excuse for not coming to a party I am giving, feigned ignorance of a wound I have lately received, three reasons offered for something that has been done when one reason would easily have sufficed. This time I am just as certain, though no disturbing subject has ever been broached. An instinct rattles: I am familiar with the rhythm of that voice when it is at ease and open, when it is unaffectedly itself. There has been intimacy between our two voices, and just now there was not—quite.

Is it possible that listening to Poe or to Gardner, to Wordsworth or Wells, produces consequences of quite the same kind? I have all but tasted the conversation of my friend on the telephone; I am running my tongue over it again this moment, trying by feel to find what has happened to the flavor. I will find it. It will come to me. Dare I hope that "taste" will come to me in much the same way?

For that official bogey that is called "taste" to come to any of us, it is necessary to behave no more unnaturally than we behaved, in the first place and probably long ago, with the friends we now know best. A friendship begins because someone seems likable. The more likable he proves, the more one sees of him. The friendship continues because the dialogue is so pleasant, and more time is made for it as one becomes more conscious of pleasure. Out of the liking and the extended intimacy true knowledge is born—knowledge that may not have been consciously sought but is now personal and profound.

Two surrenders are required: to an unaffected liking and to an uninhibited lingering. If one's liking should seem to fasten, in all honesty, on a love object as low as comedies featuring Jerry Lewis, it is surely far better to indulge it—in the greatest possible volume—than to spend years sitting restive before the films of Ingmar Bergman while secretly seething over an unfinished affair. There is never any point in being displeased and dishonest at the same time or in joining that group of men who sleep through what they go to in order to dream of what they have missed. The matter is not to be rectified by fraud.

It will be rectified by exposure. We have all long since dismissed with contempt the once belligerent phrase "I may not know much about art, but I know what I like." We know that the phrase is a bromide and the man who uses it a buffoon. But when we pause to consider what is wrong with the statement, we generally get the wrongness wrong. What is most often dismaying about the man who mouths the sentiment is not that he doesn't know anything about art but that, in point of fact, he hasn't the least notion of what he likes. He hasn't been there—not lately, perhaps not ever. Challenge him to speak for a moment about whatever he says he does like and chances are ten to one that, after a struggle with his memory, he will mention something he half liked a dozen years ago and has not submitted himself to since.

Liking does not survive an experience of the truly limited. Friendships are terminated, not always with prejudice. After a while one may come to feel that nothing new is being said, that the reservoir is dry, perhaps that it was never successfully tapped ("I never felt I could get next to him"). A novelist or Jerry Lewis may be bade farewell in much the same way—perhaps reluctantly, perhaps with a trace of remembered gratitude, perhaps in the comfortable certainty that the friend we are drifting from is already hoisting a glass with a new companion in the bar around the corner.

Taste is the product of tested affection. It comes from playing with the dog, not from studying his pedigree. When twentieth-century man goes seeking it, he generally does so in the interests of self-improvement—which is why he acquires so little of it and why that little is so chilly. What he might better do is to run after it in a spirit of self-indulgence, confident that pleasure holds within itself its own powers of growth and that quality will sooner or later smite him in the eye. As Henry Adams remarked, in the course of describing his own education, "For some things ignorance is good, and art is one of them."

☼   *. . . there must be at least two*
        Helping each other see it.
                        —W. D. SNODGRASS

One of the most disappointing things about the human condition is that the pleasures of the flesh offer no real antidote to the distresses of the mind. I may seem to have given very little attention in these pages to the fact that there are such things as pleasures of the flesh: if I have mentioned food here and there, I have generally kept my counsel about sex. It is almost as though I were determined to confine pleasure exclusively to the country of the mind, relegating physical sensation to the status of a quite unimportant border state.

There are reasons for this, and they are not meant to be prejudicial to the delights of responding to one's animal instincts. It is agreeable that man has not yet evolved into pure spirit. But, as it happens, man's mind has by this time achieved a degree of complexity even greater than that of his astonishingly complex body, which means that his mind makes demands his sensual equipment cannot hope to satisfy. Sensuality can provide him with a brief nirvana—a consummation perhaps not to be despised—but it cannot nourish what it tends, temporarily, to obliterate.

In a practical sense this should be clear enough to us from the fact that we live in an age that is highly permissive in sexual matters—our taboos are surely fewer than those that inhibited our fathers—but is also extraordinarily conscious of its intellectual unrest. The fleshpots are exactly as attractive as they always have been and no doubt are a good bit easier to come by: the visual world about us is largely made up of handsome commercial invitations to ladies, liquor, and lazy days on the beach. But the fleshpots, even when they are visited and not merely yearned for, seem to brew very little in the way of sustained contentment; they give rise, rather surprisingly, to a fury. The most disenchanted face one sees in the newspapers is the face of the playboy who ought, by the standards enunciated in all of those commercial invitations, to have had the most fun. (He has had fun, too, and let's not pretend that he hasn't. Why hasn't it been enough for him?)

The restiveness that stirs, ungratefully, in a flesh-coddled time is likely to get worse. There are two things we can be fairly sure of. One is that our work is going to get harder, not easier. The other is that its nature is going to be increasingly intellectual. As these developments continue, the disproportion between the restoration the mind cries out for and the relief the flesh is able to provide cannot help but grow. The feeling of physical well-being that follows upon the honest exercise of an honest instinct is apt to wither earlier in the day when the day is principally determined to pick a man's brains.

There is a further problem here. The athleticism of which our minds are capable is now not only more complex than that of our physical reflexes. It is also of a higher and more influential order. That is to say, the flesh becomes aware that it is being warmed in a somewhat dumb and humble and submissive way, like a kitten purring. But the mind, being a reflective instrument, is able to be inside a pleasure and outside that pleasure at one and the same time, behaving and knowing how it is behaving simultaneously; it is even able to glance down and understand a physical pleasure, whereas a physical pleasure has no talent for glancing up. Being so powerfully conscious, it is able to dominate all that is sensual—to control it and also to corrupt it. Men have spoken forever of the mind's power to control the senses in the interests of a belief; very little has as yet been said about the mind's power to corrupt the senses in the interests of a belief. Yet an unease of the mind can infect an instinct to the point where it virtually disables it.

We are aware of this, and sporting enough to make a joke of it, in isolated instances that strike us as accidents: we have discovered, by this time, that a bad state of mind can make for thoroughly bad sex. Nature is not automatically triumphant over a stubbornly agitated brain.

It may not, however, have occurred to us how extensively our present intellectual dissatisfaction—in essence, our doubt that values are real—has jaundiced our view of the very sensual experiences we profess most to admire.

We do lay some claim, in this century, to being relatively healthy in our attitudes toward sex. We do not hide it under the ottoman, as the Victorians did. We insist that its existence be acknowledged and, in the acknowledgment, honored. We do not find sex embarrassing, a sort of evolutionary hand-me-down. So far from viewing it with shame, we are ready to give three hurrahs for it: sex is an act that is beautiful in itself and beautiful in all its implications. Nor are we content any longer with the notion that it is something suitable enough for the male, whom the female must merely accommodate. The pleasures of sex are the birthright of women as well, as monthly magazine articles triumphantly announce. Meaning to honor our natures as our natures are, and to honor them in clear good conscience, we approach the subject of sex in a candid, generous, accepting, and even admiring manner.

In the course of asserting the dignity and desirability of a natural act, we have been understandably eager to free our art forms from the artificial silences imposed by Victorianism so that they should come to reflect our own new honesty and our own new joy. We have freed them. But the reflection is most strange. What do our novels and our plays show back to us? Almost without exception, an image of sex that is violent, frustrated, shabby, furtive, degrading, treacherous, and—more and more—aberrant. The heroine has taken lovers on the lawn beyond counting; she ends in an asylum. The countess requires the ministrations of a homosexual if her nerves are not to give way; his give way, and he hangs himself. The hero finds gratification with a twelve-year-old child, who is more accomplished than he is; she ends a slattern and he a convict. The virile ex-soldier is close to being spastic because he knows that all women want to "cut it off," the suburban husband is hopelessly and impossibly enamored of the baby sitter, the wife of a distinguished lawyer futilely says "yes" to a stranger in an elevator, one teen-ager is being raped near a wire fence and another is returning from the abortionist, and there is no lasting love in a summer place. The little college teacher hops on one foot outside his best friend's bedroom, asking in a piping voice, "Are they doing it?," while a girl abandoned by the sailor who has made her pregnant asks snickeringly of a homosexual friend, "But what do they *do?*" The sex act is not always unromantically conceived: it may come as a brief prelude to the disintegration of a woman's life, a fling before she turns on the unlit gas heater, or a respite for a couple who must thereafter separate, he to return to an insane wife and she to an indifferent husband. But even when the interlude serves as emotional relief, it is apt to take place in an oppressive atmosphere and a seedy environment; when it is over, its effects are at best ambiguous and at worst distasteful to the people involved. For the most part, as we spy upon sex we seem to be spying upon failure. The sky is overcast, and the woman waiting in a doctor's office to be fitted with a diaphragm is not so much an awakened partner as an outpatient of Hell.

What we proclaim as noble we present as nasty. If no Victorian ever said so much about sex, no Victorian ever said anything so unpleasant about sex. Dante made Hell itself a more comforting place than this.

Now I should like to bypass, as best we are able, any discussion of the possible ethical implications of the wild contradiction in which we are embroiled. The moralist may very well see in these self-flagellating images the unbidden stir of our consciences in a time of too much license, an instinctive insistence upon telling the real truth no matter what announcements we have been making. The moralist may very well be right. He could not, in any case, ask a better advertisement for his cause. It is doubtful that Savonarola himself, thundering from his pulpit, could have painted a starker or more discouraging portrait of the bad end we were to come to than our "entertainments," generally, now offer us.

I am not interested here in our sexual behavior. Chances are that few of us have flirted with excess to the point where the jeremiad that is hurled at us from page and stage is altogether deserved or to the point where the "decadence" set before us is instantly recognized because we were involved in just such a mess last night. As the drunken, drugged heroine crawls out of bed calling for her oxygen mask, which is brought to her by a hero who has begun his career by giving his true love a venereal disease and who is going to end it by being castrated, we probably do not lean toward our companion in the theater and murmur, "Fred should see this—I've told him and told him." Not seriously, anyway.

I am interested in an attitude, in a state of mind that accepts this nearly universal image as being more or less appropriate, about what was to be expected; in a state of mind that gives detached credence—no matter what our own experience, good or bad, licit or illicit, extensive or limited, may have been—to a landscape that looks like a nightmare. I am interested, additionally, in the lie we seem to give ourselves, one way or the other: in the fact that we give formal assent, in our pronouncements, to an act regarded as beautiful while giving formal assent, in our images, to the same act regarded as ugly. Which of these things do we truly believe; which represents our genuine conviction?

Forced to vote, I am afraid I should have to come down in favor of the mirror as being the truer record of our minds: it is much easier to spot a lie in a play or a story than it is in a conversation. Unless I have overlooked a sizable body of contemporary literature in which sex is seen to be precisely as healthy an activity as we proclaim it to be, I am compelled to conclude that no matter what our voices say when we are talking for effect, when the eye of the mind begins to do its work it photographs sex as a dubious pleasure. With the click of the shutter, there is a sound of doubt.

The eye of the mind has a bias that will not yield to rhetoric.

We have been proud to give praise to the flesh. But our paint-ings, now that we notice them, seem not to have heard us. There is very little flesh, and less really luscious flesh, in them. We shout what we think; but they show us what we know.

Or, rather, they show us the shape of our doubt. Our minds come equipped with doubt-rods as effective as divining-rods these days, especially where the possibility of pleasure is con-cerned. It is as though we had been provided with X-ray machines for detecting forgeries, as art experts are, and as though we were able to apply them, instantly and infallibly, to every promise of being pleased, or moved, or rewarded. How alert we are to the least vibration that promises to unmask a fake, and how eager we are to embrace any hint that we are really deceiving ourselves whenever we are enjoying ourselves! The pejorative phrase has not yet been coined that is sufficiently disillusioning for us; after we have gobbled up this latest one, we shall go find another.

In reviewing a volume of literary criticism, Malcolm Cowley has described some of the instructions we give ourselves:

"Never say friendship; say 'innocent homosexuality.' Never say curiosity; say 'voyeurism,' or refer to the curious man as a 'castrated peeper.' . . . Instead of self-awareness, speak of 'narcissism.' Remember that fun and games do not exist in the Freudian world except as 'the symbolic enactment of sado-masochistic desires.' Remember that family affection is merely 'a repressed incestuous longing' and that chastity is 'the morbid fear of full genital development.' A tomboy is a 'transvestite' and a writer is—what?"

Not all of these things are pleasures, of course, though most of them are at least distantly related and it comes as no surprise to find "fun and games" at their center. What the grouping does indicate, however, is the degree to which ordinarily spon-taneous, outgoing, instinctive responses are at the mercy of a mind that has reached a controlling conclusion. There is no

hiding out from an overriding conviction: not for sex, not for
fun and games, not for friendship. If the conviction maintains
that pleasure itself is unreal, it will in due time take the pleasures
of sex and climbing trees and seeing the family again along to
the intellectually-conceived graveyard. An infection begun in
the mind will reach every extremity.

Conversely, there is no solving the problem at the extremities,
neither in the flight to the bedroom nor in the flight to the bar-
room, certainly not high in the branches of the old apple tree:
the wasteland is already there, waiting. Until the mind can be
convinced that pleasure is meaningful, until it can feel that
pleasure is just, until it can quite simply and plainly be pleased
with itself, there will be cakes and ale for nobody.

It is no doubt a mistake for me to mention cakes and ale at
this point, for that is just what we conceive our pleasures to be:
desserts, things we can and should do without. (Are we trying
to convince ourselves that we should do with less sex in all
those novels and plays, that we should care less for the flesh
in all those paintings?) Pleasure itself is something more than
that. Being pleased in our minds with our minds and with our
bodies and with all that our minds think and our bodies do is
something more than that. It is an interior experience of the
rectitude of things, a seen certainty of the consonance of things.
When I become aware that I am in harmony with my own
being, I am pleased. When I become aware that I am in harmony with all other, or any other, being, I am pleased. One
often thinks of pleasure as the satisfaction of an appetite, which
it is. But what is the appetite, traced to its ultimate source, and
what does "satisfaction" mean? The appetite is for fulfillment,
completion. To "satisfy" means "to fulfill the needs, expectations, wishes, or desires of . . . to suffice, fulfill, or answer the
requirements or conditions of." Insofar as I am, I have requirements that must be met if I am to continue to be. When they
are met—when they are satisfied, as a true measurement in

architecture is said to satisfy or as a just judgment in a court is said to give satisfaction—I am made fully myself, and it is this rightness, this perfect conformity of requirement and response, that I call my pleasure. Tracing the origins of the word "pleasure," one comes upon a curious early equivalent: agreement, mutual understanding. When I am in the right place, and all the world fits me, I am pleased.

In this ultimate sense of the word, pleasure becomes one of the mainsprings of the will. Being made certain that I am not a displaced person in a universe indifferent to me, I am able to move about in it. But if I have no direct, deep experience of how much the universe and I agree, I shall doubt the likelihood of our ever coming to a mutual understanding and so become either immobilized or very angry. The immobility is linked, fore and aft, to apathy; and there is a surprising apathy in some sections of the world today. The anger, conscious that movement is still possible but convinced that it is essentially random and therefore incapable of being satisfied, explodes into activity that is, and in the circumstances cannot help but be, irrational; we read of the irrational act, whether it is a private act or a vast public one, more and more often these mornings. Being pleased is not a mere matter of our being titillated; it is a condition of our being willing to go on. "No man can exist without pleasure," said Aquinas, and we may soon bump head-on into the appalling discovery that we cannot or—if the hour has grown late—that we could not.

I do see that these remarks attach what seems an excessive importance to an experience we think of as trivial. Therein lies our greatest stumbling block just now: a profound requirement of our natures is fixed in our minds as superficial.

Just as we equate "recreation" with the recreation room and not with rebirth—which is what the structure of the word truly signifies—so we habitually speak of pleasure as though all its implications were idle. "Well, one has to get some pleasure out of life" is not a proudly-held creed; it is an excuse, uttered by way of apology for an evasion of responsibility one is contemplating but of which one is transparently ashamed. Here is life on one side, over here. It is something to be got through, and the assumption is that getting through it will in no way be pleasing. But by the time one dies, one ought to have slipped in a few odd hours of dereliction of duty. A man is entitled to cheat a little along the way.

The roots of the word "pleasure," wriggling this way and that over the centuries, have taken a variety of turns, and some of these have headed in our direction. The medical term "placebo," for instance, is an offshoot of the Latin for "to afford satisfaction or happiness," and it suits our present understanding well. A placebo is "a medicine given merely to humor the patient; especially, a preparation containing no medicine but given for its psychological effect." That indeed is how we look upon the whole matter of delight: partly as coddling, partly as fraud, altogether as something from which true substance is missing.

But now we must face up to the implications of our attitudes; it is time to be entirely honest with ourselves. We hold two attitudes, and they are deadlocked. One is that, because we have been unable to provide pleasure with a value, pleasure is insubstantial, illusory. The other—and this is where our inquiry began—is that the value we do acknowledge, the abstract value we give to the thoughtful ratios of our labor, has also, and in spite of us, come to seem insubstantial, illusory. Between two negations, between two pathways felt to be slippery, is there no firm earth we can ever get beneath our feet?

Or is it possible that firmness, security, confidence, and joy— in this most mysterious universe—depend upon our willingness always to walk both paths at once, always to advance one foot on the right side and the other on the left so that we shall keep from toppling either way, always to accept the fact that the only way we can have one world is to admit and to honor the existence of two? There is a famous Chaplin image, at the end of a film called *The Pilgrim*. Chaplin has been ordered out of one country, literally kicked over the border. But across the border he is caught in the murderous cross fire of bandits engaged in guerrilla warfare. Where to turn? Swiftly shrugging his shoulders, he decides. The last we see of him, he is deftly and philosophically shuffling away from us, straight down the border line, one oversize shoe safely planted in this country, the other safely planted in that.

I say "safely." But, of course, there is something very tentative, eternally unresolved, in his teeter-totter journey to the horizon. And there is something about tentativeness, about teeter-tottering, that we do not like to allow in our own lives. We prefer to get things straight, to get things settled, to discover a single efficient way of hitching all we must deal with into single harness. We like to be single-minded, to have one rule of thumb, to define all that is diverse in the same simple set of terms—if we can possibly do it. The world is easier to manage that way, we feel.

But what if there is no single way to manage the world, no simple way of holding onto anything quite so supple—as though we were trying to lift a cobra with one hand when it really takes two? What if the world is as solid as rock and as yielding as water at one and the same time and man is a creature who needs the rock to sit on and the water to get under? What if man himself is essentially unresolved—partly granite and partly mercury, immaterial as his thought and material as his toenails, an unfinished sum and an unfinished symphony, an eternal spectacle in the mismatched socks he is wearing—and what if it is precisely in his failure, or his refusal, to define himself absolutely and to commit himself forever that his flexibility, his power of inventiveness, and his exuberance lie?

We are now being given hints that if this were the case, it

would be an excellent thing. I quoted Teilhard a few chapters ago on the flexibility and playfulness of the kitten. I did not mention then that the very advance the kitten, along with its cousin mammals, represented in the evolutionary development of life stemmed from its superb sloppiness, its comparative inefficiency, its frisky escape from the drive toward automated perfection. It had left behind it, and well beneath it, a much better organized species, the single-minded insect. With the mammal, Teilhard remarks, "instinct is no longer narrowly canalised, as in the spider or the bee, paralysed to a single function. . . . We are dealing with an entirely different form of instinct in fact, and one not subject to *the limitations imposed upon the tool by the precision it has attained.*"

The insect had been strict with itself, honed each of its parts to a specific function, tolerated no nonsense in the process of its self-organization. Having sorted out all things safely, and having co-ordinated them toward a single end, the busy bee and the admirable spider completed themselves—and thereby froze themselves. Out of perfection of a kind came a kind of death: the insect had formed itself absolutely and was now able to sustain itself indefinitely—but it could make no further contribution to anything outside itself or better than itself. The mammal, "no longer completely the slave" of its methodology, kept a response or two open—undetermined, uncommitted, untamable, elusive—and it was the open responses that enabled it to participate in further adventures. A loose character, the kitten.

If we are to believe the paleontologists, then, the looseness we notice in the strange ambiguity of our lives is one of the luckiest things we possess: something to be cherished, *as looseness*, rather than to be regretted as awkward. If we are, at our present stage of development, forced to do some things with one tool and some things with another, forced to labor on the boss's time and make love on our own, forced to advance upon the universe with both arms open and each hand prepared to make a rather different gesture, our advance in nature and in grace is not over. Something ahead of us invites us to test it this way and that, to strike it and to stroke it, to assault it and to steal up on it. If it is complex, we are still flexible and apt to surprise it in the unexpectedness of our approach. With a roller skate on one foot and a hiking boot on the other, we can switch tactics; it is by being free to switch tactics that most engagements are won.

But if we are ambidextrous wrestlers in a multiform world, doing some things intuitively and some things doggedly, now dancing about the arena and now showing what a straight line we can walk, where in all of this uninterrupted sparring can substance lie waiting for us? Must we posit that, given our odd natures and their apparent suitability to an equally odd universe, substance exists for us in the dimension that leaps into being when the two faces of the world are seen in a shimmering superimposition, one relieving the other with shade and the other lifting its companion into light? This is admittedly an unstable image for an unstable condition: the two do not absolutely merge; we cannot have the universe whole in one fell swoop. The two meet, and shield one another, and illuminate and shadow one another, in a meeting that is not quite a fusion: it is as evanescent as an eclipse, though it may be as thrilling. Are we vouchsafed the certainty of a sun and moon only while they are brushing contours, exchanging darkness and glow, fleetingly and ungraspingly making two faces one? Perhaps it is intolerable that substance, and value, and all promise should be as impermanently and dizzyingly known as this. But perhaps it is also the guarantee of our continued mobility, our malleability, our throbbing sensitivity to impressions that are themselves throbbing with life, a guarantee of our active partnership with an active, growing, changing, hallooing universe. Here nothing is frozen, not in our heads, not in the skies. We buzz, and bend, and beam together as we play hide-and-seek until dawn.

And see where we are, if any of this is so. Suppose that an eternal, hide-and-seek, mysteriously creative duality *is* so—a duality of thinking and seeing, of abstract and concrete, of action and contemplation, of cerebration and intuition, of work and play, of profit and pleasure, of assertion and surrender—and that our confidence and our exhilaration depend upon an alternating exercise of dual tools upon a double face—an exercise so regular and so rhythmic in its alternation that we come to have a lively sense of the sustained presence of both, finding substance in their iridescent interplay.

In that case, we are, at this precise moment in time, ready to declare ourselves a bonus. We have achieved a high degree of skill in one kind of groping, the hard kind, the theoretical kind. Our futures now depend upon a most attractive activity: upon our developing a matching skill in the easy kind, the loving kind, the arm-in-arm kind. Praiseworthy as we are in the work we have been doing, and certain as it is that more work will have to be done, our freedom to grow in stature rests unconditionally upon our ability to play. To keep our minds supple and the universe in focus, we are requested, most cordially, to exercise just those intellectual instincts which tend —in their contemplative listening and their intuitive rejoicing— to produce pleasure.

Can pleasure, then, be said to have a value, a value at least half as big as the total capital available to us, a value big enough to give us permission to pursue it? Intellectually speaking, I think so. It is, in essence, the value of The Other.

How much we have neglected The Other, and how strainingly we yearn for it, is not always clear to us. It is not clear to us because we have not fully realized how much of a burden, and how unnecessary a burden, we have conscientiously placed upon The Self.

One last, short recapitulation. When we decided that all value was extrinsic, and that no value was intrinsic or actually *in* things, we accepted a private responsibility that might well be called intolerable. We said that all that was touchable and all that was visible—from the grass outside the window to the face looking up at us from a chair across the room—was neutral and that worth was something we constructed for it in the adding machines of our heads. But this meant—though we barely noticed the implication—that all that was real, all that was worth-while, all that was valuable, was in *us*—in the equations we manufactured in the busy switchboard of our brains. Whatever vitality or continuity the universe possessed came from *us*. We were its guarantor, its prop, its collateral, its claim to being. We carried it on our shoulders like a willing, though perspiring, Atlas: the moment we ceased our cerebration, the moment we stopped supplying it with fresh charges in the shape of formulas, it would drop. The world about us, the womb in which we grow, had no other source of energy, no powers of its own. Each of us, in the individuality of his thinking mind, had perforce to accept the responsibility not simply of knowing the universe but of creating it—abstractly—and of perpetually maintaining it in the sustained tension of his thought.

Without being in the least egocentric, we had got ourselves in the position of the man who does not trust airplanes and who therefore does one wholly unnecessary thing: he gets a grip under the armrests attached to his seat and helps hold the plane up.

To acknowledge the presence, the independence, the energy, and in some way the reality of The Other is to begin to put down the burden that makes us most lonely, most isolated, most exhausted—and to begin to take pleasure in the comfort, the mutual support, the "oh, *there* you are!" of friends.

The Other is that warmth in a field that would make the ground thaw and the wheat grow if I never happened by; when

I do happen by, it is waiting not for the support of my thought but for the impress of my foot. It is that moment in a conversation when, toward the end of the evening, the few who are present sit back and realize, with a quiet leap of the heart, that each has touched something in the other and not merely imposed a rattle of entertainment upon him. It is a living face noticed across the aisle in a theater in which slightly parted lips and intent eyes and head held poised all, together, speak of a completeness I could not add to; or a face carved in marble, or in oil, that lifts the marble from the earth and the oil from dead cloth. Even when he is painting a self-portrait the artist must be stunned by the otherness he has trapped: this is he, but it is different from what he had thought. The Other is in this curious book we are reading in which an adolescent we have never known and could not have imagined does very strange things, and confesses to very strange thoughts, that bring him closer in his strangeness than our own children are in their familiarity. It is in the unfathomable chase Bach leads us, so urgent that there is almost not time to space the notes, after something that will escape him with a cry if he does not hurry; but he hurries, and it is still just there. It is in the movement that is not made in a dance, because the dancer is patiently permitting the invisible to pass him. What did you think the clown was crying about? He saw perfection, and it was not in him, it was somewhere else. And did you think he was unhappy crying? No. That kind of crying is a kind of happiness.

I am pleased in that instant when I discover that I am not alone. My joy, like the discovery, is profound.